John Pym Yeatman

# The Shemetic origin of the nations of western Europe

and more especially of the English, French, and Irish branches of the Gaelic race

John Pym Yeatman

**The Shemetic origin of the nations of western Europe**
*and more especially of the English, French, and Irish branches of the Gaelic race*

ISBN/EAN: 9783741166310

Manufactured in Europe, USA, Canada, Australia, Japa

Cover: Foto ©Thomas Meinert / pixelio.de

Manufactured and distributed by brebook publishing software
(www.brebook.com)

John Pym Yeatman

**The Shemetic origin of the nations of western Europe**

# THE SHEMETIC ORIGIN

## OF THE

# NATIONS OF WESTERN EUROPE.

# THE SHEMETIC ORIGIN

## OF THE

# NATIONS OF WESTERN EUROPE,

### AND MORE ESPECIALLY OF THE

## ENGLISH, FRENCH, AND IRISH BRANCHES
## OF THE GAELIC R/ ᵕᵕ

BY

## JOHN PYM YEATMAN,

FORMERLY OF EMAN. COLL. CAMB., AND OF LINCOLN'S INN, ESQ., BARRISTER-AT-LAW ;
FELLOW OF THE ROYAL HISTORICAL SOCIETY OF GREAT BRITAIN ;

*Author of "A History of the Common Law of Great Britain and Gaul,"*
*"An Introduction to the Study of Early English History,"*
*"The Mayor's Court Act, 1867,"*
*"An Exposure of the Mismanagement of the Public Record Office,"*
*"A Treatise on the Law of Trades' Marks," &c. &c. &c.*

"MAGNA EST VERITAS ET PREVALEBIT."

LONDON: BURNS AND OATES.
1879.

TO

Ⓗⓘⓢ Ⓘⓜⓟⓔⓡⓘⓐⓛ Ⓗⓘⓖⓗⓝⓔⓢⓢ

# NAPOLEON EUGENE LOUIS JOHN JOSEPH BONAPARTE,

PRINCE IMPERIAL OF FRANCE,

*THIS WORK,*

ILLUSTRATIVE OF THE RELATIONSHIP BETWEEN

THE GALLIC AND THE ENGLISH PEOPLES,

AND

COMMEMORATIVE OF THEIR GLORIOUS POSITION AMONGST

THE NATIONS OF ANTIQUITY,

BY PERMISSION,

IS MOST RESPECTFULLY INSCRIBED.

# PREFACE.

IT is not a very pleasant task to oppose the strong current of public opinion, even in matters of science or learning. Although every one asserts, and no doubt generally believes, that he is only anxious to learn or to teach the truth, yet when the truth is discovered, too frequently is exhibited a spirit of impatience, and occasionally the discoverer is abused, and sometimes in no unmeasured terms. And although his object may be simply to show what is the right and correct view of the matter, yet if, in so doing, he opposes the views of others—and it is inevitable that he should do so—the worst motives are sometimes attributed to him, and he is accused of being "rude," "violent," "passionate," "overbearing," "dogmatic," and indeed of the very conduct which in his soul he most truly abhors; and the reason of this is obvious—it is self-interest. It is impossible to show the fallacy of certain main lines of a science, upon which, in fact, its very existence depends, without at the same time showing that its professors are wrong, and no one in such a position cares to learn this; but when, in addition to the mortification of such an exposure, these professors find that works which have perhaps cost them much time and money to compose and publish are so radically wrong that they are comparatively worthless,

although much may be good and valuable in them—a
scientific work in which some of the axioms on which it
is founded are unsound is absolutely unsaleable—it would
perhaps be extravagant to suppose that it should be possible for these writers, who, according to the fashion of the
day—and a very bad fashion it is—are also critics of the
class of works in which they themselves are professors,
to view or review a book which condemns their views
with anything like favour; and this the author found, to
his great loss and chagrin, when, some few years ago, he
published the first part of a book entitled " The History of
the Common Law of Great Britain and Gaul." This was
a work which might be supposed to offend no one, for its
main object was to prove—the result of years of study and
reflection—that the notion that our legal institutions were
of Saxon, that is, of German origin ("German" in the
modern acceptation of the word) was erroneous, and that
it was, in fact, of Keltic or Gallic origin; and any one who
will glance at Dr. Mackay's new work, "The Gaelic Etymology of the English Language," will very quickly satisfy
himself of the accuracy of this view. It is no mere figure
of speech to assert that Dr. Mackay's work will create a
revolution in English philology, and render necessary a
revision of our dictionaries; we cannot, in the face of the
facts produced, continue to ignore the importance of the
Gaelic element of our language. The author's work might
have passed unnoticed, for very few lawyers of the present
day care to understand, and still fewer to write upon, the
scientific principles which underlie the judicial system;
and, indeed, they are so buried and disfigured by what is
inaptly termed "judge-made law" that it is difficult to
apply them. But unfortunately, as the author showed in
his Introduction, this result followed. If the law were

Keltic, probably the people to whom it belonged were of that race also, and this trenched upon the sacred province of history as taught in the schools; and worse than this (though not necessarily), it might follow that the English language also, which Dr. Johnson and the Oxford School have affirmed to be German, was of the same high origin.

This was too much for certain worthy critics who are also authors, and they gave vent to their feelings, or some of them, in tolerably strong language, the direct effect of which was, that almost immediately the author received more handsome and complimentary notices than he either expected or desired—probably this is generally the case simply in proportion to the virulence and excess of unfair criticism.

The effect of these attacks was that the work fell dead from the press. The author then republished the first part of it, which was merely introductory, as "An Introduction to the Study of Early English History;" and this book, although attempts were made to stifle it, has made its way, and its utility has been acknowledged.

Dr. Charles Mackay, in his preface to his work just mentioned, thus refers to it: "Recent historical researches prove abundantly (see especially 'The English and their Origin,' by Luke Owen Pyke, M.A., 1866; 'The Pedigree of the English People,' by Thomas Nicholas, M.D., Ph.D., 1868; and 'An Introduction to the Study of Early English History,' by John Pym Yeatman, 1874) that the Keltic inhabitants of England were not exterminated by the conquerors; that the Danish and Saxon invasions, though successful on the eastern and southern coasts of the island, did not extend so far into the Midland counties, or into the west, as to make the invaders numerically

superior to the inhabitants." And he adds : "The searching critical spirit and the fuller investigation of our times
have lifted some portion of the once almost impenetrable
veil that hid from our eyes the noble forms and the
venerable speech of our British ancestors, and from whom,
at this remote day, the living people of Great Britain and
Ireland have inherited some of their finest qualities. It
has been tardily discovered that we are not quite so Teutonic a people as we have been for ages considered ; " and
he arrives at, amongst others, the following important
conclusions :—

"First, That the Gaelic and other divisions of the Keltic,
so despised by Johnson and the succeeding writers whom
his false teaching led astray, prevails to a very large extent in the unliterary and colloquial speech of the English
people, and that it continually crops up in apparently
new, but in reality very ancient, slang, or, as they are sometimes called, cant-words.

"Second, That the Gaelic underlies all the languages of
the Western and some parts of North-Western Europe,
especially French, Spanish, and Italian.

"Third, That what is called Anglo-Saxon should be
designated Kelto-Saxon, and that the word Angle is a
corruption of An Gael or The Gael.

"Sixth, That the great Keltic swarms before the dawn
of history proceeded from the heart of Asia, and peopled
Assyria, Babylonia, Egypt, Phœnicia, and afterwards
Greece, Italy, Gaul, and the British Isles."

The third of these conclusions was arrived at by the
author after he had published "The History of the Common Law," and it forms the *motif* of his "Early English
History." Further consideration of the subject only confirmed the previous view. When, happily, reading a passage

in Verstegan—that most able but mischievous and misleading writer, who is at the bottom of much of the erroneous teaching of our schools—a flood of light burst upon him, and a wider survey of the whole subject fully confirmed him in the absolute truth of the sixth proposition of Dr. Mackay's book. Verstegan writes (p. 24), that in his day a "scythe" was called in Netherlandish "saison," the same word which represents a "Saxon." Therefore it seemed to follow that Scythian and Saxon were convertible terms, and possibly the one word was a corruption of the other. The object of the following pages is to illustrate this idea, and if in the process the author has outstepped the bounds of reason, and has committed himself to some absurdities, he can only state by anticipation that this may well be so, for, as there are no aids to guide, error is unavoidable; and since this subject is so wide as to embrace, in fact, a history of mankind in all ages, and indeed to involve the necessity of weighing the truth of the separate history of each people and nation, it would be only wonderful if it were not so; and that since Dr. Mackay himself states "that the recent historians have treated the subject of the fabulous extermination of the Britons and the consequent death of their language so thoroughly as to render necessary a new history of England," and as no one has yet ventured to come forward, any one who will adventure upon the task ought to be rather encouraged than blamed, especially if, in spite of such errors, a new light is thrown upon the subject and fresh facts of importance are brought forward; and this, at any rate, the author claims to have accomplished. And besides this, he ventures to think that in some instances at least he has drawn sound and correct conclusions, though they are at variance with the views of previous writers. These views and opinions, though undoubtedly intended to be used objectively, are submitted to the learned reader rather tentatively than dogmatically. The conclusions arrived at are based upon the labours of many men in various fields of science, and it would be as presumptuous as it would be dangerous to lay down a dogmatic rule, or to make a positive assertion upon the sum and substance of all their labours, especially when the whole compound, speaking chemically, is composed of .many ingredients, each of which is possibly a compound in itself, and when the study of any one of such items may require and exact the labours of a lifetime. The historical writer is necessarily dependent upon the labours of others; but that is not all. His greatest difficulty is to determine and choose between the several parties who labour in the same field of learning. Unfortunately, uncertainty and contrariety of opinion prevails in every department of science, but more especially so in the domain of history; so that if a writer has a bias, he may without great difficulty gather proofs in support of his own theory, even from those most opposed to him; and often when he has no bias it is essential that he should do so. He who has only truth for his object, as he is subject to human weaknesses, is liable also to this danger, and it would therefore be rash on the part of any one, however eminent and however great his following may be, to write dogmatically; much more would it be rash for an unknown writer to do so. And it leaves him open to the charge of presumption and arrogance if in the course of his labours he opposes the views of others, and especially so if those views are not only generally accepted but are acceptable.

Still, however true this may be, a writer who wishes to

arrive at the truth must take his course at all risks and hazards; nor can he perpetually stop in the course of his argument to apologise to those whose ideas or systems he opposes, or perhaps the errors and fallacies of whom he unwittingly exposes. Nor can he always avoid the charge of dogmatism, for he cannot invariably give the authorities on which he bases his propositions, and unless he states them positively they lack weight and sanction. It is to be feared that many of the following pages will be thought uninteresting, and to scholars wholly unnecessary, because the proofs are stated from step to step—proofs which to many minds are unnecessary. This course, however, has only been pursued in matters of the greatest importance, and especially in those which have been most hotly contested. So various and conflicting are the views of modern writers, and so curiously are to be found points of agreement amongst some of them, that it is necessary to note a point of difference, lest the reader assume too close an approximation to the views of any particular writer or school.

The principle adopted by the author in the composition of these pages is to strive, first of all, at getting at what facts may be clear and undisputed, and to graft upon them such historical evidence and such individual opinion as may be relied upon, and, where this is deficient, to endeavour by rational deductions to complete the argument.

In many cases, the responsibility of supporting particular propositions is left to the writer whose name is cited as an authority. In a book dependent upon almost the whole range of science, it would be manifestly impossible to do otherwise; but it is not pretended that where no authority is cited that none is existing, for it would give the book the appearance of a condensed encyclopædia to publish authorities on every point.

With these words of apology, which are intended, if possible, to calm the susceptibilities of modern critics and to allay their wrath, the author would add a few words of acknowledgment to those to whom he feels indebted for aid and enlightenment in the composition of the following pages. Of the dead, he would mention with the most profound respect the name of Dr. Whittaker, who has left behind him a mine, of wealth, and, after much consideration, the author is satisfied he is the safest guide which we possess to British history, although modern writers affect to despise his works, and, at any rate, ignore them; yet it is not too much to say that they are the basis of much that is judicious and sound in many of their compositions; and both in encyclopædias and works of that kind they have been used freely, and too frequently without acknowledgment. Next in importance are the Keltic researches of the Rev. Edward Davies, of the value of which it would be impossible to speak too highly. It is much to be regretted that both of these books are so little known to the public, except at second-hand and through distorted channels, and that they are not republished with notes explanatory of facts which have come to light since their publication. Of modern classical writers Dr. Donaldson is one of the few who has attempted to throw any light upon the dark pages of history.

To living writers the author is most indebted to the Very Rev. Canon U. Bourke, formerly President of St. Jarlath's College, Tuam, who, especially in his work entitled "The Aryan Origin of the Gaelic Race and Language," has indicated very clearly the importance to the student of British history of a study of Irish records and

Irish traditions; and to Lord Arundel of Wardour for the benefit of the discovery of the value of traditionary evidence, and its infinite superiority to the more positive but uncertain proofs to be adduced from the apocryphal remains of so-called Saxon history.

Lord Arundel's work, "Tradition Principally with Reference to Mythology," is most valuable in enabling us to form a sound opinion as to the historical truth which may be imbedded in the most corrupt and apparently worthless traditions, and especially is it valuable in giving confidence to those who would venture to oppose the traditional and historical teaching of the sacred writings to the atheistic and rationalistic views of modern scientists.

The author has consulted the valuable tracts of Mr. Joseph Boult with great advantage; and to these three writers the author gratefully acknowledges the debt of personal aid and advice upon points of great interest and importance.

The author also wishes to express his deep obligation to his Imperial Highness Prince Lucien Bonaparte, whose love of philological science and deep learning are so well known, and whose kindness to men of letters is proverbial. To him the author is indebted for advice and direction upon philological points which have not yet been sufficiently dealt with by living writers, the determination of which has shaped his course in these pages. It is not pretended that the views of this book have received the sanction of his Highness, or that he will approve of them, but the author owes it to Prince Lucien that he has not transgressed certain laws known to philologists, to which the especial points referred to dangerously approached. The author would desire to express his gratitude not only for direct personal advice, but for a privilege which his Highness has not unfrequently extended to men of letters, that of consulting the Prince's magnificent library at Norfolk Terrace.

4 SUMMERHILL VILLAS,
CHISLEHURST, 17th March 1879.

---

## POSTSCRIPT.

This book was written during the last winter vacation, and at intervals down to the middle of March last, but unhappily under circumstances of great anxiety; and when, some three months since, the MS. was nearly ready for the printers, the author found himself so much indisposed as to be unable properly to complete it, and some valuable notes have not been incorporated in the book; nor was he able to cut out some repetition, or properly to arrange certain parts of it. Worse than this, the greater portion of the proofs have had no real correction; the author could do little more than mechanically compare them with his rough copy, and he fears that some ludicrous blunders will appear in the book, though, thanks chiefly to the great intelligence of the printers, they may not be very many. For the latter part of the book he is not so anxious, for, happily, a complete severance from professional labours for some months, and some respite from anxieties, and especially many happy rambles amongst the delightful scenery of this neighbourhood, have combined to restore him to health, and he is now able to read with some appreciation of the subject; and for the last six weeks or more, Mr. Joseph Boult, the author of the tracts referred to in this volume, hearing of the author's illness, most kindly volunteered to look over the proofs, and verify such of the quotations as were within his range of books, and this has given the author confidence that no absurd blunders will be found in the latter part of the work.

These lines are written not by way of pleading *ad misericordiam* to hostile critics. Men who could write such reviews as some of those published at various times of the author's different books are not amenable to feelings of mercy since they are blinded by passion; but the author's vanity requires that some explanation should be given for the presence of appalling blunders to his friends, and to those amongst his readers who are good enough to appreciate his labours in this field of learning; and he is happy to reckon amongst them many persons whom he has never seen, some of whose works he has read with delight, and who have kindly declared themselves favourable to his views, actuated to this un-English but pleasant act most probably through reading the grossly ill-natured attacks which have been made upon him.

It is perhaps to be regretted that this book has been sent to press in this crude and unfinished state; but it will probably be many months before the author will be sufficiently recovered to venture upon the sustained labour of revising it, and even then he may not be sure of having leisure for the purpose; and the book, though written in a very short time, is yet the result of a life's labours and thought; and the author felt in the first stages of his illness that he might never have an opportunity to publish it, and that, subject to such errors and imperfections as he has referred to, the book after all contained the germ of his ideas, and if published it might, through the labours of others, bring forth the fruit so much desired, and do the good which it is the author's earnest wish that he might be allowed to do in his day and generation. He felt that the main arguments were correct and well considered, and that minor matters, and especially errors in typography or spelling, were comparatively of small moment.

To the author's illness may also be attributed the fact that a list of subscribers is not published, the Prospectus bound with this volume not having been distributed. The names the author has received are too few fairly to show the number of persons who would care to identify themselves with this publication, the true use of such a list. But should a second edition be called for, the author hopes to publish one, and with that view he will be grateful to those purchasers of the present edition who will favour him with their names ; a goodly array may have great effect in compelling our teachers to alter and modify their views upon English history.

ARUNDEL, SUSSEX, 30th *May* 1879.

# CONTENTS.

XX CONTENTS.

# THE SHEMETIC ORIGIN

OF THE

# NATIONS OF WESTERN EUROPE.

---

## CHAPTER I.

### THE FALLACIES OF THE ARYANIC THEORY.

IN order to gain an acceptance for the theories of this
book, it is first of all necessary to discard the teaching of
the Oxford School of Philology, especially that presented
by Professor Max Müller, which, from want of thought,
and possibly from sheer laziness, and partly from ignorance and wilful disregard of Keltic learning, for some
twenty years has been accepted as positively true.  Alas!
this twenty years' progression has been in the wrong
direction.  In plain language, this school inculcates the
rejection of the Mosaic account of the early history of
mankind, and in substitution for it suggests the notion
of a self-created intelligence,—of a system which has
for its base the heathen doctrine that man has achieved
for himself by little and little the knowledge and science
he possesses, and that he began to improve himself from a
mental position little better than that of an ape; certainly
not an inapt description of the state of the learned world
at the dawn of modern history.  This is the pet theory of

A

German philosophers; and Professor Max Müller, who is undoubtedly a man of very great ability, has made it his special study to heathenise our ancient history and to blind our universities; and for this purpose he would discard the Mosaic account, and he starts with the assumption that the Sanscrit, to the study of which he has devoted (and wasted) his life, is the parent of all languages, and that its *situs* or home is the cradle of our race. As this doctrine, if stated too baldly, would probably shock our classical scholars, Professor Max Müller proceeds to feed them with pap, and the nostrum which he invented for the purpose is the " Aryanic Theory." It assumed a rational and inviting form, which scholars, who were absorbed in the study of Latin and Greek, were willing enough to accept, especially as it saved them from the trouble of thinking about it, and from the expense of having a professorship for the study of the Keltic, by relegating that language from its position of being the parent of several tongues to one dependent upon itself and independent of all other languages. And it must be admitted, although crowned with fable, the Aryanic theory has for its substratum many sound historical truths : it is in their application that error and confusion arise. Professor Max Müller writes :—" When Sanscrit had once assumed its right position " (*i.e.*, the parent of all tongues), "when people had once been familiarised with the idea that there must have existed a language more primitive than Greek, Latin, and Sanscrit " (observe the flattery of our classical professors), " as well as of the Teutonic " (observe the modest position assigned to the Teutonic), "Keltic, and Slavonic branches of speech, all languages seem to fall by themselves into their right position. The key to the puzzle was found, and all the rest was merely a work of patience.

The same arguments by which Sanscrit and Greek had been proved to hold co-ordinate rank were perceived to apply with equal strength to Latin and Greek ; and after Latin had once been shown to be more primitive in many points than Greek, it was easy to see that the Teutonic, the Keltic, and the Slavonic languages also contained each a number of formations which it was impossible to derive from Sanscrit, Greek, or Latin : it was perceived that all had to be treated as co-ordinate members of one and the same class." Now, putting aside the absurdity of supposing that there was a mechanical system of languages which only wanted one key to unlock it, this theory is a slurring over of the Mosaic account of the confusion of languages at the building of the Tower of Babel. The difference between languages is delightfully plain from the Aryanic key—that is, the difference between tongues is accounted for on rationalistic grounds, and the story of Moses of the confusion of languages is reduced to a figment. The theory in the main is correct, in so far as concerns the differences between certain specified forms of language, such as the Latin, Greek, and Keltic, which are all of the same family, and were never confused ; but it is utterly and hopelessly wrong, and insufficient to account for differences such as exist between languages which have been confused, like the Basque, the Sarmatian, and others, which are not members of the same family or class, but wholly and entirely different. The truth of this proposition is apparent if proof can be found of any one language which must be classed by itself—and even the infidel or Aryanic School admit that the Basque has no congeners—if the doctrine is accepted (and it must be, even with our imperfect knowledge of them) that there are numbers of languages spread over the world each of which belongs to no class but its own, then the Aryanic theory is proved to be untrue. But without this test, if it is put on the sharp index of common-sense, it collapses at once. Take its name, "Aryanic." Max Müller has not invented the term; he has only misapplied it. Aryanic means a race of people who are not of nomadic habits, or the tillers of the soil. A nomenclature which depends upon a habit of only a certain class of people is absurd if applied to all as a test of race, a confusion of ideas and tongues worse than that of Babel itself; and the result, which binds together in one family the Hindoo, the German, the Frenchman, and the Englishman, is in itself an absurdity. Learned and Christian men have adopted this Aryanic theory without seeing its meaning, and probably assigning to it a very different application. They overlook the etymology of the word, just as Max Müller has done, and they mean by it a term which expresses the language of our first parents. This is evidently the view adopted by that eminent scholar, Canon Ulick J. Bourke. It must be left to scholars to decide the question whether the language of Eden was Aryanic, Latin, Greek, Sanscrit, or Gaelic; possibly it was Hebraic, possibly it was neither. We do not know what was the primitive tongue of our first parents, but still we may consider that Adam is hardly likely to have changed his form of speech, and he was cotemporary with the following patriarchs, all of whom lived in the age of Noah—Enos, Cainan, Mahalaleel, Jared, Methuselah, and Lamech:—

| Enos lived | 695 | years | with Adam | and | 84 | with Noah. |
|---|---|---|---|---|---|---|
| Cainan, | 605 | „ | „ | „ | 179 | „ |
| Mahalaleel, | 535 | „ | „ | „ | 234 | „ |
| Jared, | 470 | „ | „ | „ | 366 | „ |
| Methuselah, | 243 | „ | „ | „ | 600 | „ |
| Lamech, | 56 | „ | „ | „ | 595 | „ |

This is based on the Hebrew version, but the argument is not really weakened if the Septuagint version of dates be adopted. So that it is clear that Noah must have spoken the very language of the Garden of Eden. We know positively from Moses (Gen. xi. 1) that even down to the building of the Tower of Babel all the world was of one language and of one speech, and we learn also that Noah survived the deluge 500 years, and lived down to the age of Israel himself, so that there is only the period during which the Israelites sojourned in Egypt that is not covered by the personal presence of the patriarchs. We know also that the Israelites lived quite apart from the Egyptians, so that their language would probably remain uncorrupted until Moses fixed it in writing. If, then, this tongue of our first parents still survives, reason points to the Hebrew; but, as a fact, there is no authority whatever for asserting that it is now in existence, still less for supposing that it was Sanscrit or Aryan, whatever that may mean. It may be conceded that Max Müller does not pretend that he has discovered what the real Aryan language was, but he insinuates that it was Sanscrit. Now this fact is apparent; looking at the diversity of the languages of which we have any knowledge—for instance, the Basque and any other—if they are simply, as the Aryanic theory teaches us, members of the same family of language, merely corrupted by time and habit, we must reject at once the Mosaic theory of our pedigree, for it would take myriads of years to create such an utter diversity. This we can prove by dates: according to the mean of Scripture chronology, the date of the deluge was 2756 B.C., the great pyramid dates this event 2790 B.C. The separation of mankind occurred some years afterwards. Now we cannot, of course, determine within a few hundred

years the date of the separation of the two branches of
the Keltic family which ultimately settled in the British
Isles, but looking at the date of the earliest Greek settlements, and at the fact that the Latin language is of
earlier date, and that the Keltic is earlier than either,
we cannot place the date of their separation at less than
2000 B.C.; quite possibly it was 500 years earlier, that is,
at least 4000 years ago, and this is very nearly approaching, if not actually, the very date of the dispersion of
mankind. Yet though the difference is immense between
them, we very easily recognise the fact that both the
Gaelic and the Cymric are of the same family : they may
be unintelligible as a matter of speech, but reduced into
writing we easily discriminate the similarity of their roots,
and without difficulty see that the Welsh and Irish are
branches of the same tongue. Time has indeed wrought
great changes, but these changes vanish when we compare
them with the changes between, for instance, the Keltic and
the Basque. We can only conclude that such changes have
been effected by a miracle such as that described by Moses ;
to account for them on Professor Max Müller's theory would
be to admit that myriads of years had elapsed since the dispersion of mankind. It does not follow from the Mosaic
account that each individual of the period had a distinct
language given to him. Looking at the two last verses of
the preceding chapter of Genesis, it would rather seem that
although mankind were of one speech, yet there was even
then dialectical differences amongst them, for prior to the
account of the confusion of languages it is stated that the
people were divided after their tongues in their lands,
after their nations, and after their families, after their
generation in these nations ; and we know that afterwards
the Israelites differed amongst each other, as in the case

of the Ephraimites and of the Galileans, showing that even thus early they corrupted their speech by contact with other peoples. The number of languages must have been either in accordance with the number of nations, or of families, or of individuals. Of the first there were sixteen and about seventy families. The Irish traditions curiously seem to confirm the latter theory, for it is stated that Gaelic was derived from seventy-two languages—the very number, by the way, of the transcribers of the Jewish scriptures into Greek, from which event possibly the tradition is taken. The common opinion is, that the number of original languages thus created was according to the number of families, and possibly this number is sufficient to account for all the tongues, ancient and modern, known to us. It is now, after the lapse of time, and the inextricable confusion created by contact and intermixture with each other, simply impossible to trace each family or language separately; and if we could, we know that language is not an infallible guide. All we can do is to trace the origin of some few nations, and this can best be done by the division by Moses of the sons of Noah. This is by far the best classification we can take; it is not so learned and ambitious as the German Aryanic theory, but it has the advantage of being simple; and at any rate, it dates from a period when we have the Mosaic writings to guide us, as well as some scraps of contemporary history.

Homer seems to have been ignorant enough to have accepted the tradition of the confusion of languages, for he applies the epithet *Meropes* to mankind, by which he intended to denote, that whereas they were at one time of one speech, their language had at some period been divided into several tongues.

Another great objection to the Aryanic division of languages is, that it recognises as a language that which is only a stage of one, irrespective of its age or family, or that which is a composition of several. The Latin, Greek, and Keltic are treated as three separate and distinct languages, whereas they are all offshoots of the same family, and probably the two former are based upon the latter. A very few years ago the common teaching was that Latin was derived from the Greek. The Very Rev. Canon Bourke, in his history of the Aryanic origin of the Gaelic race and language—a work of immense value in all that relates to that language, though singularly reticent as to the subject which it affects to deal with, namely, the history of the steps between the Aryanic or primitive language of mankind and the Keltic tongue, and, indeed, of the Aryanic language itself—states very clearly and concisely the facts which show that Latin is older than Greek, and Keltic older than either, which gives to the latter tongue an immense antiquity, dating it probably from near the dispersion of mankind; whereas German, as we know it, which Max Müller classifies with it, is a compound of many tongues based upon one, and did not exist as a language until Luther fixed it; and Sanscrit dates somewhere between the two—rather a wide margin certainly, and rather, we should think, an unscientific classification.

Dr. R. G. Latham ventures upon an approximation of the date of Sanscrit, and he "is not afraid of committing himself to the doctrine that when philologues make the Vedas three thousand and odd years old, and deduce the Latin and its congeners from Asia, they are wrong to at least a thousand miles in space and as many years in time." And this is the deliberate opinion of the first English philologist. Surely it is enough to make us pause before we discard the Mosaic account for this bran-new German revelation which our great Oxford scholars have not only tolerated but approved of.

The earliest remains of any language belonging to the same class as the Sanscrit with an approximate date are the cuneiform inscriptions delivering the edicts of the kings of Persia, ranging from B.C. 470 to B.C. 370, to the people, who must not be confounded with the earlier inhabitants of that country. Next in order of time is the language of the Caubul coins, in an alphabet written, like the Shemetic, from right to left. Then there are four coins which may be referred to the early part of the dynasty of the Seleucidæ. After these there are no definite dates until after the Mohammedan conquests.

To what do these scraps point? Only to contact with and instruction from the Shemetic races settled in Asia Minor or Syria: certainly they are no proof of race or antiquity of language. And it is upon such an unsound basis as this that the Germans build a superstructure going far back, dating, in reality, myriads of years prior to the time of Adam. We know that the Keltic, Greek, and Latin all emanated from the neighbourhood of Asia Minor, near to the spot indicated by the Mosaic account; but what possible proof is there that they came from such a distance beyond it? The course of the Sanscrit would denote, in accordance with the Mosaic account, that it travelled from the same spot eastward; and we know from sacred history that Solomon traded with India about the time of the building of the Temple, so that there is a reason why much of the learning and some of the language of the Vedas came from his neighbourhood, though it would probably take centuries of the effects of such contact before so scientific a system as that of the Vedas could be evolved; so that, taking this Jewish contact to be the source of their knowledge, Dr. Latham may be absolutely correct in his conjecture respecting the date of these writings. This is true, that when dealing with MSS. of a Shemetic or Christian character, we frequently find them much older than they are estimated, but the exact contrary is commonly the case with heathen documents, simply because, as the latter obtained their knowledge from the former, it took long years to develop it in their own fashion.

Nor is this the only objection to the Aryanic classification; it cruelly leaves out of reckoning all the languages but those of the modern great and powerful nations —a system of flattering the great which at once detracts from its value as a scientific classification. Why German, for instance, should be intruded, it is difficult to say, unless it is in accordance with the fact that the Germans as a family, tested by their blood, are entirely distinct from the rest of the nations collected together as members of the same happy family; but if so, the classification is again faulty, for the Latin, Greek, and Keltic are undoubtedly nearly allied to each other in blood as well as in language, and, comparatively to German, should be ranked under one head. If by German, Gothic is intended, the classification is more accurate; but true philology teaches that German and Gothic are not convertible terms, but are languages wide as the poles asunder, though modern German has borrowed many words and phrases, idioms and rules of structure, from the Gothic. The Aryanic theory seems to have been invented expressly to bring the German language into good company with which it has actually nothing in common, although curiously the root of the German, the Prussian language or the

Lithuanic, is unquestionably the nearest congener to the Sanscrit, and after it the Old Slavonic, which is left out in the cold. And if, as is supposed, the Slavonic is a Japhetian language, Sanscrit may be the same; and looking at the proximity of Japan, assuming the Javanese to be sons of Javan, it follows that the Prussians, at any rate, if not all the Germans, may be akin to the Indians, and so an Indo-European class of languages may be admissible, that is, an Indo-European as opposed to Shemetic-European languages. Japhetic-European would be a more accurate term than either, for Indian may be applied to a Shemetic language; but this division would not suit the German professors, for they would properly belong to neither.

They could not belong to the Shemetic-European class, because their Sarmatian or Japhetic base neutralises the effect of the Gothic or Shemetic words which their ancestors, the Sarmatians, adopted in taking possession of Gothic territory. Although they have many inarticulate or corrupt renderings of Shemetic speech, they are not entitled to rank with the Shemetic nations, any more than are entitled to be ranked with the English the natives of Africa who have been transferred to our colonies, and who have engrafted upon their own tongues many of our words. Nor can the Germans properly be classed with the Japhetic-Asiatic race, since, although they are undoubtedly as to the structure and form of their speech the nearest congeners of the Sanscrit, yet the numerous Shemetic words they have adopted have so completely altered their language that it cannot be called Japhetian.

The German speech, in truth, is a compound; it is not a primitive language, or even a national language. It is rather, to adopt an etymology which, though probably

false, suits it as a fact, the tongue of all men, or *garmen ;*
and it is unscientific to attempt to classify it with primitive forms of speech like the Gaelic or the Greek. The
philologist is too apt to disregard history : he takes a form
of speech as he finds it, and he classifies it according to
certain rules or laws of construction, and in this way
a tongue of yesterday's date—as, for instance, the lingo of
the Nigger, or that invented between the Turks and the
sailors and soldiers of the Allies in the Crimean war, if it
still survives—becomes entitled to equal rank with the
Gaelic, or the Sanscrit, or the German. This is the principle
of the Aryanic theory, and though, for the mere purposes of
teaching languages, it may suffice when it is applied, as
it is here by Professor Max Müller, as a test of race or
history, it is evidently absurd. It is rather hard that this
system should be attempted to be foisted upon us to save
the German from the disgrace of belonging to no known
tribe or race (except to the cannibal Sarmatian, who is
kept out of sight as much as possible), and as it tends to
confuse our history and to render it unintelligible, all
those who would endeavour to read it aright must incon-
tinently reject it.

Few people care to oppose the tide of current thought,
and it is pleasant to note that Mr. J. Crawford had the
courage to read before the British Association at Oxford in
1860, when the Aryanic theory was yet in its infancy, a
paper in which he insisted that the Aryanic or Indian-
Germanic theory which referred the languages with the
people speaking them to a common origin to be entirely
groundless.

Men are not so outspoken now-a-days. A succession of
British Association meetings have stamped the theory
with a mark of apparent genuineness, yet Canon Greenwell

has indirectly ventured to doubt the "savage" theory as applied to the ancient Briton, and Mr. Thurman, p. 139 of his "Crania Britannica," considers "that the present state of the linguistic question of Britain cannot be considered to be settled definitely;" and he suggests, following Pictet, "that the Irish, Welsh, and Gaulish languages require a more profound study." The author ventured to make, quite independently, the same suggestion in the last chapter of his "Introduction to the Study of Early English History." As a first step, then, in this direction, it is necessary to discard altogether the blessings of the Aryanic theory, and to launch out unguided into the ocean of uncertainty.

# CHAPTER II.

IT may appear to be degrading to the man of advanced
ideas to reject the scientific theories in which he is a firm
believer, and to follow humbly the old-fashioned views of
the book which, with perhaps the childish belief in its
sanctity, he has long since rejected; but the true philosopher will quickly overcome this feeling of repugnance
if he sees that there is, after all, sound wisdom in the older
theories which he had overlooked, and especially if he
accepts the views set out in the last chapter of the
unscientific and unsatisfactory nature of this pet scheme
of modern days.  If reaction sets in, he may be tempted to
accept even more than is required of him; but in this
work, at least, all that is insisted upon is, that, for the
period which the history of Moses covers, there being no
other guide, we ought gladly to accept it, especially as
there is no rational doubt of the antiquity and genuineness of the work; for, happily, it is the possession of a
Church that does not seek for proselytes, and has therefore
less temptation to exaggeration; and from its character of
being everything but a flattering account of the people
whose history it relates, it comes to us with the best
possible recommendation in favour of its veracity.  Happily
the Pentateuch was never the subject of any quarrel between the Jews and the Christians; and in the Septuagint,

assuming we possess that work, we possess a copy of it made at least 200 years prior to the period when it is asserted attempts were made to alter and falsify the prophetic portions of the sacred writings. The Jews, of course, retort upon the Christians that they are authors of the variancies which appear between their books and the Septuagint, but, happily for the historian, this controversy does not affect the Pentateuch; both Jews and Christians alike agree in their estimate of it—both admit it to be the genuine writing of Moses himself. The Greek version, of which we probably possess an accurate copy, dates from the time of Ptolemy Philadelphus, some two or three hundred years before the Christian era, and the history of that translation, the great political price the king paid for it, the magnificence with which the seventy-two interpreters were received and entertained, and the whole story of its reception, mark it as the most wonderful literary event that has ever occurred—proof, if any were wanting, of the veneration and respect which the books possessed at that date. If Philadelphus regarded this work as the crown of his magnificent library, and went to such cost to obtain it, surely it is worth while to weigh it attentively, and to endeavour at least to gain some historical knowledge from its contents. It is only as an historical record that it is proposed for consideration. We require little proof since the era of Christianity that we possess a true copy of this document, and from the date of Ptolemy to Josephus we rest on the evidence of Aristeas, Aristobulus, and Philo.

Josephus, who, of course, was at variance with the Greeks as to the genuineness of their version of the prophetical writings, admits that they possessed a true copy of the laws.

It is confidently asserted that, for the first stage of history, the works of Moses are the only guide, and that any departure from his classification or from his account of mankind is sure to land us in some muddle, like that of Professor Max Müller's pseudo-Aryanism. Dr. R. G. Latham in his "Comparative Philology," which is the best book extant upon the subject, has happily ignored the Aryanic theory, but by discarding the grand lines laid down by Moses, his work, which otherwise would be a great contribution to the subject, is in terrible confusion, although, taking each section separately, much learning is contained in it, and much knowledge may be gleaned from it. He would be a bold man indeed who would endeavour to write positively of the history of the human race without reference to Moses, for, with the exception of the Israelites, no nation has preserved any reliable un-broken history extending more than 600 or 700 years before the era of Christ; and even in the sacred books, all we can hope or expect to do is to pick up here and there at second-hand a few facts relative to the history of other people than the Israelites. We occasionally do so in the Mosaic history, and we also sometimes may do so in profane writers; but they are so fragmentary, and in the latter case so obscured by fiction, that little or no consecutive history can be gleaned from them. We must be content, therefore, with picking out a landmark here and there, and advancing by induction from ascertained facts to learn something of the history we desire to obtain.

Although we have no history of an early kind, yet we can, from facts to be so gained piecemeal, make out a tole-rably consistent history of our race from the age of Solo-mon, or about 1000 years B.C., but we cannot get back any earlier, except in the most crude and general manner, and

that without any degree of exactness, except we resort to
other classes of facts from which we may induce a reasonable belief in a much greater and more glorious antiquity, one uniting us with the earliest races of mankind,
and that by a chain of evidence clear and conclusive,
though, it must be confessed, at times depending upon
presumptions or philosophical deductions; yet presumptions of such a character that they are, in some respects,
better than a positive chronicle, since that might be
deemed to be unreasonable, and as it must be without
collateral evidence to support it, it would be open to the
objection of being a concoction.   First, then, we resort to
the region of positive history for proofs ; and secondly,
to the evidence to be obtained from the language, habits,
and general history of our race.

Of the sources of positive history, those we must per-
force put the greatest faith in are the records of the Jewish
nation, but these unfortunately are of a very meagre description.   The sacred books of Moses cover the period of
the history of mankind for 2500 years, and for nearly 1200
years after the date of the Flood; and the first book alone,
consisting of a very few chapters, deals with the whole of
that period, with the exception of the last 200 years, of
which we are without any positive history.

Moses in the first book, although he relates circumstantially the personal history of the Israelitish family,
gives only the barest details of the collateral branches.
These facts are so few, and of such importance, that it
may be worth while to set them out, as they are the
first links in the chain from which we deduce our history.
We need not refer to that which relates to the sons of
Ham, for it is assumed that we deduce our origin either
from the sons of Shem or Japhet.

B

In the tenth chapter of Genesis, second verse, we read, that "the sons of Japhet were Gomer and Magog, and Madai and Javan, and Tubal and Meshech, and Tiras ; and that the sons of Gomer were Ashkenaz, and Riphath, and Togarmah; and the sons of Javan, Elishah and Tarshish, Kittim and Dodanim, and by these were the islands of the Gentiles divided in their lands, every one according to his tongue after their families in their nations," the islands here intended being those distant countries which were reached by ships, from which it is frequently inferred, though apparently without any authority, that the first settlers of the distant parts of the world were the sons of Japhet. Of the children of Shem, other than the Hebrews, even less information is given, for the Mosaic history is confined to that of the Israelites, only a section of them. At verse 21 of the same chapter we read "of Shem also, the father of all the children of Heber, the brother of Japhet, the elder sons were born, Elam, Asshur, Arphaxad, Lud, and Aram ; and of Aram, Uz and Hul, Gether and Mash." This is all that Moses tells us, excepting the fact that each of the family, in direct descent from Shem to Abraham, had other sons and daughters, and that Heber, the father of all the Hebrews, had two sons, Peleg, from whom the Israelites are descended, and Joctan, who was the father of twelve sons; a few names are given of the brother of Abraham and of his descendants, and the names of the sons of Abraham by Keturah. There the Scripture account may be said to end, nor have we any other account from any other writer of authority, except from Josephus, who lived 2700 years afterwards, and from whose accounts it is clear that he had no authority for any statement except the barest and most unreliable tradition, or most assuredly

he would have adduced it; from which it is clear that no
consecutive history of mankind can be expected, unless it
should turn out that in the unknown inscriptions of the
East accounts may yet be forthcoming; but for these we
must be content to wait, for at present, although we hear
of boasted discoveries of the secrets of these hieroglyphics, so far no practical result appears to follow from them.
Of what value, then, is the Mosaic account, since it must
be admitted to be of the very slightest, and since it must
be admitted also that its accounts are not certain, either
as to the names of the tribes and nations, or of their
residences, and especially since the history of the Jews
teaches us how readily whole nations and tribes changed
their residences, and travelled from one country to another, supplanting and possessing each others' countries
and names, to the utter confusion of boundaries ; and this
is supplemented by the facts of positive history, which
teach us the same thing ?

We, at any rate, learn these facts, that mankind was
divided into three great families, answering generally to
the three great divisions of the human race—the white
race and the black, and those who belong to neither of these
two divisions. It may be said that through admixture
of races there are infinite shades and degrees of mankind,
and that such a division is absurd, because we have no
means of determining to which class any particular race
belongs.

Granted that it is impossible to determine positively
the proper classification of every race and tribe, the kin
and family of some races of people may be easily determined: no one can doubt but that the Jew belongs to the
former, and the Negro to the latter, and the Chinaman or
Javanese to the middle class. Hence we learn that the

Jewish type is Shemetic, the Negro Hametic, and the
Japanese Japhetian.  That is sufficient for our purpose,
which is not to classify all the races of men, but to prove,
if possible, the right of the people of Western Europe to
class themselves under the first great family of nations,
which Moses calls the family of Shem.  Assuredly they are
neither black nor of a neutral tint ; and some of them, the
Gaelic race, at any rate, have not mixed with either of the
former races.  Moses gives us the names of some of the
younger branches of this family, as, for instance, the five
sons of Shem, the sons of Aram and Joctan, from whom
it may be assumed that some of the great nations of the
earth derive their origin; and he relates the fact that
others had families, which should teach us not to assert
too positively our relationship to any one in particular.

But we learn more than this ; we learn as a fact that
at a certain period there was a confusion of languages, a
fact which is confirmed by the traditions of many nations,
and which Homer especially asserts ; and we know that
this was confined to only certain of mankind, and that
the patriarchs of the Shemetic race were not included in
this visitation.  We may be quite certain, therefore, that
all nations who in the early ages spoke a Shemetic dialect
were of the Shemetic race; and if the Keltic can be shown
to be such a dialect, the Keltic race are necessarily a
Shemetic people, since it is against reason to suppose
the possibility of a people of the patriarchal age assuming
a language not belonging to them.  This argument is addressed solely to those who believe in the inspiration of
the Sacred Scriptures ; to them it must be absolutely convincing.  It will be the aim of these pages to prove,
chiefly by means of the Scriptures, that the Keltæ were of

Shemetic origin. To those who do not give credit to the Scriptures, the arguments addressed are simply useless.

The account that Moses gives of the Shemetic race, bare as it is, is much more satisfactory than that given of the children of Japhet or of Ham, for whilst he gives some account of the issue of Shem for ten generations, down to the time of Abraham, showing that at each step of the pedigree there was other issue born besides the chief line, with only one exception, that of the children of Ramah, he has traced the children of Japhet and Ham to the third generation, or to the very date of the dispersion of mankind, as if to give us only the names of the families who, at the dispersion, received different languages, and, as separate families, subsequently became separate nations. We seem to have here the true division of mankind into individual nations, and we should be able to trace historically the name of each; and, as if this was the intention of the scribe, the children of Canaan, the younger son of Ham, whom tradition relates to have been involved with his father in the curse, are already named, not as individuals, but as nations.

If this idea is correct, we should have no difficulty in showing the utter falsity of the appropriation by Josephus of the persons named in the Sacred Scriptures to the nations existing at his date. For instance, Javan, instead of being the father of the Greeks, would be the progenitor of the Javanese; Mesech, instead of being the father of the Cappadocians, would be assigned to the Muscovites; Ross to the Russians; the Paphlagonians to Peleg rather than to Riphath, and so forth; in fact, we should only have to trace the ancient name of a nation to ascertain its origin. This would involve the difficulty of determining whether a particular name originally belonged to a nation or was adopted by it from the locality into which it settled, unfortunately a difficulty frequently arising. We have direct proof of this in the history of the Israelites themselves, who were styled Canaanites on account of their living in that land. Zophar, the grandson of Esau and uncle of Job, was called a Naamathite because his predecessor in his estate, a Cushite, had been so called, and numerous instances are given in the Mosaic writings of people adopting the name of their predecessors.

The Mosaic writings, unfortunately for the historian, are open to the objection of narrowness; they are not cosmopolitan in the primary sense of the word. They profess to relate, and they do so, to the history of the Israelites, and outside the chronicle of this people they give no information except such incidental facts as are necessary to illustrate it; so that, apart from the general scheme of the distribution of mankind in the primitive period of history, we can only glean here and there a fact of importance; but as containing a system of chronology these writings are simply invaluable, for, with all their imperfections—using that word in its primary sense—they are the only reliable records of time that we possess. What would history be without them? We have only to look at the history of the Greeks for an answer. They are unquestionably the first of living peoples (counting the Phœnicians, the ancient Assyrians, and peoples of that age as past and gone), and their history would be a mere chaos had it not been for the succession of the Lacedemonian kings upon which to depend; and even with the support of this undoubted chronology, learned men of our own day would discard the earliest Grecian history as fabulous, just as they have endeavoured to sweep away all British history until a few centuries prior to the Christian era.

Blot out from our minds the chronology of the Old Testament, and what of certainty should we have to supply its place ? The prospect is appalling. Nothing certain before the time of Herodotus, and even that grand old writer in these sceptical days most unfairly named the father of lies. Homer and Hesiod, although only dealers in old scraps, are too mythical to be absolutely relied upon ; Sanchoniathon and Menathon, both of them too wicked. What have we to cover the long period antecedent to Herodotus, during which all history was fixed? With care and trouble we can trace clearly back to him; but then we are at the end and not at the beginning of things. The scraps and odds and ends to be gleaned from old tombs, from inscriptions, and from other sources open to us, are useless without a true system of chronology upon which to engraft them. Scientific men very recently had constructed a beautiful and scientific theory of periods somewhat in imitation of Hesiod, but Dr. Schliemann's discoveries on the site of Troy and other means demonstrate the absurdity of relying upon the theory of progressive development. One school proves conclusively the progress of man through the ages . of stone, bronze, and iron, whilst another equally conclusively reverses the process.

We are afflicted at every step we go with a variety of laws, scientific and otherwise—mostly otherwise—in imitation no doubt of Grimm's Law, Bopp's Law, &c.; indeed, it is fashionable to reduce everything to a system. Mr. Hepworth Dixon, summarising the efforts of Sir John Lubbock, Mr. Mill, and Mr. B. Gould, the leading workers in this field, thus writes :—

"Every one who has read the annals of our race—a page of nature with its counterfoil in the history of everything having life—is aware that in our progress from the

savage to the civilised state, man has had to pass through
three grand stages, corresponding, as it were, to his child-
hood, to his youth, and to his manhood. In the first stage
of his career he is a hunter, living mainly by the chase;
in the second he is a herdsman; . . . in the third stage he
is a husbandman. . . . These three conditions of human
life may be considered as finding their purest types in
such races as the Iroquois, the Arabian, the Gothic in its
primal stage, but each condition is in itself and for itself
an affair of development and not of race. The Arab, who
is now a shepherd, was once a hunter. The Saxon, who
is now a cultivator of the soil, was first a hunter, then a
herdsman, before he became a husbandman. Man's progress from stage to stage is continuous in its course, obey-
ing the laws of physical and moral change. It is slow, it
is uniform, it is silent, it is unseen; in one word, it is
growth. . . . These three stages in our progress upward
are strongly marked, the interval dividing an Iroquois
from an Arab being as wide as that which separates an
Arab from a Saxon." Lord Arundel (on Tradition), in
showing the inconclusiveness of the examples adduced,
points out that the theory is unsound by suggesting other
examples rather nearer to the point; that, for instance, Cain
was a husbandman whilst Abel was a shepherd; and that
Herodotus, speaking of the Scythians, divides them into
those who apply themselves to the culture of the soil, and
those who neither plough nor sow but keep cattle; and to
this might be added the case of the Egyptians, who cultivated the soil but who despised the keepers of cattle.
Special reasons of soil, locality, religion, or manners make
people take up one or other of those modes of life, as
amongst ourselves; and even at the present day they are
all compatible, and may be carried on simultaneously; yet

our scientists would deduce from them laws which shall teach us the history of our race. In sober truth, we do not develop very much from the natural-development theory. If, then, in general history we have no chronological guide except the Hebrew writings, what guide have we in ethnology except we rely upon them? The science of comparative philology is tardily admitted to be useless as a guide for such a purpose. That had been used to prove the identity of race between the Greeks, Latins, English, Goths, and Germans. The fact that its influence was confined to these dominant races ought to have shown its folly; but great scholars, and notably Dr. R. G. Latham, have shown conclusively that although the German language has much Gothic in it, the German people of to-day are of Sarmatian, and not of Gothic, race; and consequently that language is not an invariable test of race, but possibly is only a proof of contact.

Hence, as there is positively nothing to vie with the Mosaic writings, no evidence of any sort to contradict them, and the history of the Israelites positively to affirm them, it would be worse than folly to disregard them in the pursuit of history. To show their immense value—and it is indeed a curious fact, but it is true—those who are most strongly opposed to the evidence afforded by the Scriptures in matters of history yet invariably base their system upon them, and that through the aid of a Jewish writer—Josephus. No one denies, but, on the contrary, every one is ready to admit, the Japhetian origin of the Aryan nations. The Greeks, Latins, Thracians, Goths, French, English, and Germans, are all said to be descended from the sons of Japhet. The Keltæ or the Galatæ are all Gomerites or the sons of Gomer, whilst the Greeks themselves are said to be descended from Javan, and the writings of Joshua are invoked to confirm it.

Tracing backward through successive historians for the first promoters of the Japhetian theory of our origin, we invariably find ourselves remitted to Josephus, and Christian writers, at least of our day, have accepted his testimony without cavil or investigation; but a very cursory examination of the facts will show that it is to be regarded with extreme suspicion, and that perhaps the only safe rule to be followed with regard to Josephus is only to follow him implicitly when he relates anything against himself; this was the canon laid down by St. Ambrose, and to follow it, at any rate, is a safe precaution. But this implicit trust in a man whose learning was known to be profound, and who was the custodian of writings of the highest value, is not to be wondered at; for even at his date no historian besides him had any pretension of being able to give an early and consecutive history, and to gain any fact at all men were obliged to adopt his fables.

# CHAPTER III.

## THE FABLES OF JOSEPHUS, AND THE TRUTHS TO BE LEARNED FROM HIS WORKS.

It may shock many right-minded people to read this title, and if it will only draw their attention to the truth, the writer's object will be obtained; for unquestionably Josephus has been relied upon implicitly, and he is an author who cannot be perfectly trusted. On reading the history of Moses, the mind would be prepared to find that at any rate the race of Shem would have a respectable portion of mankind assigned as their representatives, and a fair share of the globe assigned to them for a possession; but if we believe Josephus, the direct contrary is the fact. According to him, the sons of Japhet, and especially the issue of Javan, hold the first position amongst nations, and possess all the habitable portions of the globe. This fact alone should warn all believers in the inspiration of the Bible from putting any confidence in Josephus, and even those who only believe in it as at best an historical book, can only regard his evidence with extreme suspicion.

Josephus was himself a Jew, and the son of the high priest of the Jews. His position was remarkable and his opportunities great, but a cursory glance at his work is sufficient to satisfy us that we can gain nothing of value from it, and that, in fact, he had little or nothing to tell.

His work, as regards the early part of it, is simply a para-phrase of the books of Moses, and the fact that he does not carry the early account a step further, whilst at the same time he professes to bring it down to his own day, shows that the Jews of his date had, like their neighbours, broken the chain of ancient lore; and they, too, were in little better plight than the Greeks, who, for want of a true history of themselves, had adopted a heterogeneous mass of fable and superstition.

Josephus in his work admits that he had simply translated these antiquities from the sacred books, and he adds, "No one had been bold enough either to add anything to them, or to take anything from them, or to make any change in them;" and he is writing truthfully, for it is a fact that the pedigrees of Josephus, though interlarded with moral observations and some quaint reasonings, are in reality as bald and as deficient of information as the pedigrees of Moses. They throw no light whatever upon the interesting subject of the place of residence of the patriarch Noah and his descendants down to Terah, nor do they give more information re-specting the settlements of the younger branches of the family. Josephus has simply taken the names recorded by Moses, and, without supplying a single link, connects them severally with different nations existing in his own day. It is perfectly apparent from the animus exhibited, not only in the preface but in the body of the work, and especially from the subsequent book against Apion, that Josephus was most anxious to give all the information possible relative to his own people, and at the same time to malign and vilify his opponents. In his work against Apion, which was written some twenty years afterwards, perhaps about A.D. 100, the motive is more clearly apparent.

He was endeavouring to vindicate his race from the contemptuous and even cruel aspersions of his cotemporaries that they were of Egyptian origin, and had been driven out of Egypt because of their uncleanness. Although the exodus from Egypt had occurred some 1600 years previously, the traditions of that event were clear and distinct, and the Jews had only to appeal to the Book of Genesis to relieve them from this odious stigma. Clearly they had not preserved any other account, and as that related to a period so many hundred years earlier, it was of course impossible to invent one without transgressing the canon laid down by Josephus; and fortunately the proof is clear that Josephus did not attempt to add one jot or tittle to that word, but taking the account of Moses as it stood, and without adding fact or figure to it, he endeavoured to make it fit in with his malice and hatred of the Greeks by simply stating that the nations of his day were descended from the persons mentioned by Moses. He expressly states in his preface that he wrote his work for the benefit of all the Greeks. Whiston would have it that he uses the word, in the sense of Gentiles, to include not only the Greeks but the Romans —in fact, Gentiles as opposed to Jews; but there is no warrant for this supposition, and the fact that in the previous sentence the Romans are especially mentioned, proves that he wrote, as he expressed, for the benefit of the Greeks alone.

Messrs. Besant and Palmer, in their book upon Jerusalem, p. 12, supply us with a fact which would indicate how bitter and deep-rooted was the hatred between the Jews and the Greeks about this period, for they relate that in the time of Florus the Greeks added fresh matter for wrath by ostentatiously sacrificing birds in an earthen

vase as the Jews went to the synagogue, to signify that
they had been expelled from Egypt on account of their
being lepers, a calumny that nearly deprived Josephus
of his reason, for he made it the occasion of writing so
bitterly against them, that he would rob them of all glory
of antiquity, and of everything but present power.　He
sneered at them for their ancient ignorance, stating falsely
that they had not the use of letters till long after the age
of Homer, whereas modern researches prove their use even
in their colonies prior to his date.

And he endeavoured to retort upon them the libel of an
Egyptian origin, for nothing could be more bitter, in the then
degraded state of the Egyptians, than such an aspersion;
and in employing this *tu quoque* form of argument to the
Greeks, he desired at the same time to relieve his own
countrymen and to fix the aspersion upon his opponents.
He writes that Pherinedes the Syrian, Pythagoras, and
Thales—and he intimates the same of Hipparchus—with
one consent agree that they learned what little they knew
of the Egyptians and Chaldeans, and wrote but little.
Now undoubtedly the Egyptians pretended that they had
imparted their science not only to the Greeks but to the
Chaldeans, from whom, no doubt, they as well as the
Greeks and the Hebrews really learnt it; and Josephus
almost admits as much, for he writes in one place that the
first leaders and ancestors of the Jews were derived from
the Chaldeans, and that the Chaldeans had recorded the
relationship in their writings.

But this claim the elder Greeks repudiated, although,
perhaps, the modern Greeks, believing the aspersion of
Josephus, did not oppose the idea; or possibly it may be
that, knowing that they were of mixed origin, they were
not certain of their true relationship.　Hipparchus, who

claimed to have discovered the precession of the equinoxes, repudiated the notion that he had learnt the idea from them; and although it is clear that the builders of the great pyramid were well acquainted with it, it is not clear that the Egyptians themselves were acquainted with it previous to the teaching of Hipparchus. Indeed, the ignorance displayed in the building of the lesser pyramids would seem to indicate that they had no such knowledge. It is, however, extremely likely that the Chaldeans retained their knowledge and taught it to the Greeks— more likely than that the Greeks discovered it for themselves. The Greeks honestly confessed that they had obtained their knowledge from a foreign source, and the East is pointed to as the source from whence they obtained it; and from the East came the knowledge which designed the great pyramid and which enlightened the world. All historians agree that the science of the Egyptians was meagre and its influence weak and indeed, harmless (G. W. Cox, History of Greece, p. 25).

But in his account of the veracity of the Greek authors Josephus is still more bitter, and certainly most unfair. He writes: "I should spend my time to little purpose if I should pretend to teach the Greeks that which they know better than I already, what a great disagreement there is between Hellenicus and Acusilaus about their genealogies, in how many cases Acusilaus corrects Hesiod, or after what manner Ephorus demonstrates Hellenicus to have told lies in the greatest part of his history, as does Timeus in like manner as to Ephorus, and the succeeding writers do to Timeus, and all the later writers do to Herodotus."

Josephus was fond of the *tu quoque* argument, referring to the reproach of the Greeks that the Jews were only a

modern nation, a reproach which could not have been
possible had they not, as these records show, nearly lost
all knowledge of their history.  He writes, and especially to refute Agarthacliedes, Manethon, Cheremon, and
Lysimachus, that men should not attend to Grecian
accounts, since "almost all that concerns the Greeks
happened not long ago; nay, any one may say is of yesterday only.  I speak of the building of their cities, the
invention of their arts, and the description of their laws."
And he retaliates upon the Greeks on the score that the
Greek writers had not vouchsafed a bare mention of the
Jews by retorting that other nations had hardly mentioned
the Greeks.

It hardly requires the evidence of these facts to prove
how utterly the Jews had lost the art of recording their
own history, and the very fact that Josephus found it
necessary to write his history in defence of their antiquity proves that their origin was more than doubted.
That he did so in such temper warns us not to place
any reliance upon him when he is writing against his
opponents.

Now certainly it may be inferred from the similarity of
the religion, laws, language, literature, science, and arts
practised and known by the Greeks and Phœnicians that
they were of the same race, and the same may be inferred
of their relationship to the Israelites; and clearly they
all learnt at the same fount.  It was probably because this
kinship was more than hinted at that Josephus determined
to add to the sacred writings his views of the connection between the persons mentioned in Genesis with the
nations of the day in order to disprove it.

The ignorance of Josephus of any fact of history outside the sacred writings may be inferred from his mistake

in supposing the pillars of Seth, the son of Sesostris, to have been erected by Seth, the son of Adam. It is surprising that he could have believed in the existence of any antediluvian remains; and especially did he display his ignorance in confounding the occupation of Egypt by the Shepherd kings with the sojourn of the Israelites. (Sir Isaac Newton fell into the error of supposing the Hyksos to have been in Egypt long after the Israelitish residence—another extraordinary mistake in history.) The discovery of the true date of the pyramid of Ghiza by Piazzi Smyth, the Astronomer-Royal for Scotland, puts this question at rest by fixing it at 2170 B.C.; but Josephus' statements regarding the relationship of the Greeks and the Jews admit of no plea of ignorance, for he wrote with the Book of Maccabees before him; nay, in part of his History he actually records as a matter of sacred history, which he could neither discredit nor deny, that some of the Greeks, at any rate, and undoubtedly the first people amongst them, had not only asserted, but had been allowed by the Jews themselves to be of their stock, and this at the instance of the Jews themselves. Only 144 B.C., Jonathan, seeking to renew his league with the Romans and the Greeks, sent letters to them in the same form, and this form was saluting them as brethren. The letter is so curious and important, and so conclusive in proof of the Shemetic origin of the Greeks, that it is necessary to transcribe it; for not only does it show that the Greeks were of this race, but as the Spartans are, in fact, the very race from whom the Llogrians of England derive their origin, every fact relating to them is of interest to us.

The words are as follows:—"Areus, king of the Lacedemonians, to Onius the high priest sendeth greeting. It is found in writing that the Lacedemonians and Jews

C

are brethren, and that they are of the stock of Abraham.
Now, therefore, that this has come to our knowledge, ye
shall do well to write unto us of your prosperity." It is to
be observed that he only claims relation through the stock,
and not through the seed of Abraham, so that it may be that
the Lacedemonians were descended from Assur or Aram,
or from a younger son of any of the patriarchs in the line
of Abraham ; for we read that all of them had sons and
daughters, though no account whatever is given of their
settlements or history, which is not very remarkable,
seeing that the Mosaic account is equally silent as to the
habitation of all the patriarchs until Terah, and no intimation whatever is given whether they remained in Armenia,
sojourned like Abraham in Chaldea, or settled in Egypt.
This matter is recorded by Josephus, who had previously
written that all the Greeks were of Japhetian origin, and
not of the stock of Abraham, and he gives no explanation
of it, although he records that the Jews answered thus
(Antiq. v. 8) :—" We joyfully received the epistle, and were
well pleased with Demelites and Areus, although we did
not need such a demonstration, because we were well satisfied about it from the sacred writings, yet we did not think
fit first to begin the claim of this relation to you." The seal
used by King Areus was an eagle with a dragon or ser-
pent in its claws, the symbol of the tribe of Dan.

It seems very probable that Dan, the son of Jacob, was
one of the fathers of the Greeks, and gave his name to
the Danai, as well as to the river Danube, by which they
traversed Europe towards Scandinavia and the west, so
that whatever may be the origin of the Lacedemonians,
they have left their name through Europe, and especially
in the south of England and Ireland. The whole west
country of England was peopled by the Damnonians, as

was Ireland by the Tuatha de Dannans, or, as they were also called, Damnonians; the Tuatha probably meaning "from the North," and the " de " godlike or royal.

It is to be noted that Jonathan fully endorses the statement of Areus that the Spartans were of the stock of Abraham, for he expressly states that "we therefore at all times without ceasing, both in our festivals and other days whenever it is convenient, remember you in the sacrifices that we offer and in our observances, as it is meet and becoming to remember brethren." And this is further to be noted, that the first reminder of this relationship came from the Jews, for the letter of King Areus is clearly an answer to a letter similar to that of Jonathan's. This letter has been used recently to prove that the English are of Israelitish origin. It clearly fails to prove this, for the statement is that the Lacedemonians and Greeks were both of Abrahamic stock, and so they would have been if of the family of any of the race of Shem—of the Persians, Assyrians, Chaldeans, Sidonians, Trajanites, Armenians, Bactrians, or Messanians, all of whom Josephus admits to have been of Shemetic origin; so it may mean that they were descended from any of the younger branches of the main line of Abraham, of whom, with the exception of Joctan, the brother of Peleg, whose sons' names are given, no mention whatever is made except of the fact of their existence.

Josephus, in relating the history of the Greeks, is entirely silent as to this important evidence, although he sullenly sets it out in his history ; but he does refer to the fact that some of the Greeks had aforetime taken considerable pains to learn the affairs of the Jewish nation ; that the second of the Ptolemies was peculiarly ambitious to obtain in the Greek language a translation

of the Jewish laws and of the constitution of their govern-
ment, only a slight reference to the historical fact that
Eleazarus the high priest sent seventy-two interpreters to
King Ptolemy, who translated the Hebrew Scriptures into
Greek; but still sufficient to satisfy us regarding the
quarter from which the admission comes.

It is a curious fact in history that the Greeks, with this
evidence before them, ignore the fact of their relationship. Perhaps it was that when they found their claims
to relationship spurned by the Jews they suppressed all
mention of their thoughts upon the subject—a thing not
difficult in those days, when libraries were few and copies
of books scarce. Hence they submitted in silence to
Josephus' remarks, and they so passed current, and have
survived to this day to confound our knowledge.

Bearing in mind the intense hatred of Josephus to the
Greeks, and his desire to debase them, and to substitute
for their Shemetic a Japhetian pedigree, we will now see
what he writes concerning the origin of mankind; but
first it may be as well to notice that, as if to account for
the untruth he was about to publish, he writes that
some of the nations who were dispersed at the building of
the tower of Nimrod retain the denominations which
were given them by the first founders, but some have lost
them, and some have only admitted certain changes in
them, that they might be more intelligible to the inhabitants. It is difficult to see how this could be the case.
Time and ignorance work these changes; but there is no
evidence of people deliberately corrupting their names for
the benefit of their neighbours; and Josephus knew this
very well, for he presently gives another account, for he
writes, "The Greeks were the authors of such mutations;"
and he gives the reason for so doing, though it is rather

difficult to apply it. He writes, "When in after ages they grew potent, they claimed to themselves the glory of antiquity, giving names to the nations that sounded well in Greek, that they might be better understood amongst themselves, and setting agreeable forms of government over them, as if they were a people derived from themselves." This charge is somewhat borne out by some historians, who deduce the whole of the Keltæ from the Greeks; but, in fact, we owe it entirely to the Greeks themselves that the names of the nations conquered by them have been so accurately preserved, and certainly none of them have the same name as the Greeks. Even undoubted Greek colonies took different names, and the Greeks themselves not only differed from each other, but each tribe had several names: the multiplicity of their names is remarkable. It is Josephus, and not the Greeks, who have changed and moulded names. He tells us that the seven sons of Japhet inhabited so that, beginning at the mountains Taurus and Amanus, they proceeded along Asia as far as the river Tanais, and along Europe to Cades, and first peopled those parts. He is entirely silent as to whether they remained in these possessions, or whether they were ever driven out of them by men of a Shemetic race. Indeed, he only adds to the Mosaic account by giving the corruption of the names, which he alleges that the Greeks had made for their own purposes, whatever these may have been.

The Galatians, who were identical in blood and race with the Galileans, he declared to be the sons of Gomer. But he does not (and of course he cannot, for the Galatians and Galileans are Jews) produce any proof in support of the statement. In the same way he asserts that the Scythians were sons of Magog. In the same way the Medes

are said to be derived from Madai, and similarly he
deduces the Greeks from Javan; and no doubt Greece is
mentioned by that name in the sacred books, but called
Javan because the Greeks were worshippers of Juno,
and not from a supposed relationship to the son of
Japhet. So Tubal is father of the Iberes; Meshech of the
Cappadocians; Tiras of the Thracians, which again is not
the name of a race, but of a country; Ashkenaz was father
of the Rheginians; Riphath of the Paphlagonians; Togarmah of the Phrygians; Elisha of the Etolians; Thirsas
of the Cilicians; Cetim of the Cypriotes,—all statements
made without a shadow of proof, and in the face of every
probability, philological and historical. Josephus, indeed,
is aware of this, for he adopts the old stage-trick of the
orator to distract attention. He adds, "And so many
nations have the children and grandchildren of Japhet
possessed, and when I have premised somewhat which
perhaps the Greeks do not know, I will return and explain
what I have omitted, for such reasons as are premised
here, after the manner of the Greeks, to please my reader,"
—a promise which, of course, he did not fulfil.

In reference to the children of Ham, he does not pretend to possess such extraordinarily accurate and sound
information, and he admits that some of their names have
utterly vanished, quite unlike the Japhetians, every man
named amongst them, except Dodanim, being represented
by great nations, though curiously none of the issue of the
patriarchs who are not named by Moses have, according to
Josephus, become the fathers of nations. Others of the
Hametic race, he admits, must have had their names
changed and another sound given to them, so that they
are hardly to be discovered; yet a few of them there are
which have kept their denominations entire, and of these

few names he adds (as we should expect) that he knew nothing of them beside their names.

Of the race of Shem he is bound, as a Jew, to be more particular, but he confined his accounts to statements which were too well known to be disputed, and to regions which did not affect the question. Elam, he writes, is father of the Elamites or Persians, Assur of the Assyrians, Arphaxad of the Chaldeans, Lud of the Lydians, Aram of the Syrians, who were subdivided into Traconites and Damascenes, representing Uz, the Armenians, the descendants of Ul, Gether being the parent of the Bactrians, and Alesa of the Messanians. He omits to tell us where the younger children of the following patriarchs resided, viz., those of Arphaxad, Salah, Eber, Peleg, Reu, Serug, and Nahor; and of the thirteen sons of Joctan, he only says that they inhabited from Cophen, an Indian river, and part of Asia adjoining to it.

He also wholly omits all mention of the Edomites and of the youngest sons of Noah; yet they, as well as the other descendants of the race of Shem, were of the same blood as the Israelites; and we have only to remember the instance of Job, who is reputed an Edomite, to see that they were of the same way of thinking. Job or Jobab, king of Uz in Arabia-Petrea, was not a descendant of Aram. The Mosaic account relates that Edom dwelt in the land of Uz, but was a son of Zerah, the grandson of Esau (Epiphanius adv. Hær., lib. i. p. 10; Jerome, Quæst. Heb. in Gen.; Theodoret, Quæst. in Gen.; and see the notes to Bellamy's Bible). So of the other persons mentioned in his history. Eliphaz the Temanite was also an Edomite; Bildad the Shuhite was a descendant of Shuah, son of Abraham by Keturah; Elihu the Buzite was a son of Nahor, Abraham's brother. The Sabeans who plundered

Job's folds descended from Sheba, son of Jockshan, son of
Abraham by Keturah, as the Chaldeans were descended
from Chesid, son of Nahor.    How is it that Josephus had
no knowledge of the descendants of these people ?    That all
the Shemetic races were existing in the days of Solomon
and David is evident from the fact that the Israelites
were forbidden to marry with them; yet they did so, and
Solomon himself took wives of the Moabites, Ammonites,
Edomites, Zidonians, and Hittites; so Ahab, king of Israel,
married a Zidonian, the wicked Jezebel; and the Israelites
through these marriages worshipped their gods, Astoreth
and Bel of the Zidonians, Chemosh of the Moabites, and
Milcom of the Ammonites.

That the whole of the Syrians were of Shemetic race
there is little doubt, as it is clear they were in close
alliance when David attacked the Ammonites (2 Sam. x.
6).    They hired the Syrians of Bethrehob, and of Zoba
20,000 footmen, and of Ishtob 12,000; and when David
attacked the king of Zoba, the Syrians of Damascus
came to their succour, and David slew 22,000 of them;
and they were not destroyed like the Hametic races, but
became tributary to the Jews, David putting garrisons in
Syria of Damascus.

Mons. D'Ankerville asserts that the Sacæ were the first
people who made nations conquered by them tributary to
themselves, though he does not, and cannot, of course, find
any evidence in support of the proposition; but assuming
that they were of Shemetic race, of which there is no
doubt, their knowledge and science, habits and customs,
would be the same, and this amongst them would be a
common habit or custom.    It is expressly stated in
Samuel that the Syrians so subject to David brought gifts;
and it is recorded that Adoram was over the tribute, as

he continued in the days of Solomon. This officer seems to have died in Spain, while he was probably collecting tribute, as it is there recorded in Hebrew characters. Unfortunately no accounts exist of Hebrew colonies or dependencies, or better evidence would be forthcoming of the spread of the Shemetic race, but it is sufficiently clear that the Israelites colonised extensively throughout the world. The Mosaic writings give evidence of the fact, and the traditions of various nations confirm it. There is little doubt but that, under the name of Phœnicians or traders, were comprised Israelites as well as Tyrians and Sidonians. The first settlers of Gadis were probably Gadites, as the first settlers of Denmark were said by their traditions to have been of the tribe of Dan. The prophets relate that the whole of the tribe had taken to ships, *i.e.*, had become Phœnicians. Besides, through the offspring of the Shemetic race, other than that of the Israelites, there were long before the time of Josephus many distant settlements of Israelites. It speaks volumes for the ignorance of Josephus that he does not mention one of them, nor does he enumerate more than a few of the descendants of the other Shemetic races. He relates at second hand, on the authority of Alexander Polyhistor, that Cleodamus writes that Sarun was the ancestor of the Assyrians; Apper and Japheus peopled Africa, and they were auxiliaries of Hercules when he fought against Lydia, and that Antæus Hercules married Apper's daughter, and begat Didones, who begat Sopher, the father of the Sophocians.

Now, considering that Josephus was expressly writing the history of the Jews, it is rather singular that he knew nothing of the history of the Shemetic race, and yet was so extremely positive concerning the history of the Greeks, which he was not writing.

But a more serious objection still exists. Assuming for a moment that his etymologies are correct, that the Gomerites are identical with the Galatæ, the Iberi with Tubal, the Cappadocians with Meshech, and so forth, it by no means follows that, in the absence of any proof of identity, these persons can be held to be identical with the race of Japhet; for it is a fact that, in the few pedigrees which Moses gave, it was a common practice for several families to adopt the same name. Cain had descendants named Enoch, Mehajael, Methusael, and Lamech; and Seth had also Enoch, Mahalaleel, Methuselah, and Lamech; and Cain had a descendant Tubal, as had Japhet; Shem had a son Aram, so had Nahor; Joctan a Shemite, Ramah a Hamite, and Joctan, son of Abraham, had each of them a son, Sheba; and, more curious still, both Joctan and Jockshan had each of them two sons called Sheba and Dedan. In fact, so frequently does the same name occur, that no argument is to be drawn from similarity of name; and when Josephus naïvely admits that in the case of Shem and Ham he had no information beyond the mere names, he cannot be believed in his statement regarding the sons of Japhet, unless he can produce some evidence in support of it. This he utterly fails to do; and he admits that his statements are against the traditions of the people themselves (indeed they are utterly opposed to them); yet, unfortunately, Josephus' statements have been accepted as true by all English ethnologists without any attempt to question them, and this in face of the fact that all the time there are people to be found in different parts of the world bearing the very names he has misappropriated, and answering far more to the description of the children of Japhet. More than this, Josephus shows no shadow of reason why the children of

Shem should not have peopled other countries besides those they no doubt at one time inhabited, or why they should remain in them for ever. There can be little doubt that, just as the Jews supplanted the Canaanites and were supplanted in their turn, the modern Persians no more represent the Shemetic race of Elam than do the Germans of to-day in many parts of Germany represent the Germans of Tacitus. Nations have been migratory ever since the world began, and passion must indeed have blinded the reason of Josephus before he could endeavour to write such manifest errors and misstatements. But adopting the idea of St. Ambrose, and believing him only when he speaks against himself, at any rate the Chaldeans, Persians, Assyrians, Syrians, Lydians, Traganites, Armenians, Bactrians, and Messanians must by this day have become the fathers of many nations, as they certainly were the fathers of the Thracians, Spartans, and other Greeks ; and yet our modern ethnologists, knowing full well that the present denizens of these countries are aliens in race to the Shemetic family, confine the issue of Shem to a very small population beside the Jews, who, of course, only represent two of the twelve tribes of Israel. That the other tribes are existing somewhere no one who believes in the sacred writings can doubt, but no one can state positively which of the nations now possess or represent them. To do so requires the gift of prophecy. Before asserting who are the Israelites, it must be determined which amongst modern nations are the Elamites, the Assurites, Ludites, and Aramites, which the younger descendants of the whole race of patriarchs, which the children of Joctan, of Nahor, and which of the younger sons of Abraham. Although it is clear that the fact of a name of a place coinciding with that of a race is not conclusive evidence of their settlement, or the Israelites would be Canaanites, yet it is probable proof that the race once dwelt there, and probably had there its primary settlement; and it must be obvious that the race of Shem had their settlements somewhere; that as the Canaanites increased in numbers and power, the Sethites, or Shemetic race, would seek other countries in order to avoid them is equally clear; and hence we may safely conclude two things: first, that the Shemetic race had originally settlements in Asia, and that they subsequently found it necessary to send out colonies (as we know certain of their number were chosen by lot) to settle in other countries. The Welsh traditions aver that their ancestors left their home in the East to avoid war and bloodshed, and to take possession of lands by peaceable means.

Even Josephus admits that the descendants of Shem were not absolutely extinct in his day; and although he gives no intimation of the localities of their colonies, he does intimate their original homes in Asia. He could not indicate any of the known peoples of his age as colonists from these countries without at the same time showing their affinity to the Greeks, whom he abhorred, and whose birth and origin he wished to decry. His evidence upon this point is especially valuable, coming from such an opponent.

It is quite clear that the Jews established many colonies, for we find from the Scriptures that many lived in Parthia, Media, Elam, Mesopotamia, and Lybia, and so large a number as 50,000 were slain at Alexandria at one time. If, then, the Jews could colonise, why not the other Shemetic families? According to Josephus' account, they appear originally to have occupied the greater part of the habitable portion of Western Asia; why should they be

confined to these spots? Josephus admits that in his
days the ten tribes were dwelling in Medea, a countless
multitude. Now, if it can be shown that any one of the
Shemetic nations which Josephus admits were existing in
his day had colonies in Europe, his testimony as to the
posterity of Japhet is at an end, especially if some of
the nations actually credited to Japhet are in reality of
Shemetic origin; and nothing is easier than to prove this,
for Moses has taught us this grand lesson in ethnology,
that we have only to trace back a nation to the parent
stem to know at once to which of the three sons of Shem
it belongs. He has given us that amount of information
in his genealogies, and no more; and that is sufficient, for
with patience and industry almost every nation of the earth
may be traced back to this necessary period. It would
take many volumes to do this work properly, and in this
book but only a slight indication of the task can be attempted. Taking Aram by example, Josephus asserts that
the Syrians are descended from him, and these he divides
into Armenians, descendants of Ul; Bactrians, of Gether;
Messanians, of Mesa; Traconites and Damascenes, of Uz.
The most important of all these to ourselves undoubtedly is the settlement of Hul or Chul in the country of
Armenia; from this country, by different routes, came the
races which ruled once more in the British Isles and in
Gaul. Armenia is probably derived from Aram, which
is the same as Syria, old authors including under that
name Mesopotamia as well as Syria Proper. Jacob in
the Hebrew is called an Aramite, though in the English
version the word is translated a Syrian. In the name of
Chul or Hul we have probably the root of all the forms
of the names by which the Kelts first styled themselves,
as Keltai, Celtie, Galati, Galli, Gael, &c., &c.

So as obviously from Gether are descended the Getæ. The Bactrians, whom Josephus asserts are his descendants, are clearly of the same race as the Mesogoths or Mesæ, the descendants of Mesa, the father of the Messanians of Mesopotamia, who were of the same Getic race as the Thracians, and the fathers of all the Goths, as the Mesæ of Syria are connected, under the name of Scythæ, by Homer and Hesiod with the Mysi of Bulgaria.

Uz founded, according to Josephus, the country of Damascus and Traconitis, from whom the Trojans were descended, probably extending to the Red Sea or to the borders of Egypt, for Edom is said in Scripture to have lived in the land of Uz.

Tradition asserts that the Ark rested upon Mount Ararat, which is again the same name as Armenia, and as the Araxes undoubtedly takes its name from this district, for it has another name, or that of Kir, before it falls into the Caspian Sea, this spot was probably the cradle of the race of Shem, as it was undoubtedly afterwards that of the Sacæ or Scythians, or the Sacasani, as they called themselves, or, as we call them, the Saxons.

To the Persians, according to the testimony of Herodotus, the words Sacæ and Scythæ were synonymous, or at any rate, they styled all the Scythæ Sacæ, and the Scythæ, according to the same authority, styled themselves Scoloti, from whence came these several words. Philology is helpless and unable to assist us.

The Prince Lucien Louis Bonaparte, to whom the author is indebted for much light upon the philological questions of this thesis, positively asserts that the words Sacæ, or Saxon, and Scythæ, cannot possibly be derived from the same root; that by no law of transmutation can such a change have been effected; that the words are radically and essentially different. It is presumptuous, in the face of so distinguished a philologist, to suggest the contrary; yet this is evident, the Sacæ were Scythæ. Leaving the question of the roots of these words, can we derive any aid from their meaning? Take the word Scythæ or Scythian. The Greeks who presented it to us are unacquainted with its meaning; they did not invent it, they only recorded its existence. From whence did it come and what does it represent?

As Professor Newman has observed, no term has been used with such infinite license as that of Scythian. The ancients reckoned fifty nations or more as Scythian, probably including those nations under tribute; but they distinguished the Scythians proper as Royal Scythians. Possibly the De of the Scythians of Ireland, the Tuatha de Dannans, may mean this same word royal. Mons. D'Ankerville (Huguet), in his valuable and most learned work, "Recherches sur l'Origine, &c., des Artes de la Grece" (vol. i. p. 44), argued that the idols made by Terah, the father of Abraham, were necessarily Scythian, since the Scythian religion was the only religion then in existence; and on the authority of St. Epiph. adv. Hæres (lib. i.), he divides what he terms religious errors under four heads or divisions:—First, Barbarism, a system which existed before any religion whatever; secondly, Scythism or Scuthismos (Mons. D'Ankerville seems to have followed Goropius in the use of this word, as in many other things); thirdly, Helenism, which succeeded it; and, fourthly, Judaism. Perhaps Jews and Christians alike might quarrel with this classification, on the ground that religion number four was first of all, and preceded the religion of barbarism, which may be taken as another form of Canaanitism; and this being so, Judaism or Deism would be identical with Scythism or Scuthismos; for although Hellenism, or the religion of the Greeks, was undoubtedly founded upon the worship of the first Scythian monarchs and heroes, it is admitted that originally the Scythians worshipped but one God, and that He was not identified with humanity, or the degrading thing-worship of the Egyptians. But unsound as perhaps Mons. D'Ankerville may be on matters of religion, in matters of science, subject to such errors, he is undoubtedly a giant, and in this absurd division of religious errors he may unwittingly have enunciated a great truth, and presented to us the germ of the word, the solution of which we require. For granted that Scythian is a term not of nationality but of habit or custom, what more likely than that it represented the grand difference which then as now existed between men, although in those days not of such infinite variety and form as at present? What more likely than that it did represent the religion of the people, and designated by that word the grand distinction between nations? And if this is so, we shall find from a closer investigation of the manners and customs of the Sacæ, and contrasting them with those of their neighbours not of Shemetic origin, that the religion of the Sacæ Scythians was, as we should expect from their locality, that of Shem, or rather that of Seth—that they were Sethites, as opposed to their Canaanitish neighbours. It would seem that no philological shadow need come between us and an absolute identity of these two words, Sethism and Scythism. Perhaps the logical conclusion to be drawn from Mons. D'Ankerville's argument is literally and absolutely correct, and in the former we find the germ of the root of the latter.

There is, however, a derivation at hand much more pro-

bable, and that is, that the word Scythian is only a form of
the word Goth or Getic. We get this word from the Greeks,
and they have no meaning for it. The German derivation from the word Scytan, to shoot, is as absurd as their
meaning of the word Welsh. A Welshman is a foreigner
to a German, therefore, they argue, he is so to all the world.
The Scythians were great shooters, and gave their name
to the art, therefore their name is derived from it. This
is the childish form of reasoning which passes current in
our great universities, and it is flat blasphemy to hint that
it is not entirely satisfactory. But take the Greek form
of Scythæ, and you have *skuthes* or *sguthes;* discard the
letter *s,* which the Greeks often add, and you have *guthes,*
which is certainly very much like Gothes or Goths. According to this reasoning, the Scythians· were the sons of
Gether. We know the Bactrians were a Getic race, and so
were the Mesogethæ, and so all the Scythian races ; so
were the Parthians ; probably the Spartans added the *s,*
as the Greeks frequently did. Now the Greeks undoubtedly
had amongst them various peoples who were clearly descended from the Getic or Thracian people, so the Spartans were unquestionably Shemetic (whether Parthians
or not), so they had colonies from Messania, from Lydia,
from Traconitis and Damascus—in fact, from every part of
Syria ; yet Josephus assigns the Thracians to a Japhetian
origin, and so with all the Greek tribes. And if it is true
of many Grecian nations, it must also be true of Grecian
colonies, and they undoubtedly colonised the whole of the
Mediterranean coasts, great parts of Italy, and much of the
continent of Europe ; as, for instance, the Spartans colonised
Liguria, and· Liguria colonised France and England ; the
Goths or Getæ spread over the whole of North-Western
Europe and returned to settle in the south. Yet Josephus

D

avers that all these nations were of Japhetian origin. The question arises, What then became of the progeny of the Shemetic races? and no answer can be given to it. This is alone sufficient proof of Josephus' malice or ignorance, probably of both.

The Book of Maccabees affords the strongest evidence that the Grecian colonies were regarded by the Jews as of Shemetic race, for Jonathan sent similar letters to those addressed to the Spartans to some of the Romans, and to other places besides Sparta.

Mr. Hemming writes respecting the trustworthiness of Josephus :—"An historian put to his choice between two discordant accounts must reject one of them. Now Josephus has in his History given us an account of the seventy-two interpreters in their separate cells, producing each a distinct translation that agreed literatim and verbatim one with another. Is it to be supposed that he believed what he had heard respecting this miraculous Greek work, or did he mean to impose on the credulous by making what he knew to be knavery appear like inspiration? If the latter was his motive, it deserves the severest censure and contempt; and if he credited what he had been writing, his understanding must have been defective. . . . But it cannot be said of Josephus that above all things he regarded truth, for his work is filled with legends " (ix.).

"Josephus stands alone and unsupported by any corroborative testimony, either scriptural, astronomical, or historical, and this even when, instead of consistent, he is contradictory throughout " (x.).

The author is not ashamed to avow that, before he looked into the history of the feud between Josephus and the Greeks, on which much more hinges than the mere science of history, he believed that the Japhetian theory of our origin was the correct one; that he adopted it, as other writers have done, without so much as questioning its truth; that he wrote and acted upon it as if it was unquestionably sound. The only marvel is, that it has so long remained not only unchallenged, but has actually been adopted as the basis of history by all writers and parties alike, and this, as it has been shown, without either probability or evidence to support it. There is no account of the origin of nations which is not based upon it, and therefore it is quite open to us to speculate upon the true history of our race, and to discover it if possible.

# CHAPTER IV.

## ON THE SOURCES OF POSITIVE EVIDENCE.

THE author has endeavoured to demonstrate in his "History of the Common Law" and his introduction to the "Study of Early English History" how little reliance is to be placed upon the generally received sources of evidence; that, especially in the case of British history, the positive evidence is most untrustworthy; that the magnificent collection of charters formed by Mr. Kemble are none of them taken from authentic documents, but from transcripts of doubtful value; and that if any Saxon charters are brought forward at this date, since the Saxons themselves did not employ writing in the transfer of land, and so great an antiquary as Selden had never seen one in his day, we could only regard it with the gravest suspicion. The writer has also demonstrated that the so-called Life of Alfred by Asser is in reality a concoction by Archbishop Parker, who took a poor tract of that title, which contained nothing of real value, and interlarded it with legends drawn from various suspicious sources. This is no libel upon the character of the Archbishop, for he has left behind him at Oxford the actual proofs of. his forgery. No doubt he himself believed that he was only adding to it what was in his day believed to be another of Asser's works, but which has since been demonstrated to be the work of another and much later author.

Striking out of Parker's Life of Alfred by Asser all

the interpolated passages, nothing remains except a Latin
equivalent (probably the original) of this portion of the
Saxon Chronicle; and as the whole of the preceding
portion of this work is simply an abstract of Bede and
Eusebius, &c., and the subsequent work down to the time
of Marianus Scotus (who was clearly the author of it, as
is demonstrated in the writer's book on "Early English
History") consists of a few poor dry records extracted from
monkish registers of little practical value. This much-
vaunted Saxon Chronicle, which so many writers have
tried to glorify, and on which so much of what is called
English history depends, is a record of the eleventh
century of little authority—so little, that William of
Malmesbury hardly so much as mentions it, or, if he
does, he describes it in such terms of contempt that, for
its character's sake, it had better have escaped all mention. And if bitter disappointment awaits the historical
student who honestly endeavours to sift the evidence of
the so-called Saxon histories and charters, still greater
disappointment awaits him who, if the passage in Bede
is not a forgery or interpolation, would endeavour to
discover the dooms of the kings of Kent, enacted, with
the advice of the wise men of the time, after a Roman
model, if indeed the so-called Saxon codes really are
intended to supply the documents adverted to. The
whole of the Saxon codes are dependent upon a single
MS. of the twelfth century of a somewhat suspicious
character, and there is powerful evidence against the
authenticity of any of them, as the writer has fully
pointed out in the fact, amongst others, that they were not
forthcoming, as they should have been, when William the
Conqueror instituted his inquiry concerning the Saxon
laws. In fact, there is scarcely a document of any kind

whatever, if we except a few clerical writings of a date
prior to the Conquest, that can be relied upon; and the
reason is obvious.  The Roman occupation had destroyed
the Keltic literature of the island, and had left nothing
to replace it.  With the destruction of the Druidical order
learning perished.  This was happily not the case in
Ireland, because the Romans had no power there; and
hence we find that Ireland, after the departure of the
Romans from England, stood out as the most learned country
perhaps in the whole world; and to Ireland, at any rate,
the whole of Europe was indebted for the learning which
survived the decay of the Roman Empire.

Those who have invented the Saxon literature which
is the basis of modern English history had an object
in view.  It was originally hatred and contempt of the
French people that suggested the notion of creating a
history independent of them.  It was subsequently a
desire to flatter a German dynasty that actuated writers
to ignore the truth and to refurbish the ancient fables; but
as, in fact, the English and French have a common origin—
common too with the Scotch, Irish, and Welsh, each wave
of people settling contemporaneously in each country—
it was necessary to invent very largely to form a completely independent history; and very largely have these
inventions been created, the offspring of passion and
hatred fostered by prejudice and ignorance.  The result
was a history of a people which was no history, for it did
not account for their origin or place of residence, or for
their very name.  No one pretended to state from whence
the Angles and Saxons were produced, except that it was
asserted that they came from a country from which they
borrowed their name, which was physically incapable of
supporting them or of affording them sustenance—a

theory so wild and improbable that it refutes itself. In his previous publications the author pointed this out, and was called to task by the critics for being in a fog concerning their origin, a fact which he honestly avowed. Recent research has made it evident that the so-called Saxons had no history of their own, simply because they were in no way separate from the rest of the British people; and if they were, the last-comers were derived from the same sources as their predecessors. This being so, the author was right in stating that if the character of the Saxon Chronicle were destroyed, as it has been, there was nothing left to represent what has been boastfully termed Saxon literature, since every previous writing of authority, including the Life of Alfred by Asser, was written in Latin; and inasmuch as it is admitted by the Anglo-Saxon professors that Anglo-Saxon, as it is called, has, unlike any other language, but one stage, or rather that it has no stages or periods of improvement or variation, the oldest and most archaic writings being undistinguishable from the latest, it follows that the alleged total destruction or loss of Saxon literature was a fable; that there was no destruction and no loss because it never had any existence; and, as the author suggested, the so-called Anglo-Saxon language was probably only a written language after it had ceased to be spoken, and that when spoken it was only the patois of a single district; that the whole of middle England, and the north, south, east, and west, were inhabited by people who spoke a language almost, if not entirely, in accordance with our modern English, and that this tongue was not German or Saxon, but English or Keltic. But because we are destitute of written evidence of our early history, it by no means follows that we do not possess any. We

have still traditions, and some of them have been recorded
by our neighbours the Welsh and Irish; and as they
rightly belong to us as much as to themselves, we may
still derive much aid from them in the composition of
our own history.

## CHAPTER V.

### ON THE VALUE OF TRADITIONARY EVIDENCE.

THE histories of most nations and peoples are founded upon some substratum of truth, and although it may be disfigured by fable or exaggerated by fancy or design, their traditions may yet be made available and of real service as the proofs of a nation's origin; and these evidences cannot be safely thrown aside as wholly useless and unreliable. Direct evidence of an absolute and undeniable character we cannot hope to obtain. No people except the Jews can boast of such a possession, and their history, after all, is confined to particular epochs, and is more an account of their moral system and of their laws than a record of the calamities and the events which have befallen the race. Their personal history is chiefly to be found in the Pentateuch. Many facts of value no doubt are to be gathered from the sacred books besides those written by Moses, but they are principally of a chronological and dry nature, and lack the wonderful and abiding interest of his work, which has a beauty and a freshness unequalled in the wide domain of literature.

The early histories of most nations lack this vitality, and are generally dull and uninteresting; but reading them by the light of sacred history, this dulness vanishes, and the highest interest is excited by the discovery that, under the guise of new, and it may be of uncouth names,

the ancient chronicler is endeavouring to describe the
history of our first parents, of their fall, of the sin of mankind, and of the Flood which ensued upon it; and, spite
of erroneous names and facts, a patient investigation
will enable us to discover that the first founder of the
race is alleged to be the patriarch Noah, he who repeopled the earth after the overthrow of mankind at
the Flood.

The science of tradition, or, as it is often called in these
scientific days of comparative mythology, like the sister
science of comparative philology, is in its infancy, but
happily, unlike that science, it has not made a false start,
and is not at present trammelled by forms and errors
which prevent its proper appreciation and culture. At
any rate, there are good books upon the subject, and
foremost amongst them is the very able and learned work
of Lord Arundel of Wardour, "Tradition Principally
with Reference to Mythology," which in a small compass
places before us a view of the early traditions and myths
of mankind, contrasted with the facts of sacred history,
of which they are mere contortions, and which invests
those myths with an interest they had hitherto wanted.

Who would care to study the dry details of a nation's
mythology for its own sake? What interest is it to read
that the first progenitor of the race was not merely a
hero, but was invested with godlike attributes? If only
the old chroniclers following Moses would have kept
these heroes human, we might have read of their prowess
with interest; but the love of the marvellous engrafted
upon ignorance and credulity has robbed their actions of
all interest, and we turn aside from their musty accounts
with derision or disgust; but this disappears at once if
we find that there is a reality about these personages after

all, and that their identity may be made manifest by the
science of comparative mythology.

If we find that the persons of Noah, Adam, the fact
of the Deluge, and other great events, can be identified
by reference to the mythology of the Chinese, of the
Egyptians, of the Assyrians, and other nations of the
greatest antiquity, and later in the Greek and Latin
mythology, we may hope to find these personages and
events typified in our own histories; and if we do, it raises
a still further hope that by means of these myths we may
gain something in the way of fact which shall throw a
clear light upon our origin, and pave the way for greater
and more important discoveries.

A writer has observed that we are wont to regard
the Grecian mythology and its many-coloured world of
fables only as the beautiful effusion of poetry or a play-
ful creation of fancy, and we never think of inquiring
deeply or minutely into its details, or of examining its
moral import and influence. It is the more natural that
the mythology of the Greeks should produce this impres-
sion on our minds, and that we should regard it in
this light, as all the higher ideas and severer doctrines
of the Godhead, its sovereign nature and infinite might,
on the Eternal Wisdom and Providence that conducts and
directs all things to their proper end, on the infinite
and Supreme Intelligence that created all things, and
that is raised far above external nature: all these higher
ideas and severer doctrines have been expounded more
or less perfectly by Pythagoras or by Anaxagoras and
Socrates, and have been developed in the most beautiful
and luminous manner by Plato and the philosophers that
followed him.

But all this did not pass into the popular religion of

the Greeks, and it remained for the most part a stranger
to these exalted doctrines; and though we find in the
mythology many things capable of a deeper import and
more spiritual significance, yet they appear but as rare
vestiges of ancient truth, vague presentments, fugitive
tones, momentary flashes, revealing a belief in a Supreme
Being, an Almighty Creator of the universe, and the common Father of mankind.

Mr. Gladstone (Homer and the Homeric Age, vol. ii. sec.
1, p. 8) takes a higher view of the matter. He suggests, writing upon Homer's poems, " That if they contain a picture,
even though a defaced picture, of the primeval religious
traditions, it is obvious that they afford a most valuable collateral support to the credit of the Holy Scriptures, considered as a document of history." This may be necessary
to some minds; but inverting the reasoning, and assuming
the Holy Scriptures to be true—and the author is so un-
learned that he knows of no possible grounds upon which
to assail them—how very valuable these proofs become in
throwing light upon contemporaneous history; and the
more defaced and deformed the mythic account may be, so
much the more credit may generally be attached to it, as
it is some evidence, at any rate, of its having been handed
down separately, and not borrowed, like the German
myths, of its neighbours. No sort of interest attaches to
German legends, simply because they are bad copies of
the Scandinavian; but the highest interest attaches to
the Scandinavian, because they are unlike the myths of
any other country, and form within themselves a complete
mythology. Unless we claim a share in the Scandinavian
system, the English have no myths but what are common to the Gaelic branches of the Keltic family, the
Irish and Gaelic, and we are not entitled to a share of

that fund, if our modern historians are correct, and we are Saxon in the sense of a German people.

In English historians we are unfortunate. Our greatest historical writers, Gibbon, Hume, and others of old date, and many of the present day, are too learned or scientific to believe in the sacred histories, and of course, therefore, as they have no standpoint from which to estimate the value of the old traditions, they have no course but to reject them; and accordingly our early histories are treated as too ridiculous and foolish to be taken into account, and our historians usually commence their histories at the most obscure epoch of our whole history, when, through the violence and ignorance of the age, we have actually nothing tangible to guide us. Of late years, indeed, some men have ventured to act upon the idea that, after all, our nation may have had some more brilliant origin than " the backwoods of a German forest," and that the earlier history, which at one time was read and cherished in every library, may contain the germs of truth; and certainly, by comparing them with the certain landmarks of the Sacred Scriptures, many facts may be gleaned which make it obvious that a severer study may be attended by greater success. Putting aside for the present the old British view of the Trojan origin of our ancestors—a myth shared by the French before they became too learned to believe in anything—take the Welsh tradition of a descent from Hu Gadarn. Comparative mythology shows at a glance that this is another name for Noah, and, very curiously, very similar to the name known to the Assyrians, who were derived from the tribes of the Scythians, who, it is believed, were living adjacent to those who were the progenitors of the Cymric race. The Syrian name for Noah is Hoa, which is readily

obtained from Noah, N'oah, Oah, Hoah or Hea (see the
account of Hea or Hoa in Rawlinson's "Ancient Mon-
archies," i. 152). That this is truly derived from the
word Noah is apparent from comparing the changes in
the word ship: Latin, *navis;* Greek, *naus.* In Armenia
it is Naw, as nearly Noah as we could expect; and in
Bas-Breton it is Neau. Dropping the first letter, Hau or
Hoa becomes Heau or Hu; and that this is a correct
deduction is proved by facts which accompany the
tradition.

This similarity of names by which the ancient Welsh
and the Assyrians both designated Noah, if it is not a
direct proof of a connection between them, is strong presump-
tive proof of it, and would be sufficient, in the absence of
all other, to indicate the line of search. It, however,
does not stand alone, for the record brings the nations
back to the same spot; not, indeed, to the Assyrian
home, but to the East, and, as will be shown presently, to
the very spot from which the Assyrians and their brethren
wandered—a remarkable indication, and one well worthy
of the closest study and investigation. The subject of
the tradition of Noah and the Ark is of importance in
proof of the origin of the Welsh, and it is worth while to
seek the ideas of learned men upon the subject. It would
seem that the fact of the Flood is a tradition of nearly
every nation who is possessed of a separate history, though,
of course, each nation appropriates the event to itself and
to its own territory. Lord Arundel upon Tradition, in
which, anticipating the objection that his theory supposes
a chronology altogether out of keeping with modern
discovery, and to the popular idea that modern science
has an historical basis to which not even the Septuagint
chronology can be made to conform, writes (page 55):—

"This really is not the case; but assuming it to be true, I must still remark, that if facts of primeval tradition have been established, the long lapse of ages will only enhance our notions of the persistency of tradition; or if the lapse of ages is disproved, this tradition will be in recognition of a truth to which tradition testifies."

Lord Arundel shows, from an examination of the chronology of the principal nations whose annals profess to go back to the commencement of things—the Indian, Persian, Greek, Roman, Babylonian, Chinese, Phœnician, and Egyptian—that there is a general concurrence in the history of each people of there having been a great Deluge, and that at a period which practically is dated near to the epoch denoted in the Mosaic writings.

The reader must be referred to the curious evidence adduced by this author in support of this view. It is not only satisfactory, it is convincing.

But the most important testimony to the fact of the Flood is afforded by the Greek traditions. As we should expect, the pupils and children of the Phœnicians, although they had somewhat defaced and degraded the story, yet retained its most salient points. The Greeks, as Lord Arundel points out, like nearly all other nations, post-dated the event and located it; and this is so invariably the case, both as to time and place, that, in accordance with the custom of modern science, it may be said to be reduced to a law—the law being that every nation applied to its own history those great points of history which belong to all mankind, and that every true event is certain to be post-dated, just as all fabulous traditions have a fabulous antiquity assigned to them.

The Greeks post-dated the Deluge by more than 1200 years. They assigned it to the year 1528 B.C., which was

probably an important era in their history—possibly the
real date of the immigration of the Pelasgii, who doubtless,
as the descendants of Shem, brought this tradition with
them. This is the date of their expulsion from Egypt.
When we remember that the first year of the Olympiad
is only 776 B.C., or only a trifle more than half the
period assigned to the Deluge from the Christian era,
it will be obvious that this date is only one guessed at
long after the event.

Deukalion, the father of Helen, the great eponym of
the Hellenic race, according to Greek traditions was,
with his wife Pyrrha, saved at the Deluge in a chest or
ark, which he had been forewarned by his father Prometheus to construct, and after floating on the waters he at
length landed on the summit of Mount Parnassus. Zeus,
upon his prayers for companions, directed him and Pyrrha
to cast stones over their shoulders; those cast by Pyrrha
became women, and those by Deukalion men. (This is
the etymology adopted by Grote, upon the authority of
Hesiod, Pindar, Epicharnius, and Virgil.)

Lord Arundel points out the very curious identity
between the words *man* and *stone*, not only in Greece,
but throughout the world.

He instances this by reference to the Latin *homo* and
French *homme*, which are from the same *humus*, the
ground or soil, but also from the Keltic *man*, the meaning
of which throughout Wales, Brittany, Cornwall, &c., is
stone, to which may be added the term Saxon, which also
represents a rock or stone. Max Müller, who derides the
myth of the creation of man by throwing stones as utterly
ridiculous, as it may be to one who rejects the Mosaic
history of the formation of man, has fallen into a vastly
more ridiculous error of deriving *man* from the Sanscrit *ma*,

to measure. *Man*, a derivative root, means to think; as if one word could have two distinct and almost opposite derivations. It is simply childish to give a choice of derivations, and it violates the rule or "law" which Max Müller dogmatically lays down, that wherever in Greek or its congeners you find a word exactly like it, in Sanscrit you will find it a totally different word. In this case the rule is sound, for this reason, that the Sanscrit is a different language from the Greek and its congeners. It is not, like them, Shemetic, but probably Japhetic. If this law were general, and applied to the congeners of a language, it would apply to the Greek when considered in relation to Latin and Keltic, but it does not.

Nor is the word *stone*, for man, confined to the Shemetic races. In Syriac *stone* signifies equally a stone and a child. Bunsen gives the word *man* as Egyptian for rock, stone. Sir William Jones (Asiatic Researches, i. 230, Rawlinson's Bamp. Lect., ii. 67): "From Manu the earth was repeopled, and from him mankind received their name, Manudsha, and in later Sanscrit Manuskya;" and Bunsen (Philosophy of Universal Hist., i. 169): "The divine Mannus, the alleged ancestor of the Germans, is absolutely identical with Manus, who, according to ancient Indian mythology, is the god who created man anew after the Deluge, just as Deucalion did"—which, if correct, would prove the Hametic origin of the Germans.

That the Greek tradition is truly the Mosaic story is apparent from the cause, which is similar in both instances: the enormous iniquity with which the earth was contaminated—Apollodorus says by the then existing brazen race, or, as others say, by the fifty monstrous sons of Sykoron—provoked Zeus to send a general deluge. Grote (Hist. of Greece, vol. i. chap. v. pp. 132–134)

E

affirms that the idea of the Deucalion Deluge was blended
with the religious impressions of the people and com-
memorated by their most sacred ceremonies.

Lord Arundel points out (p. 231) that the tradition of
the Deluge, which is allowed to be as old in Greece as the
fifth century B.C., is in reality of long antecedent tradition,
and must have been brought by the Greeks themselves
from Asia; and he cites the opinion of Varro, according
to whose calculation the deluge of Ogyges occurred 400
years before Inachus, *i. e.* 1000 years before the first
Olympiad, which would bring it to 2376 B.C., not very
far from the true period; and Lord Arundel accounts for
the double tradition of Deucalion and Ogyges on the
supposition that probably the Greeks brought the one
account with them from Asia when they first left it,
and that the other is the result of after contact with
Asiatics.    Possibly one account reached them by way
of Egypt.

Lord Arundel (chap. xi.) gives a very interesting account
of certain ceremonies which were common to Grecian and
antique Pagan countries, as well as to the Mandans of
North America and to the tropical regions of Africa,
which all closed in bacchanalian scenes of riot and de-
bauchery, typifying the Deluge, and, finally, those deadly
events which terminated in the curse of Caanan.    There
can be no doubt that Bacchus personifies Noah, the first
planter of the vine and maker and drinker of wine.

Hu Gadarn, the patriarch of the Welsh, had many
names and glories apportioned to him.    He is called
Dwyvan, and his wife Dwyvach, also Nevydd nav Neivion,
the lord of the waters; Dylanail mor Dylan or Dylau,
son of the sea, from *dyglaniaw*, to land or come to shore,
from whence Mr. Davies conjectures Deucalion may be

derived. Jolo Goch, the bard of Owen Glendwr, thus addresses him—

> " Hu Gadarn, the sovereign, the ready protector,
> A king distributing the wine and the renown,
> The emperor of the land and the sea,
> And the life of all in the world was he ;
> After the Deluge he held
> The strong-beamed plough, active and excellent."

That Hu Gadarn is clearly intended for Noah is evident from the following triads :—

"One of the three awful events of the island of Britain was the bursting of the lake of waters, and the over-whelming of the face of all lands, so that all mankind were drowned except Dwyvan and Dwyvach, who escaped in a naked vessel without sails, and of them the island of Britain was repeopled.

" One of the three chief master-works was the ship of Nevydd nav Neivion, which carried in it a male and female of all living, when the lake of waters burst forth."

Of course it may be objected that the Welsh incorporated the Mosaic traditions into their history; but the question arises, How did they obtain them prior to the Christian era ? And unquestionably Hu Gadarn is a creation of greater antiquity, for he was the god of the British Druids, and well known and worshipped throughout Britain and Gaul at a time when it is admitted the Druid worship was confined to Britain, and to those countries who learnt from the Britons.

There are many particulars relating to Hu Gadarn which are worthy of the deepest study, for they show that the ancient people the Cymry do trace back their origin to the patriarch Noah ; and although many of them typify the events recorded by Moses, many of them are

at this day inexplicable, and relate evidently to purely
local matters, which, if they could be ascertained, might
prove to be of the greatest historical value.

It is very remarkable that although Hu Gadarn stands
prominently forward in almost every capacity, he is never
represented as actually being in Britain. He is the first of
the great regulators of the island, but his services are
distinctly confined "to bringing the race of the Cymry
out of the land of Hav, which is called Defrobani, into
the isle of Britain." As the first benefactor of the race of
Cymry, he is renowned for teaching the method of cul-
tivating the ground when the race of Cymry were in the
land of Hav, before they came into Britain; as the first of
the three primary sages, he collected the race of Cymry
and disposed them into tribes. One Geogdden Gauhebon
was the first man in the world who composed poetry, yet
Hu was the first who adapted poetry to the preservation
of records and memorials, and he was of course the first
of the three pillars of the race of the island of Britain;
yet, in describing the names of the three happy controllers
of the isle of Britain, Hu is not mentioned, and the palm
is given to Prydain, the son of Aedd Mor. This Prydain
is clearly shown to have been the leader of the Ligurian
or Llogrian emigration from the mouth of the Loire or
Liger, the race of "Aedd the great" being the Aedui, the
principal race of the Gauls, who were represented directly
in England by the Hedui; and Davies identifies him with
the Aides of the Greek mythology, their acknowledged
patriarch.

That such a leader probably headed that emigration
is most probable, and the fact that he was literally and
actually there whilst Hu was only figuratively a leader,
gives force and weight to the narrative.

This strengthens the importance of the inquiry as to
the place from whence they came — the land of Hav,
which is called Defrobani. Davies admits (p. 165) that
Hav and Defrobani are very obscure names, but asserts
that commentators of the middle of the twelfth century
stated that it was where Constantinople now stands, that
is, the Euxine; but Davies asserts "that Hav would be
Ham in the old Welsh orthography, and that Defrobani
may mean either Dyvrobanau, the land of eminences or
high points, Thrace in general, or else Dyvro Banwy,
the land or vale of the Peneus, Thessaly, Harmonia."
Now, taking this literally as the land of Ham would lead
us to the territory of Uz, the son of Aram, or to the land
of Egypt.   It has been asserted, but wrongly, that the only
place known in Jewish history as the land of Ham is a
city of that name, or a territory or city anciently called
Ham, which, in the days of Abraham, was in the possession of the Zuzims or Zamzummims, who may have taken
possession of it on the departure of the children of Aram.
This city (Deut. ii. 19, 20), we read, after the possession of the Zamzummims, became the possession of the
Ammonites; their principal city was called Rabbah, a
word simply meaning great or populous; and Stephanus
asserts that it was also known by the name of Ammana,
a name which was supposed to have been derived from
the Ammonites; but inasmuch as they clearly called it
Rabbah, and the name accords much more closely to that
of Am or Ham, it is far more likely to have been derived
from the older name.   It was in after ages taken possession of by Ptolemy Philadelphus, king of Egypt, and by
him repaired and beautified, and honoured with the name
of Philadelphia.

The city consisted of two parts, one particularly called

Rabbah, and the other " The city of waters." We read
in 2 Sam. xii. 26, 27, that it was called the royal city.
"Joab sent messengers to King David, and said, I have
fought against Rabbah and taken the city of waters. . . .
And David fought against it and took it; and he took
their king's crown from off his head, the weight whereof
was a talent of gold, with the precious stones; and it
was set on David's head; and he brought forth the spoil
of the city in great abundance." From all this it is quite
clear that it was a city of great extent, and probably a
place of great natural beauty and many advantages, and
likely to have been the home of the house of Uz before
their departure from Syria, for it was a place of great
natural strength (Num. xxi. 24); and this would seem
to be the reason why the Israelites did not previously
possess it, for when they took the land of the Amorites
from Arnon unto Jabbok, they were stopped by the
border of the Ammonites, " for the border of the children
of Ammon was strong."

It is very remarkable that this is the only place known
in Jewish history as the land of Ham, except where Egypt
is poetically so described in Psalm lxxviii. 51, in describing the plagues of the Egyptians : " And smote all the first-
born in Egypt, the chief of their strength in the tabernacles
of Ham." The meaning of this is rather the race than
the land of Ham. However, in Psalm cv. 23, David writes
distinctly, " Israel also came into Egypt, and Jacob sojourned in the land of Ham." And Psalm cvi. 21, 22:
" They forgot God their Saviour, which had done great
things in Egypt, wondrous works in the land of Ham, and
terrible things by the Red Sea." In Plutarch Egypt is
called Chemia, and there are traces of the name of Ham

or Cham in Psochemmis and Psillachemmis, both of which
are cantons of Egypt.

It is observable that if Egypt had been intended to be
designated, the form Cham would rather have been used
than Ham. That the writer of the triads had Egypt in
his mind is perhaps clear from his adding to the name
of Ham the description of "Defrobani," or the land of
eminences or high points, to distinguish it from Egypt ;
for it cannot possibly refer to that country, which is
generally a remarkably low country, unless indeed it
refers to the pyramids. But, on the other hand, the only
place known by the name of Ham is Rabbah of the
Ammonites. That place is certainly nowhere called the
land of Ham, but it answers more strictly to the description of a land of eminences or high points, and two of the
titles of Hu Gadarn seem to be taken from it. He is called
Nevydd nav Neivion, the celestial one, the lord of the
waters, which was poetised by the Welsh bards into
Dylan, son of the sea. The waters of which he was lord
may well have been the city of waters of Rabbah. But
whichever place is the true one, it matters very little, for
in the days prior to the time of Abraham the children of
Aram possessed both of them ; and just as Ptolemy Philadelphus made Ham his summer abode, the children of
Aram may have ruled Egypt from thence, for there is little
doubt but that they were the Shepherd kings who built
the great pyramid of Gheza. There is one event which
occurred near that place, which was of so fearful a nature
that, if the Cymry came from it, we should expect to find
mention of it in their traditions, although it occurred
after their departure ; for the possession of Ham by the
Zamzummims in the time of Abraham fixes it at an earlier
period ; yet as the emigration from Syria into Britain

lasted at any rate down to the time of the Phœnicians, they would have had tidings of it, and would doubtless be greatly affected by it: that is, the destruction of Sodom and Gomorrah by fire. There is a triad of the three awful events of the island of Britain which probably refers to it. The first, of course, was the drowning of mankind at the Deluge; the second was the consternation of the tempestuous fire, when the earth split asunder to Anugu (the lower region), and the greatest part of all living were consumed. To the inhabitants of Ham this would seem to be the case; that the event is localised in Britain does not detract from its merit.

Another triad pointing to an Eastern origin, though the event is again localised amongst the chief master-works of the island of Britain, were the stones of Gwyddon Gauhebon, on which were recorded the arts and sciences of the world. He also was the first of the human race who composed poetry, though Hu Gadarn afterwards applied it to memorials and records. From this it is clear that the Triad relates to the Sethite knowledge, which distinguished the race of Shem from the Canaanites. As in the time before the Flood memories would be perfect, there would be no necessity to form a system for the preservation of the memory of events, and in all probability Noah or Shem may have invented such a system. The exact division of the genealogies of the race of our Lord seems to point to a poetical arrangement of the kind, and the reference to the stones on which were engraved the arts and sciences of the world refer to the pillars of Seth, or more probably to the pyramid of Gheza.

The traditions of Ireland may be examined for the purpose of throwing light upon the early history of the Gaelic race with advantage.

The Irish records have been systematised and reduced into order by the Four Masters. In one way this is an advantage, in others a danger; for at the time its version was arranged but little was known of comparative philology, though that little was not so utterly erroneous as the science which now passes muster for it. The Four Masters assert that the Tuatha de Dannans left Greece after a battle with the Assyrians, and went to Norway and Sweden, then to Ireland.

General Vallancy (Essay, Ancient History of the British Isles) asserts that the Irish MSS. "contain a more perfect account of the emigration of the Armenians, Scythians, Persians, &c., from the banks of the Caspian and Euxine seas to the islands of the Mediterranean, to Africa, to Spain, and to the Britannic isles, than any history hitherto known. The details of these emigrations perfectly correspond with the Punic accounts translated out of the books of King Hermsal's library for Sallust and the traditions of the Bubere or Showah." If this be so, it is a pity that Irish MSS. have been so long neglected, and that they are not made accessible to the general reader. There can be little doubt but that much general history would be gleaned from them.

The concurrent testimony of these traditions undoubtedly points to an Eastern, and many people think to an Israelitish origin, though a little consideration will satisfy a reasonable mind that there cannot possibly be certainty on this head, and that all that can positively be proved is a Shemetic origin. That these traditions, and especially the Irish account, are directly taken from the Hebrew Scriptures—are, in fact, incorrect versions of the history of the Israelites—is not to be denied; but they are not to be summarily rejected on this account, especially if the leading facts can be corroborated by undoubted historical evidence. It is worth while to inquire if this can be done. This fact is noteworthy, that if these traditions were mere inventions, they would probably have a common origin. It is irrational to suppose that three distinct peoples, the Irish, the Welsh, the Breton or the French, could separately invent one and the same story. Of the antiquity of the Irish tradition there is no doubt. The history of Scotland, though very poor, yet in a manner corroborates it, at any rate sufficiently to satisfy the mind that such a tradition existed from a very early period, certainly some centuries before the Christian era. The Welsh traditions cannot be dated much later than that period, for they were cut off from England and France by the Roman occupation, and their accounts certainly date from that separation. The French accounts, as we should expect, have been more altered than the others, and have become more tinged by military romance. They lead rather to Troy than to Jerusalem. Not that the Irish records have any avowed connection with the latter place, only the record fits in more completely with the theory of an Israelitish origin.

In considering these traditions, it is obvious that no true chronology is to be gathered from them, and all that we can hope to obtain in that direction is the recital of successive events which may, by reference to some great event or to each other, enable us to arrive at some definite notion on the subject; and unfortunately the history of each country in which the stage of the events recorded is laid is itself in terrible confusion. The earliest fact we have in history which confirms tradition is the connection between Britain and Ireland with Phœnicia. What do we know of Phœnicia? Nothing except what has been filtered through a Grecian source, or through Carthage from Roman writers; we do not even know the nationality of this people, or whether it was with them a name not of nationality but of habit; that is, whether it meant more than the word merchant or trader. The Syrians were Phœnicians, so were the Israelites, and so probably were other nations. But if we know little of the Phœnicians, we know much of their warfare from Roman annals. We know little of the history of the Carthaginians; so of the early Spanish colonists we know they were mixed Phœnicians, Syrians, and Hebrews, and afterwards Carthaginians, but we know positively little more; history and tradition alike are lost. We have only philology to guide us, and a dangerous guide it is.

This then is the first fact that we can positively assert, that both Britain and Ireland were visited by Phœnicians and Carthaginians, and the traditions of both countries relate, as the history of the Phœnicians and Carthaginians would lead us to expect, that both settled colonies in these countries. Who were these colonists, and at what time did they first settle there? The Irish records positively assert that various colonies of pirates from Phœnicia and Africa (of course pointing to Carthage) settled there, and the history of the Phœnician connection with England is too well known to require repetition. So Irish and English traditions concur in the statement, which also reason would teach us, that both countries were peopled from the Spanish coast, as well as from the Cimbric Chersonesus.

The particular tradition of the Irish occupation is actually Hebraic. It relates that the Scoti or Scythi, under Nial, son of one of the kings of Scythia, settled in Egypt and married a daughter of that Pharaoh who was drowned

in the Red Sea.    Nial had a son, Gaddhal, who gave the
name of Gadelians or Gaels to the Scots.    These Gaels
were expelled from Egypt and returned to Scythia under
Eber Scot; that they then went into the Mediterranean
under a chief, Breogan, who founded the kingdom of
Brigantia in Spain; and the Spanish traditions would
seem to agree with the Irish story, if, in fact, it is not
taken from it; a very doubtful matter, however.    There is
a Spanish tradition which is summarised by Peter Ponada,
writing, about one hundred years since, a synopsis of the
genealogy of the most ancient and most noble family of
Brigantes or Douglas, which is interwoven with the traditional history of Scotland, related on the authority
of Hector Boetius, a Scottish historian, who was born
A.D. 1470, and of Polydore Virgil, an Italian cotemporary
who also indulged in historical speculations, that the
Irish were descended from Cecrops, the first king of the
Athenians, whose son Gatheles fled into Egypt and
served under Achorus, the son of that Pharaoh who was
drowned in the Red Sea, and married his daughter, Scota,
and having been compelled to leave Egypt through the
tyranny of the Egyptians about the time of the return of
Moses to Canaan, he with his companions set sail westward, and after a long voyage passed the Straits and
landed at a place afterwards called Portugal, or the Port
of Gael, and founded Galicia.    Here again is the same
tradition filtered through a Scottish source, diversified
considerably, but still substantially the Hebrew story.

Nial, who is said to have conducted the first colony
into Egypt, planted his followers on the borders of the
Red Sea, where they are known to have dwelt at the time
of the crossing of the Israelites.    In this statement the
Irish records are supported by the testimony of the Rabbi

Simon, who states that, after no long residence in this position, the Phœnician colonists were expelled by Capercheroth, the grandson of Pharaoh, upon which they returned to their mother country. They then sailed to Gades in Spain, where they were permitted to possess themselves of a maritime position; thence their posterity embarked for Ireland, of which country these emigrants have long enjoyed the merit of being the discoverers.

Occa Scarlensis gives a tradition that the Saxons were originally a people of India in Africa, and being constrained by lot to emigrate, fought under Alexander of Macedon in Asia, on his death returning to India, and in the year 3670 landing in the Cimbric Chersonesus.

This tradition concurs with the main features of the traditions of Scythia and of Greece. The settlers under Nial may have been either Phœnicians or Aramites under the protection of the Shepherd kings, and their expulsion from Egypt and return to Scythia would seem to point to the expulsion of these kings and the invasion of the isles of Greece; and the subsequent settlement in Galicia is of course the old Phœnician story so well known to readers of history; so that, putting aside the embellishments, this account may be substantially the true account of the settlement of the Gaels or Phœnicians in Ireland.

# CHAPTER VI.

## THE POSITIVE FACTS OF BRITISH HISTORY.

IN order to prove the Shemetic origin of the English race, there are two distinct sets of propositions to be proved, and two parties of objectors to oppose. First, there is a class of writers, now happily dying out, who assert that the inhabitants of these islands were prior to the Roman occupation mere savages; and, secondly, those who assert that this early race, whether savage or otherwise, were stamped out and extirpated by the Saxon. To the first class nearly every writer belonged until the labours of Pearson and Creasy showed the contrary to be the truth; to the last even Pearson and Creasy and their school belonged, although some of them, notably Professor Freeman, admit, though without showing the slightest evidence in support of the distinction, or indeed of the fact, that the extermination by the sword or otherwise of the ancient British was not complete, and that the women were spared. Nothing is said about children, and hence, it is alleged, is to be found a small amount of Welsh in the English language.

The present chapter will be devoted to the proof of the first proposition, that the early inhabitants of the British isles were not savages; and in absolute proof of this we have the actual remains of the people themselves, and their baubles and trinkets are the best possible evidence of their knowledge and progress in the arts and sciences. And curiously the contents of British barrows again illustrate the folly of Mr. Hepworth Dixon's school, for they show that whilst the later burials supply evidence of error and superstition and of a small amount of civilisation, earlier barrows prove that the farther we go back the more skilful and intelligent were our ancestors, confirming the truth of Dr. Schliemann's account of the decline of early civilisation exhibited in the successive cities built upon the site of Troy. For the purpose of this investigation England and Ireland will be treated as the same country, and no attempt will be made to prove which of them had the honour of being the parent of the other. Like Tyre and Sidon, they may each safely claim to be the parent of the other; probably they are similarly indebted to each other for much that is valuable in their possession. Taking the case of Ireland first, Mr. Wilde, in a lecture on the ethnology of the ancient Irish, divides the people of the earliest primeval barrows into two races, the descendants of which he somewhat rashly asserts are still to be seen in particular districts of Ireland, and these correspond both in physical attributes and order of succession to the two primitive races of Denmark of Professor Eschereck, the first possessing brachycephalic or round skulls, and the second dolichocephalic or longer crania; and writing of the latter he adds, "The skulls of these long-headed aborigines of Ireland present the same marked characters in their facial aspect and the projecting occiput and prominent frontal sinuses as the Danish;" and he does not confine himself to the more unsatisfactory description by comparison, but he states that they are chiefly characterised by their extreme length from before backwards, or what is technically termed their antero-posterior dia-

meter, and the flatness of their sides.    He also found the
same characteristics in skulls found in Gloucestershire.

Professor S. Neilson, agreeing with Professor Retzius
of Lund, divides the primitive inhabitants of Scandinavia into three classes, agreeing with the Irish order: the
oldest brachycephalic; the second he thinks were agri-
culturists, and possessed a lengthened and oval skull,
having a narrow and prominent occiput; and the third
are intermediate: and he considers that the present inhabitants of Scandinavia are an entirely different people.
The third class he thinks were Celtic.

Dr. R. G. Latham considers that the Celtic are pre-
eminently a dolichocephalic race.

Professor Daniel Wilson, writing concerning Scotland,
whilst admitting that the data are much too few to
justify a dogmatic assertion of any general inference,
yet thinks the order was first primitive dolichocephalic;
second, brachycephalic; and third, Celtic; and he thinks
that "not the least interesting indications which these
results afford, both to the ethnologist and the archæologist,
are the evidence of native primitive races in Scotland
prior to the intrusion of the Celtæ, and also the probability of these races having succeeded each other in a
different order from the primitive races of Scandinavia."

We do not obtain the same positiveness in the result of
the labours of British craniologists, although Mr. J. B.
Davies, in a separate preface to "Crania Britannica" which
he published in conjunction with Dr. Thurnam, asserts
that we "possess materials for solving the secret problem
of primeval man in at least as pure, abundant, and satisfactory a form as they are to be found in any other land,
Britain being a world by itself."    Yet, he adds, and
especially points out, "Our materials are far too slender

to enable us to determine whether any physical peculiarities distinguish the different Anglo-Saxon tribes among themselves, and to ascertain in what they consisted" (p. 211).

He considers that most of the central districts of England still retain a mixture of aboriginal British blood, which he thinks is proved by the prevalence of dark hair and eyes and dark complexion, as well as by a medium stature (p. 212). And he adds, " If we revert to the size of the brain as a test of the mental capacity of the race, we shall find that the results embodied in the tables fully support the high position claimed for the ancient British " (p. 237).

Canon Greenwell gives no uncertain sound in his valuable work upon British barrows, just published, to which the learned reader is referred for full information upon the subject. He distinctly states as a fact that two orders of people were buried in these tombs—those in the earliest or stone and bronze period, which he asserts is well marked, being dolichocephalic; and those in the iron or later period, brachycephalic, thus fully corroborating Professor Wilson.

The conclusion to be drawn from these facts is, that whilst in Scandinavia and in Ireland the first inhabitants were a round-headed race, possibly of Japhetian origin, the race of Shem settled primarily in England, and were its first inhabitants; that they were intruded upon by the round-headed race of the Continent and of Ireland, probably the Belgæ or Firbolgs; that both were succeeded by the second dolichocephalic wave, who may be identified as that of the Damnonii or Tuatha de Danann, and both subsequently by the last race of the Celtæ or the Saxons, the last word being applied solely to that wave, to render this phase of the matter more

F

intelligible, the probability being that some if not all of
these races were of the same family, though possibly some
of them more or less mixed with other races.

So much for the people themselves; a few words upon
their belongings.   We know from the earliest Greek
writers something about their dress and appearance two
or three centuries before the era of Cæsar; and that great
man has written a few lines concerning the appearance of
the British in his day which have puzzled antiquarians,
since they confound and contradict previous writers; but
nevertheless his loose words have generated what may
be termed the blue-paint school, which has found many
admirers.   As the British had not degenerated in learning, for they were still the teachers of Europe in his day,
it is unlikely that they had degenerated in their personal
habits; and Canon Greenwell's book affords evidence of
their state not 200, but possibly even 2000 years, before the time of Cæsar.   He dates barrows in general as
belonging to a period before bronze was in common use.
Canon Greenwell, p. 32, remarks, " The wardrobes of this
ancient people were by no means slenderly provided;"
and he adds, "The people, as might be expected, notwithstanding the popular notion about our naked and painted
ancestors, wore clothes, and sometimes, if not always, they
were buried in them."   They had fastenings of jet, bone,
and stone highly decorated.   The barrows are found to
contain examples of almost all the stone implements which
occur elsewhere.   Vessels like those used by the Greeks
and the Etruscans are frequently found, and amongst
them incense-cups, which he asserts are common to both
England and Ireland, and he conjectures that they were
used for the purpose of burning incense, aromatic oils,
and perfumes.

This subject may best be concluded in Canon Greenwell's eloquent words : " Without the wondrous museum of gold and silver, and iron, and precious stones, and glass, and bronze, and ivory, which the cemeteries of Kent, of East Anglia, and of Middle England have so carefully preserved for us, what should we have known of English progress in many a development of artistic workmanship ? How should we have become cognisant of their wondrous skill in goldsmith's work, their tasteful application of metal, stone, and glass to the enrichment of personal ornaments, their knowledge of glass manufacture in beads and vessels of that material, their high cultivation in art, their great practical acquaintance with the mystery of the smith ? " (p. 58).

This evidence must set at rest for ever the ridiculous assertions of the blue-paint school of history.

# CHAPTER VII.

THE COMMERCIAL INTERCOURSE OF THE EARLY BRITISH
WITH PHŒNICIA.

IT cannot be denied that the facts stated in the last
chapter prove conclusively that a people the shape of
whose skulls proves them to have been of a Shemetic type,
and whose dress and personal ornaments, vessels, and
utensils prove them to have been highly civilised, lived
in Britain some 2000 years before the period when Cæsar
libelled the people of that country. The next step in the
argument is to ascertain whether it can be shown that
any ancient people had relations with them, and who the
British represented themselves to be. These two inquiries
mutually aid each other.

The earliest name by which the island of Britain was
known to the inhabitants was Inys Vel, and Ireland Inys
Fail. It is possible that these names were identical, and
that both are different forms of the name by which the
first people who are known to have traded here were
known, and they were the Phœnicians.

The Phœnicians were the inhabitants of Palestine, or
the land of the Palli, Phali, or Shepherds. This word is
another remarkable instance of the similarity of the Irish
and Punic, *pal* or *phal* being in Irish " shepherd" at this day;
*palno*, sheep-ground. As Ireland has always been known
for its beautiful pastures, always celebrated as the Eme-

rald Isle, as Green Erin, it is more reasonable to suppose
that this is the meaning of the name than that it should
represent "the island of destiny," or some unmeaning
phrase of that description. The greatest objection to this
derivation is that it was adopted by General Vallency;
but although some of his views are wild and visionary, he
was a man of undoubted talent and unwearied industry;
and putting aside the absurdity of the particular hobby
he was endeavouring to ride, which was to prove that his
countrymen were Canaanites, there is undoubtedly great
weight in some of his reasoning, and he made valuable and
learned historical researches. Mr. Nevins in his "Ireland
and the Holy See" states that in the Annals of Innis-
fallen the Plain of Fermoy is called the Plain of the
Phœnicians. Kildare, amongst other Irish towns, had
an undoubted Phœnician name, Laberno-lahab-era, a
flame in a cave. The round tower of Kildare, the proof of
Phœnician worship, is still existing. That England was
equally the land of the shepherds, and that the same
learned race, the Druids, inhabited both islands, is perfectly clear. Thus, by the same argument, England also
was the land of the Pali or shepherds, although Mr. Davies
in his "Celtic Researches," p. 190, on the authority of
W. Arch, vol. ii. p. 1, states that Inys Vel means Island
of Bel, and he gives a fragment of a Druidical prayer in
which the word appears to be used in this sense; but it
does not follow from this that it may not originally have
had the other and older meaning; and, at any rate, the
Irish word Fail cannot be translated Bel also, or Jacob's
stone at Westminster, the Lia Fail, would lose its character
for sanctity.

Now this is perfectly clear: if we believe the Pali of
Ireland to have been Phœnician, we should expect to find

the Phœnicians traded with the inhabitants and formed colonies upon the coast.

A curious proof that illustrates the idea that Ireland was largely colonised by the Phœnicians is to be found in the fact that the Phœnicians were termed Scuits or sea-wanderers—*scuit* coming to mean a ship. This word is engraved in Runic characters on the Lia Phail, or stone of the Phali. M. Beuley asserts that the Phœnicians were originally Scythæ. So General Vallancy considers them. Phœnician remains have been found in Ireland; a bronze figure of a sailor was found in an Irish bog, made according to the principles of Etruscan art, and many other articles. Bronze swords have been found in Irish bogs, precisely similar to the swords of the Carthaginians found in the field of Cannæ, now in the British Museum.

Mr. George Smith, in his able little book, "The Cassiterites," shows tolerably conclusively that no other country but Britain was worked for tin in the early stage of the world's history, and that, consequently, the tin used by the Phœnicians and Greeks must have come from Britain. Sir George Cornewall Lewis, the great opponent of the theory that the Phœnicians traded with Britain direct, that is, round the seas, is yet constrained to admit that they obtained their tin from these islands, and all history proves the fact, and the very name of the island, which was Baratanac to the merchants, proves it. Baratanac is Punic for the land of tin, and the Greeks, when they succeeded to the Phœnician trade, translated the word into their own tongue, and called the British isles the Cassiterites, which name is still applied to certain fossils found in Devon and Cornwall. That the Carthaginians traded here for the same purpose is a matter of history.

and that their trade commenced at a very early period there is no rational doubt; and this is also tolerably clear, that the tin used by Solomon in the construction of the Temple was obtained here through his friend and kinsman, Hiram, king of Tyre, who was his great merchant-carrier; in fact, his Phœnician, for Phœnician meant trader. To clench this argument, we have only to show that Phœnicia exchanged her marts for British tin, and this is proved by Canon Greenwell and other authors from the evidence of the barrows.

From whence did the British and Irish obtain their ivory, their gold and silver, and their glass? Phœnicia was famous for all these manufactures, especially for that of glass; and it is not too much to say that the fact of glass being found in a country at that date is evidence of a trading, directly or indirectly, with Phœnicia. There is evidence of a direct trading in the Irish word for glass, which is actually Punic. Whether is it easier to believe that all these articles were native manufactures or bartered from a country known to manufacture them? The raw material of some of them, such as the articles of ivory, must have come from the Phœnicians, for there were no other traders at that day with India. This suggestion, it must be admitted, rather detracts from the force of Canon Greenwell's eloquent panegyric upon the intelligence of the ancient inhabitants; but it does not detract from the argument of the British being civilised and in communication with civilised beings. But if it does, so let it be; it is better that the truth should be known; and it is going some way to prove civilisation to show intimate intercourse with such a people as the Phœnicians. That the Phœnicians had colonies in the island is proved tolerably clearly from the fact that remains of mining in the Phœnician fashion are still found; nay, the very moulds into which spear-heads and other implements were cast have been found.

It is clear also from the traces of Phœnician worship, which are discoverable throughout England and Ireland, that the worship of Baal was practised here; and, as we have seen, whether it was the primary meaning of the word or not, the native name of Britain was at one time the Island of Bel, and no doubt Bel, or Apollo, was the great god of the Druidical system.

Traces of direct Tyrean worship have been found not only in Cornwall, where the tin-workings were established, but at Colchester, and even in Northumberland. Dr. Todd discovered an altar to the Tyrean Hercules at the former place, and two altars were found at Corbridge in Northumberland inscribed with Grecian characters, one to the Tyrean Hercules and the other to Astarte. Hiram, king of Tyre, built two temples in the time of Solomon, which he dedicated to these deities.

Mr. James Barrington, in the "Archæologia," vol. iii. p. 331, endeavoured to account for these altars by suggesting the marriage of a Roman soldier with a Syrian bride! As well suggest a union with a Hottentot Venus. The inscription being written in Greek characters affords no presumption that any Greek or Syrian brought them hither, but rather that they were native; for Cæsar assures us that the British themselves used the Greek characters, which they doubtless learnt in the course of their trading with the Greeks. At Chesterford, on the borders of Essex and Cambridge, a Hercules was found (Jour. Archæ. Ass., vol. iv. p. 375). One was found at York (ib. ix. p. 88).

Traces of Baal-worship are to be found everywhere in Ireland, and the name of Astarte has become fused into everyday life. The word "astore," which the Irish lover addresses to the Venus of his affection, is the same word.

So, too, unquestionably, it would seem the round towers of Ireland were built for the purpose of Baal-worship. T. M. F., the author of " Polythéism Analysé," asserts that the monuments of Bel had a tower which served at once for a temple and for an observatory; and we know that the Druids were great astronomers, and possessed all the learning of the Chaldeans. Ireland may well have been called, as it was, Ir of the Chaldees and the Holy Island, for Bel-towers are to be found in every part of it; and her people, too, are of a deeply religious nature. A relic of the worship of Bel remains in the name of their May-day, which in Ireland is still La Beltine.

The letters, language, and customs of the ancient Irish are said to be of a Phœnician character. General Vallancy asserts that there are 2000 words in Irish similar to the Chaldean, Hebrew, and Hindoo languages. The Phœnician letters and characters are found in ancient MSS. The Irish Boboleth characters are like those of the Phœnicians, Carthaginians, and Egyptians.

There are, says Canon Bourke, p. 293, only seventeen letters in Gaelic, just the number of the letters used by the Greeks before they had lost the digamma; and these letters, he tells us, are identical—twelve consonants and five vowels. Now it is clear that the Greeks had lost their sixth letter or digamma some 3000 years ago, long before the age of Homer; therefore it is clear that the Irish Gaels, if they learnt their alphabet from the Greeks, must have done so at or before the arrival of the Tuatha de Danann, certainly not later. Now they spoke the same language as the Firbolg, who preceded them, and who probably possessed the same letters. They can hardly have learned

them from the Milesians, for they did not arrive in Ireland
for fully two hundred years later; and if they came from
Greece, as they could not very well have been all that
time upon the way, they must have brought only the sixteen Homeric letters.

Canon Bourke is a disbeliever in the Phœnician theory,
or possibly he only objects to General Vallancy's idea of a
Canaanitish origin. His opinion, whatever it is, is entitled
to the greatest possible weight; but still facts must be
balanced, and the deduction drawn which could seem
fairly to arise from them; and it appears to the writer
that there is great weight to be attached to the Irish
tradition of such an origin. That the Tuatha de Danann
were called Scythians, like the Phœnicians, is clear beyond
doubt; that they were possessed not only of the letters
but of the very arts in which that people were most skilful is also admitted. The Phœnicians were great colo-
nisers, and for some reason they left their own country:
some of them, no doubt, settled in Carthage, and some in
Cadiz, from which place a settlement on the Irish coast
would be most natural; but the strongest possible corro-
boration is to be found in the round towers of Ireland.
Canon Bourke has combated in a masterly manner the
various views as to the origin of these buildings which have
been put forth by various writers, and it would seem he
has most successfully demonstrated their insufficiency and
errors. He himself propounds a theory: the only fault
which can be found with it is that it is too vague. He
summarily disposes of the idea that they were built either
by Danes (that is, since the Christian era) or by Christians,
and he suggests that they were the work of men skilled
at the very earliest period in the Cyclopean style of architecture. It is in style, he contends, similar to that dis-

played in the Cyclopean buildings in the East, in Persepolis, Ecbatana, and in Babylon, as far as can be known; in Thebes, and in the pyramids along the Nile; and he affirms, with great precision and distinctness, that in the slanting doorway, in the style of arch, in the material used, in the cement, in the shape and size of the stones, and in the manner in which they are laid, are architectural features which are nowhere to be found except in the Cyclopean edifices of the earliest historic period.

Mr. Moonson asserts that the round tower of Dysart bears a strong resemblance to the Etruscan masonry of Italy and the early Greek churches (Petrie, p. 362). Canon Bourke proves that five hundred years prior to the arrival of the Tuatha de Danann the Irish had wonderful skill in the art of building, as well as in that of dyeing and of painting, both of which arts surely flourished in Phœnicia, if we have read aright our accounts of the products of Tyre; and he leaves the question of the time when these masons built the tower to the imagination, rather leaning to the earlier than to the later period; and in this, perhaps, he has exercised the soundest judgment, although there are not wanting Irish historians of credit who assert that they were the handiwork of the Tuatha de Danann.

The solution of the question rests, perhaps, in the use and object for which these towers were built. Canon Bourke suggests that they were built and used only for securing hostages. But this surely would not account for the purpose of their construction; a square dungeon would answer such a purpose equally well.

Le Brun, "Voyage to the Levant," p. 494, asserts that Jacob's Tower, near Bethlehem, was twenty feet high, and exactly resembling the Irish towers. In Trinity College,

Dublin, there is a MS., H. 2, 18 f. 157, a. b., in which is an annual payment for fire mentioned. A most careful examination of ancient Irish MSS. has led to no discovery to corroborate the idea that the towers were used as beacons (Petrie, 373).

Is nothing to be gained from the name? They are called Bell towers. Does that word give no sound? Bell towers either mean the Tower of Bel, the god, or of the church bells. But few of them are built near churches; but in such cases, no doubt, the Christians used as far as they could their towers for their own worship, and the only use was to employ them as Belfries. But what is the meaning of the word "bell," as applied to the implement used for calling together the congregation? Does it take its name from the tower, or supply it? Surely the former. The Keltic word for bell is *clock* or *cloggen*. But if we conclude that the implement takes the name from the towers, we ask, Who could have been the worshippers of Bel?—and the answer is clear and decisive. Bel was the great god of the Phœnicians, and these towers were most probably raised by them for his worship.

We read in history that the Sidonians, who were of a most happy genius, were a branch of the Phœnicians. The Druids were known to the Greeks by a name very similar to theirs—Saranides—said to be compounded of the Gaelic words *sar dhuine*. It is possible that this name is a corruption of the former.

It is at all events quite certain that the Irish Druids and poets had written books before the coming of St. Patrick in 432 (Canon Bourke, p. 280).

The "Saltair of Tara" was completed by Cormac Mac Art, son of Corm, in the third century. He died 266 A.D. (O'Curry; and see Petrie's "History of Tara Hill").

There is no doubt at all that the pre-Christian Gaels of Ireland wrote in Ogham (Canon Bourke, p. 281).

Dr. Graves says that the concurrent authority of the most ancient MS. histories prove that an alphabet called Ogham was invented by the Scythian progenitors of the Gael race, and was introduced into Ireland by the Tuatha de Danann about thirteen centuries before the birth of Christ.

H. N. Coleridge, "Introduction to the Study of Greek Classic Poets," says, "Of one thing there can be no doubt, that the Greek alphabet is essentially of Oriental origin."

Herodotus asserted that the Greeks obtained their letters from Phœnicia, because he saw in the Temple of Apollo at Thebes letters which the priests called Phoinika or Cadmeian. Euripides and Æschylus deny this.

Irish and early Scotch Gaelic MSS. are written in a hand resembling that made use of by the Anglo-Saxon tribes. Both received it from Rome, and Ireland gave it to Germany.

The Irish had a knowledge of illuminating at a very early period. The Book of Kells is more decorated than any other existing copy of the Gospels, and it is the most beautiful MS. in existence of so early a date, and the most magnificent specimen of penmanship and illumination in the Western world (Canon Bourke).

Long before Byzantine art had time to deviate much from its ancient traditions, and even while it maintained an easy supremacy over the Western Empire, a formidable competitor for the leadership in the art of illuminating had sprung up in the extreme West, in the island homes of the Keltic race.

The general character of the decoration of all writing previous to the origination of the Keltic style in Ireland

had been limited to the use of different coloured golden
and silver inks on stained purple and white vellum grounds;
to the occasional enlargement of and slight flourishing
about initial letters; to the introduction of pictures, generally square or oblong, enclosed in plain or slightly bordered
frames, and occasionally to the scattering about throughout
the volume of a few lines and scrolls (Wyatt, p. 18).

The earliest MSS. of Greece and Rome show nothing
like the distinctive Keltic art; nor the Italian museums,
nor the wall-paintings of Herculaneum or Pompeii, beautiful
as are the representations of the human figure found there;
nor does Byzantine art afford any similar type. From
whence, then, did the Irish, the acknowledged founders
of Keltic art in Europe, derive ideas of ornamentation?
This is one of the historical mysteries, which, like the origin
of the round towers, still awaits solution. One must travel
a long way, even to the far East, before finding the decora-
tions of the ancient Hindoo temples anything approaching
to the typical idea that runs through all Irish ornamentation. It is, however, an incontrovertible fact, and one
proved to demonstration by Mr. Westwood's learning,
labour, and researches, that at a time the pictorial art was
almost extinct in Italy and Greece, and indeed scarcely
existed in other parts of Europe, namely, from the fifth to
the end of the eighth century. A style of art had been
originated, cultivated, and brought into a most marvellous
state of perfection in Ireland, absolutely distinct from that
of any other in the civilised world, and which, being carried
abroad by Irish and Saxon missionaries, was adopted and
imitated in the schools of Charlemagne, and in all the
other great schools and monasteries founded by them upon
the Continent (Lady Wilde).

It is no idle boast to say that the Irish were the teachers

of Europe from the seventh to the ninth century in art and religion. Mr. Westwood has visited all the great libraries of England and the Continent, and found abundant evidence that Irish art, or Hiberno-Saxon art, was diffused over Europe during that period. The Greek and Latin MSS. are not illuminated, but are adorned with intercalated pictures. Irish art differs from them in many respects; among others, in having the figures and rich ornamentation printed on the leaves of the book itself (Canon Bourke).

Digby Wyatt observed that in delicacy of handling and minute but faultless execution, the whole of palæography offers nothing comparable to the ancient Irish MSS., especially the Book of Kells, the most marvellous of them all. He attempted to copy the ornaments, but broke down in despair. In one space about a quarter of an inch superficial, he counted, with the aid of a magnifying glass, no less than a hundred and fifty-eight interlacements of a slender ribbon pattern, formed by whole lines edged by black ones upon a black ground. " No wonder," says Wyatt, "that tradition should allege that these unerring hues should have been traced by angels." Whence did the native race derive this knowledge? Either they invented it, or, as Lady Wilde seems to divine, they had it from the East. The science of comparative philology bears out Lady Wilde's views. These views appear the best and truest (Canon Bourke, p. 335).

The art was known before the arrival of St. Patrick. It did not come with him from Rome, for the Romans themselves did not begin to practise that art till about that period, or a century later; and when they did begin, they had nothing so beautiful or grand as the illuminating school in Ireland even at the earliest period produced (Ibid.).

All writers admit that the Keltic race were most tenacious of old rights, old customs, and traditionary knowledge (Ibid.).

Zeuss and Constantius Nigra bear ample testimony to this special trait of character. "Morum priscorum semper tenacissimi fuerunt Celtici populi" (Grammatica Celtica, Leipsæ, p. 915).

Lady Wilde says, "The Irish adhered with wonderful fidelity to their peculiar art ideas for at least eight hundred years. While the Saxons coquetted with Frankish art, the Irish continued their exclusive devotion to the ancient and national Keltic type. They gave ideas to the world, but received none in exchange."

The intimate acquaintance of the ancient Gaels of Erin with the cardinal colours in their highest degree of purity, and with a great variety of other shades and tints, can be clearly established by existing evidence of a very certain character (W. K. Sullivan). Whenever amongst the early MSS. in foreign libraries one is found surpassing all the rest in the singular beauty and firmness of the writings, then at once an Irish hand is recognised as the writer, or an Irish intellect as the teacher. The borders of the pages in Irish MSS. seemed powdered with crushed jewels (Lady Wilde).

Another Phœnician habit found in Britain is the British use of war chariots armed with the scythe. Cæsar mentions the fact of the British using war chariots, and he describes how expert they were in the use of them, but he does not mention the fact of their being armed with the scythe. He does refer to its use at Pontus in his war with the Pharnaces. The fact, however, that the British armed their chariots is tolerably clearly proved by the evidence of Mela, who speaks of falcatis axibus. See also Frontinus (Strateg., lib. 2, c. 2, ex. 18; Lucan, lib. I, c. 426; and Silius Italicus, lib. 17, c. 417).

The inhabitants of Palestine, the Canaanites, Hittites, and Philistines, Shemetic people all closely allied to the Phœnicians, used war-chariots.

Again, the name of Phœnician, and as somewhat associated with rebellion, as it would be in the mouth of a people who regarded the race as intruders, is still in use in Ireland in the revered word Fenian. From whence does that word come, and what does it mean if not Phœnician? Nor need we doubt that the Phœnicians had power and the means to settle colonies. The history of the Mediterranean shores is a history of Phœnician settlements. Spain was a combined Phœnician and Hebrew colony. Strabo asserts that the Phœnicians possessed the better part of Iberia and Lybia before the time of Homer, and continued masters of those places until their empire was overthrown by the Romans.

Festus Avienus, writing in the fourth century of the Phœnician voyages made 500 B.C., states that they visited the Holy Island, once so called, as well as Albion.

In the Periplus of Scylax, writing about 558 B.C., it is asserted that from the Pillars of Hercules on the European coast there lay many settlements of the Carthaginians. There was found a tablet fixed in a temple at Carthage, on which it was inscribed that about 500 B.C. Hanno set sail with sixty vessels containing 30,000 colonists, men, women, and children. This would give an average of 500 souls for each vessel. It is well known that they had vessels capable of carrying a great number of people, which were managed by the most ingenious machinery.

In the "Æconomicus" of Xenophon, who wrote 400 years B.C., a Greek is represented as having said, "The best and

G

most accurate arrangement of things I think I ever saw
was when I went to look at the great Phœnician ship, for
I saw the greatest quantity of tackling separately disposed
in the smallest stowage.  You know that a ship comes to
anchor or gets under way by means of many wooden
instruments and many ropes and sails, and is armed
with many machines against hostile vessels, and carries
about with it many arms for the crew, and all the
apparatus which are used in a dwelling-house for each
mess; besides all this, the hold is filled with cargo,
which the owner carries for his profit; and all that I
have mentioned lay in not much greater space than
would be found in a chamber large enough for ten beds,
although they lay in such a way that they did not obstruct
one another, so that they needed no one to seek them,
and could be got together, and there were no knots to be
untied and cause delay if they were suddenly wanted
for use."   It is not difficult to suppose that such a people
could colonise both Ireland and England if they chose.
It would be done quite in accordance with their customs
and in their interests, a combination of events quite sufficient for their inclination.

Dr. Latham admits the probability of Iberian settlements both in England and Ireland, and this would be
quite in accordance with the Punic system.  Phœnicia
settles a colony at Carthage, which 1100 B.C. founds Gades,
and Gades subsequently founds other colonies.   But
probably Gades had long been a colony before the alleged
date of its foundation; or if not, Ireland and England had
been colonised directly from the mother country.

It is curious to observe the double method by which
both France and Britain have been colonised.   The Gauls
came by sea, while the Scythians or Cymbri came over-

land, and that was the difference between them. Both were originally Scythians or wanderers, nomads, hippomolgi; but just as Dan subsequently took to ships, part of the Shemetic race did the same, and part of them remained a pastoral people, and retained the name of Scythian which the others lost. But still both retained their ancient Sethite knowledge; they only applied it differently; and this, above all things, distinguished them from the Canaanitish and Japhetian races settled around them.

And the wanderers by the sea, becoming traders, were called Phœnicians; and they still kept up their intercourse with their brethren, for how otherwise can we account for the use of metals, of glass, and of other Phœnician manufactures, amongst the nomad tribes of Asia? Is it possible that they also were manufacturers? Both have been credited with the invention of music and of musical instruments, because both were in possession of Sethite knowledge. Who shall say to which of them these inventions properly belong?

Canon Bourke, has given the writer a good reason why the early inhabitants of Ireland, and it would follow of England also, were called Phœnicians though of purely Scythian or Gaelic race. In a letter written to the author 10th January 1879 he states :—

"Many Scythians mixed with the Phœnicians on the coast of Asia Minor. The inhabitants of Tyre and Sidon, and all down the entrance into Egypt (along the coast), were of a half-Keltic class, and hence some of the old writers could have said that the Gaels were Phœnicians; that is, the Gaels (or Kelts) passed through that country just as the Northmen passed through Brittany, or after landing in England passed through after settling in Wales. The word Scythian at that time meant (like Jew

and Gentile) any one not a Phœnician, or not a merchant
of the then merchant world; at least this is stated, and
facts go to show that in the early ages Scythian had that
meaning.    Many of these (Scythians), emigrating from the
East, came at a very early date to North Germany (all
admit this).    The Keltic branch too had come, and hence
both could be called Kelto-Scythian."

## CHAPTER VIII.

### PHŒNICIA, ITS ORIGIN AND PEOPLE.

As it is clear that we possess no safe guide in Josephus, although we may gain valuable hints and occasionally explanations of matters which were doubtful, we must ascertain whether ancient history will not supply us with the information we desire.

As tradition and positive evidence both point to the Phœnicians as the first traders with, and settlers in, the isles of Britain, or Baratanac, as the Phœnicians, according to Bochart and other writers, called these islands, it is only following out a reasonable clue to ascertain who the Phœnicians were, whether their language, habits, laws, literature, science, and arts accorded with our own; in other words, whether we are of them and who they were.

There is perhaps no people of ancient history so well known as the Phœnicians, and of whom so little is positively known. It is recorded of them in turns that they were of Shemetic, Hametic, and Japhetian origin; not that they were supposed to be a mixed race, but it would seem that no one knew who they were, and so every one jumped at the conclusion most pleasing to himself.

That the country of Phœnicia was called Chna or Canaan is so well known that it is idle to refer to it. Heccateus and Stephanus Byzantinus both assert this fact, and so does Jewish and all history. Euptolemus,

apud Euse, 6 Pr. Ev. 917, makes Canaan to be the progenitor of the Phœnicians; but with equal truth the Phœnicians might be called Aramites because their country was
once called Aram, or Assyrians because their country had
been known as Syria, or Philistines or Pali because it is
also well known as Palestine or Palistan, *i.e.*, the country
of the Pali. That Phœnicia was in the time of the Greek
dominion of Syria, and continued to be called by the
name of Canaan, is evident from an inscription upon a
Phœnician coin, which is "Laodicea, the mother of Canaan;" and later St. Augustin, writing of the Carthaginians,
says (Augustini, Ep. ad Rom., opera iii. 932), "Interrogati
rustici nostri quid sint Punici respondeat Chanani;" but
this only proves that they had adopted the name of their
territory, just as have the Germans of to-day. Sanchoniathon states that the name of Chna was changed into
that of Phœnix, a form of it which is to be found in
Finnish or Finland, as well as the Fingalian and Fenian
of Ireland. Why it was so changed, or what is the real
meaning of the term, does not appear. But there is evidence that Phœnician means a trader, as well as a native
of the country, and there is little doubt it was applied to
the Hebrew traders as to the Syrians; and as the Phœnicians were essentially a commercial people, this may be the
origin of the name, although it may be a consequence. It
has been said of the Phœnicians, that though living in
Phœnicia they were not of it. They resided there to carry
on their commerce, but they did not extend their conquests inland, nor did they care even to colonise anywhere
except for the purpose of extending their commerce. Their
settlements were invariably chosen in order to further
their occupations. Professor F. W. Newman (History
of the Hebrew Monarchy, p. 8) asserts that Canaan or

Chna is interpreted by many writers as the low country, as opposed to Aram (Syria), the high country; but however this may be, we learn from Moses that many Canaanitish tribes settled there. Herodotus, in spite of the bad name Josephus would give him, is far more trustworthy than his traducer, and he states that the Persian writers relate that the Phœnicians came from the sea called the Erythra, and settled in Chna; and in proof of this, three places are pointed out on the Persian Gulf bearing similar if not identical names with those of Phœnicia, Tyrus or Tylus, Aradus, and Dora, in which were temples resembling in architecture those of Phœnicia, and the inhabitants of which claimed the Phœnicians for their colonists (Kenrick's Phœnicia, p. 48). Dionisias the Periegete also states that the Phœnicians are descended from the Erythreans; and, as we have seen, they have been called Scuits and Scythæ. It is thought by some that the name is derived from one Phœnix, but this was the result of the common delusion of a certain date, that all tribes and nations were named after their leader, and unless better proof be forthcoming in support of it, it may be dismissed without further consideration. This is an etymology worthy of the faith of the Oxford school of history.

Others derive the name from *phonis*, a palm or date, a tree which abounded in that neighbourhood; but this is putting the cart before the horse with a vengeance. Possibly a palm was called *phonis* from being so plentiful in the country of that name. This, however, is a form of the name very near to that of the Irish Fenian. Others, more sagacious, think that Phœnicia is a corruption of Edom, though by what process the one word can be said to be derived from the other it is difficult to determine. True it is that the Edomites fled hither in the days of

David, but we read subsequently of their utter destruction
as a nation, whilst we know that the Phœnicians remained
prosperous long afterwards. Solomon's dealings with King
Hiram of Tyre are ample proof to the contrary.

Bochart tells us that the most probable derivation is
Phene Anak, the sons of Anak. This derivation has only
to be examined to be summarily disposed of. Anak was
the son of Arba (Joshua xv. 13), and his city was Kirjath-
Arba, but Joshua gave it, under the name of Hebron, to
Caleb, the son of Jephunneh the Kenezite. The Anakim
were cut off and utterly destroyed, with their cities, from
Hebron, Debir, and Anab, and from all the mountains of
Judah, and from all the mountains of Israel, although
they remained in *Gaza*, in *Gath*, and in *Ashdod*, all cities
of the Philistines, which fell under the dominion of David;
and all this time and long afterwards the Phœnicians lived
and flourished in their own territory.

Notwithstanding Professor Newman's distinction of the
inhabitants of the world into Canaanites as dwellers in the
low country, and Aramites or dwellers in the high country,
there is grave doubt whether there was any distinction
whatever between the dwellers of the low and high country, or at any rate whether the Phœnicians were not called
Aramites as well as their neighbours. It is clear they
were both called Syrians, as were many of the neighbouring countries. Villanuava, p. 100 of his valuable book,
" Ibernia Phœnice," thus writes of the Syrians :—

"Syri vocati sunt Aramæi seu Aremin a Aram majoris
Asiæ regione cujus incolæ maratime fuerent Phœnices
quorum præcipuæ urbes Tyrus et Sidon. Hæc autem
regio nomen sortita est non a Aram filio Camuel ex
famile a Nachor (Genesis xxii. 21, 23) sed a Aram filio
Sem quinto quo nomine hujus oræ incolæ gloriabantur

nam abiis Shur quod est Ashur vel Assyria detractâ
Syllaba et confusis nominibus Suria Syria Aram vocatur
est unde et Syri in continente terræ Chanaan habitantes
et Phœnices incontinii Aramæorum nomine semper dignosci
voluerunt Græci eos appellabant Lyres sed illi se ipsos
Aramæos quod Josephus (Antiq. lib. 7) et Strabo (lib. 13)
asserunt et veteris testamenti mos est Aram pro Syria
et Arami pro Syro ponere."

A very learned writer, Goropius Becanus (Indo-Scythia,
lib. 5), gives valuable testimony upon the point. He
writes, "Hieronimus et plerique Hebræorum omnes Aramæos Syron esse credent ab Aram filio Semi genus et
nomen sortitus quod quia bis per omnia eum ·antiquorum
pugnat sententiam quam Plinius e monumentis vetustis in
lucem revocavit viz. ultra suæ Scytharum populi Persæ
Mos Sacas in universum appellare a proxima gente antiqui
Aramæos quo tamen ubique parte sit satisfactum conce-
demus Aramæos alios esse ab Armenis et eos quidem
quos Græci Syrus vocant Hebrorum lingua Aramæos
ab Arami dici Mos autem quis Scythas nominarum anti-
quitas dictos et illos quidem Aramæos esse verum am
Hebraicum sed sua id est Scythia lingua confitendum erit
a Judais totam Scythiam Armeniam vocari."

Goropius has detracted from his ·merit, and indeed
brought ridicule upon himself, by endeavouring to prove
that Flemish was the language of the Garden of Eden;
and so it may have been if a dialect may stand for a
language; but the idea is absurd, not less so than General
Vallancy's idea that the Irish are Canaanites simply
because their ancestors passed through the land. He
too has lost a great reputation by this foolish mistake.
Another great genius, and almost equal to these two,
is John Pinkerton. His books are most learned, and

his industry in searching the original authorities unwearied. Few writers have ever equalled him in this
respect, yet all his vast learning and industry is disre-
garded and lost because he too had a bee in his bonnet,
and his bee was the Germanic theory. His proofs of
the descent of the Goths from Thrace is perfect, but his
identification of the Goths with the modern Germans is
foolishness. He forgot that the German race were cannibal Sarmartæ or Saroumartæ, who seized upon the
Gothic possessions on their departure for the sunny south,
and assumed with their territory much of their language
and some of their character — proof that these savages
came in contact with some of the Goths and intermingled
with them, or otherwise the Gothic civilisation had died
out in Germany, and it had been called Sarmatia.

It has been said that great wits are allied to madness, and
these three men, Goropius, Vallancy, and Pinkerton, are
absolute proofs of the fact; but this should not make us
despise their works. They are most valuable, and abound
with hints and ideas, and are filled with facts, any single
chapter being more than equal in these respects to a
volume of the present day; and if we only discard their
folly, we may derive the greatest benefit from their
learning.

That Syria is an older name for the country than Aram,
would appear from the fact that in the time of Strabo the
inhabitants were said to have been called Aramites, who
were formerly called Syrians. It is supposed that Assur
was the progenitor of the Syrians and Assyrians, ancient
writers using these names indiscriminately, and the country
from Assyria to the sea-coast having borne the name of
Assyria or Syria at an early date. At that period the
Aramites were probably confined to the country north of

the Syrians, and along the Euphrates to the Erythrean
sea; but being of the same Shemetic race, and encom-
passing the Syrians on every side, they would readily
incorporate themselves together.  There is little doubt
but that the Aramites, travelling round Syria, went into
Egypt, and through their water communication in that
land, running down the Nile, settled on the coast of Syria,
founding the great cities of Tyre and Sidon.  Indeed,
Syria seems to have been a centre around which they
settled, as if to approach as nearly to it as possible; and
so mixing together, they would be known indiscriminately
as Aramites or Syrians; and since they are both of Shemetic
race, no confusion could occur in consequence.  This idea
is rendered more probable from the fact that the Scythians
mixed more largely with the Phœnicians or Syrians.
Villanuava would deduce the name Scythian from Phœnicia.  He writes: "Mihi probabilius est ne dicam indubiam Scythes a Phœnicibus hoc nomen sortitus ex quo
illis admixti sunt magnam Syriam partem occupantur et
illos sic vocasse quonium eorum tribates viderunt ad id
tempus per agros et sylvus discurrentes et per incultas
solitudines et asperos montes errare solitus eorem Phœniciis."  Now it is clear, as will be presently shown, that
the Scythians sprang from the Armenians, who are admitted by Josephus to have been the descendants of Ul or
Chul, the son of Aram.  And looking at the map of Armenia, and its water communication with Syria, it is very
easy to see how naturally the Armenians would overflow
their country; and the proof that they actually did so is
to be found in the history of the Keltai or Galatai, who
settled north of Syria, and gave their name to that part of
the Mediterranean.

In Tylor's "Primitive Culture," Arabs, Jews, Phœni-

cians, and Syrians are all accounted of Shemetic origin.
That the Phœnicians proper did not colonise the country
inland more may be accounted for by this very fact, they
could not do so without displacing their own brethren.
They therefore settled on the coast; and just as the
Armenians, then called Gaels by the sea, or Galileans,
sent forth their colonies to people the earth, it is quite
possible that no true Phœnician ever settled in the British
isles, and that the so-called Phœnicians who did so were
the Gaels who passed through their country.    Canon
Bourke would seem to be of this opinion.

Josephus, of course, is in difficulties in the distribution
of the territory to the issue of Shem, and to satisfy the
sons of Shem he distinguishes between the Assyrians and
Syrians, assigning the first to the issue of Assur and the
latter to Aram ; and by this means he, in fact, gives the
Aramites the double name, for undoubtedly many of the
sons of Ul, Uz, Gether, and Mesa all settled in Syria.
But as clearly that name was derived from the Assyrians.
Virgil, writing of Tyrus, says, "Sarrono dormiat ostro,"
Tyrus formerly being called Sarræ, which is probably
derived from Assur or Assyria; and Sidon is probably
derived from Saria and don—the men of Syria or Saria.
However that may be, there is ample evidence that the
Phœnicians were not Edomites, as many writers have
contended, but originally Assyrians, and recruited from
the ranks of the Aramites; and the best proof of this is
in the fact that they were possessed of the Chaldean
learning—were in learning Sethites as opposed to the
Canaanites, though they subsequently lapsed into idolatry.
If this were a proof of their Canaanitish origin, on the
same principle the Hebrews would be Canaanites also.
The Phœnicians were Canaanites only in accepting that

idolatry. Some proof of the Shemetic origin of the
Syrians may be gathered from the fact that the Arabs
have always and still style their country that of Shem.

It would seem that the wicker boats covered with
hides, which our Keltic ancestors in England and also in
Ireland adopted, were used also by the Assyrians and
Aramites upon the Euphrates.

Hesiod and Homer both prove that the Syrians were
Aramites, and many writers of antiquity testify to the
same fact; so that it follows that if this is the fact
Josephus is convicted of one false statement; and if it can
be shown that he is in error as to the issue of one of Shem's
sons, his authority is utterly gone.

Josephus himself asserts that the Phœnicians are
Scythians, but he alleges that the Scythians are sons of
Magog. He is probably right as to the former statement,
and that is admitted by the Irish themselves. Francis
Plowden (Historical Review of Ireland) writes that "the
ancestors of the Irish were undoubtedly Scythians, as
they were afterwards called Phœnicians." That the Scoti
were Scythians there can hardly be a doubt. It is curious
to find how individual facts in Irish history corroborate
the idea. The Formorians, who were probably settlers
from England, claim to have been of Shemetic race; and
if so, so were all the Irish races, for they all spoke one
language with the English of the period, and that undoubtedly a dialect of the Shemetic form of speech.

Mr. Kenrick writes (p. 48),"The threefold character under
which the Phœnicians appear to us in their earlier history,
navigators, merchants, and pirates, have always belonged
to the nations of the Arabian peninsula, and these attributes were united in no other nation of equal antiquity.
The Babylonians were not familiar with the sea, the

Egyptians abhorred it." And he adds, the Phœnicians were never more than settlers on the coast of Syria, without root in the interior; so they began, so they ended. It is indeed singular that this character so exactly accords with the character of the British at this day. The traditions of the Babylonians represent their civilisation as coming to them from the head of the Persian Gulf, the original home of the Phœnicians—a country which really lies to the south-east of Babylon, and which a writer in Palestine or Egypt would very appropriately designate the East.

Combining these facts with the belief of the Phœnicians themselves, Mr. Kenrick considers that there is a body of evidence in support of the idea that their original home was upon the Erythrean Sea which it would not be safe to set aside.

The term Erythrean Sea is, however, rather vague. It has been applied to a great part of the Indian Ocean, and repeatedly by the Greeks to the Arabian Sea, which was named the Sea of Edom, Hebrew for the Red Sea, because the country of the Edomites was situated upon it, and the term Erythrean signifying "red" in Greek also, the two became confounded; hence also, probably from this circumstance, the Phœnicians have been mistaken for the Edomites, who may possibly be the ancestors of our Turkish allies.

The part of the Erythrean Sea inhabited originally by the Phœnicians was the mouths of the great rivers Tigris and Euphrates—a position of great commercial importance, and one which a people like the Phœnicians would struggle to secure. It is probable that the majority of them came down from the land of Aram to inhabit it, and that they are truly Aramites; and this is highly probable, for the Aramites would naturally become a maritime people, as

they occupied the greater portion of the country watered
by both these rivers; and their locality would account for
their connection with the Chaldeans, and it would account,
too, for Abraham traversing their country, and dwelling
so long at Haran. Now whether they had traversed the
mainland which separates the high country of Aram from
the coast—a very inconsiderable space—or whether they
had arrived at it through the ancient canal between the
Arabian Sea and the Mediterranean, is a matter of small
moment. Either route would be easy to them, and again
either would be natural, inasmuch as they would spread
in both directions, by land as well as by sea; for the sons
of Aram inhabited all the country from Chaldea to the
Sea of Askenaz, from which they would take ship for the
Crimea, their next settlement northwards; and again they
would as easily approach it by sea from their settlements
in Egypt, for many facts conduce to the belief that the
Hyksos, or Shepherd kings of Egypt, were of this race.
Again, we find them extending into the country, and gradually settling in it, by using the great water-communica-
tion. Sesostris is said to have been the first to dig the
canal which connected the Nile with the Red Sea, which
was no doubt restored by Ptolemy, and again by Trajan;
but so little reliance can be placed upon Egyptian accounts,
that it is far more likely to have been the work of the
Phœnicians, since it terminates at a town called Babylon,
and it had a city of Succoth on the way; and, moreover,
it is called the Canal of Amram, which is probably a corruption for Aramenian. The traditions of the Egyptians
themselves exactly tally with the notion that the Shepherd
kings were Phœnicians or Aramites. It is known that
the Hyksos dwelt at Memphis, though it is not exactly
known where this is situated, though probably near ancient

Babylon, since their residence must be connected with the great pyramid of Gheza, which was unquestionably the work of these Shepherd kings. Piazza Smyth would therefore give the date of 2170 B.C. as that of their occupation, and Salatis is the first of these monarchs who is said to have built it; how long before and how long after this date is matter of conjecture, but this date at any rate may be considered a true one.

Manetho states that the Shepherd kings reigned in Egypt 511 years, and it is also stated that there were only six of them. This would rather point to the patriarchs themselves as the rulers, for what other people lived to such great ages? Josephus confounds them with the Israelites, but this is clearly an error, for their departure from Egypt, according to the best authorities, was in the thirty-seventh year before Abraham was born, or 2054 B.C., some few years after the building of the great pyramid. From this date agreeing so closely with that of the great pyramid, it must be clear that the date recorded on the building is that of its completion, for it is a monument that must have in all probability taken some centuries to complete, possibly the whole of the five hundred years that the Hyksos reigned in Egypt, in which case Salatis, the first founder, may well have been the son of Arphaxad, and Memphis may have been the residence of the patriarchs. Josephus relates that "the Almighty permitted certain men to live a longer time upon earth, because He was so pleased with them for their virtue, and the good use they made of their astronomical and geometrical discoveries, which would not have afforded the time for foretelling the period of the stars unless they had lived six hundred years, for the great year is completed in that period." The fact that men lived for near a thousand years at this time is, according to Josephus, vouched for by Manetho, Berosus, Mos, Hestinus, Hierom, Hesiod, Heccatæus, Hellinicus, Acusilaus, Ephorus, and Nicalaus. Men would require a great age to conceive and carry out such enormous works as that of the great pyramid, and it may well be that it was the work of the patriarch Noah and his sons, some of whom may have dwelt in Memphis and others in Chaldea, or even in more distant countries.

Some Egyptian accounts assert the Hyksos to have been Arabians, but Phœnicians coming from the Arabian Sea may well have been so described. This much is tolerably clear, they were driven out or left Egypt in the reign of Thethmosis. Bunsen (lib. 3,p. 48, Geza) extends the occupation of the Shepherd kings to 929 years, and he supposes that the fifty-three kings mentioned by Appollodorus (Lyne, pp. 147, 279 ; ed. Diod.) to be the Theban kings who were contemporary with the Shepherds.

It is curious that all historians—Herodotus, Manetho, Diodorus, and others—disagree as to the builder of the pyramid—some declaring that Cheops built it, others Souphis, others Chemonis; while Pliny and others declare that the builder is unknown. The Egyptians themselves state that it was built by one Philitis, whom historians have attempted to identify with Melchizedek of Scripture. All accounts concur in stating that the Egyptians hate the building, although they have attempted unsuccessfully to copy it, and claim it as their own; and all agree that they hated the people who built it, as well as their occupation of shepherds. This fact seems to indicate that the Hyksos must have been a nomad tribe, just as were the Phœnicians, the Chaldeans, and the Hebrews. The fact that Josephus makes so curious a mistake between the Israelites

H

and the Hyksos, if nothing else were wanting, shows that
he is no authority as to the antiquities of the nation, and
knows nothing of their history but what is contained in
the Mosaic records, though, notwithstanding, the tradition
may have a foundation in fact ; for if the Hyksos kings
were indeed the patriarchs, they were the ancestors of the
Israelites.   This is the only hypothesis that can be reconciled with Josephus, but it is not his meaning, and he
clearly intended to indicate that the sojourn of the
Hyksos was that of the Israelites.   He well understood
the division of mankind into the followers of Cain and
those of Seth, for he writes that Cain was the author of
measures and weights, and that he changed the world into
cunning craftiness; whilst the Sethites, who answer to
the Chaldees, were the inventors of that peculiar sort of
wisdom which is concerned with the heavenly bodies and
their order; and Seth, he declares, made two pillars, and
inscribed these discoveries upon them, which remained in
the land of Syria to that day,—forgetful of the fact that
Seth lived before the Flood, and that the two pillars in
question were alleged to be, and possibly are, the work of
Seth, the son of Sesostris, king of Egypt.   He also states
that the descendants of Seth (he must mean Shem) continued to esteem God as the Lord of the universe, and to
have an entire regard to virtue for seven generations.
This exactly tallies with the statement in Joshua, that
Terah, the father of Abraham, fell away to the worship of
idols.

   That Abraham was a good man is vouched by many
historians.   Berosus is said to have referred to him when
he stated that in the tenth generation after the Flood there
was amongst the Chaldeans a man righteous and great,
and skilful in the celestial science.   Heccateus, Josephus

asserts, left a book about him. Nicalaus of Damascus in the fourth book of his History states that Abraham reigned at Damascus, being a foreigner who came with an army out of the land above Babylon called the land of the Chaldeans, but after a long time he got him up and removed from that country also, with his people, and went into the land then called the land of Canaan, but then the land of Judea. The name of Abraham, he asserts, was still famous in Damascus, and there is shown a village named from him "the habitation of Abraham." The sons of Abraham by Keturah, and their sons, Josephus asserts, he contrived to settle in colonies, and they took possession of Troglodites and the country of Arabia the Happy as far as it reached to the .Red Sea. Abraham is recorded by Moses to have gone down into Egypt to avoid a famine in Canaan, so that at his date, not so far removed from the so-called expulsion of the Hyksos, the race of the Hebrews must have been held in good estimation, otherwise he would not have dared to intrude.

Mr. Kenrick (Hist. of Egypt, ii. 192) asserts that the account given by Apollodorus (ii. 1, 3), that Egypto, the son of Belus, brother of Agenor king of Phœnicia, came from Arabia and conquered Egypt, unhistorical as it is, may have had its origin in the invasion of the Hyksos, who are called both Phœnicians and Arabians, and who settled in Palestine on their expulsion from Egypt.

The connection of the myths of Isis, Osiris, and Typhon with Phœnice, of the Tyrian with the Egyptian Hercules (Herod. ii. 44), and generally of the Phœnician with the Egyptian civilisation, will be best explained by the supposition that the nomad tribes of Palestine were masters of Egypt for several generations, and subsequently returned to the same country, carrying with them the knowledge of

letters and the arts, which they were the instruments of
diffusing over Asia Minor and Greece. Phœnicia has evidently been the connecting link between these countries
and Egypt, which directly can have exercised only a very
slight and transient influence upon them.

It may well be that all that has been asserted of the
Hyksos is correct; but to state anything positively of
what happened at such a period would have no basis at
all to found it but for the wonderful remains at Gheza, no
doubt the ancient Memphis, or near to it. Memphis is
stated to be at Abaris in the Sethroic nome, or Saite in the
Typhonian region.

Mr. Kenrick assumes, upon the very slightest evidence,
that the Phœnicians were Jebusites, simply because of the
accounts which are given of their alleged expulsion from
Egypt; and adds, that thereupon the Phœnicians settled at
Jerusalem, and the Israelites, when they settled there 500 or
600 years later, found the Jebusites in possession; as if the
Phœnicians might not have left in the meantime, or perhaps
have never been near to it. Little better is his assumption
that Manetho mistranslated the Hyksos Phœnicians because
they were Canaanites. Surely the Canaanites would be
well known to the Egyptians, who were of that very race.
However, it is tolerably clear that the Phœnicians were
very early settlers in Palestine, although it is impossible
wholly to credit their own chronology. Herodotus was
very curious to learn the date of their temple dedicated
to Hercules at Tyre, and he was told by the priests there
that it was built 2750 B.C. Their system of chronology,
by the way, he asserts, differed entirely from that of the
Greeks or the Egyptians.

Mr. Kenrick objects to Sanchoniantho's history upon the
ground that it is in fact a history of the human race since

the earth was repeopled by Noah; but so it naturally would be if the Phœnicians were identical with the Chaldeans; and this date for the building of the temple of Hercules is, in fact, very nearly the date of the Deluge—actually within six years of the mean period—a proof not of the antiquity of the temple, but of the true chronology of the Phœnicians. Sidon is claimed for an older city than Tyre; but it would appear that this is, like many other such claims, untenable, for a Phœnician coin of the date of Antiochus IV. has been found, which has on it an inscription of Tyre, the mother of the Sidonians; and again, in the Mosaic writings Tyre is always named first.

The fact is important, as showing a relationship between the Israelites and the Phœnicians; which may account for the fact that neither of them encroached upon the territories of the other. That neither Aco, nor Ecdippa Byblous, nor Sidon came into the possession of the Israelites is quite clear; but it is not clear how much of the territory of each was occupied by the tribes of Naphtali, Asher, or Dan, though it is clear Dan copied the ways of the Phœnicians and dwelt in ships; and from the letter of King Hiram to Solomon it appears that they intermarried. That the Phœnicians behaved badly to the Jews is no proof, but rather the contrary, that they were not related. Joel the prophet accuses the Phœnicians (800 B.C.) of selling Jews to the Greeks, their relatives; so Amos complains that they sold Israelites to their relatives the Edomites. Moses does not pretend to give the history of the other members of the Shemetic race, hence he only records the doings of the Israelites, and of the rude tribes and peoples who opposed them. He is even, as has been observed, totally silent as to the doings of Noah and the patriarchs; nor does he ever refer to the great pyramid, though he must have been well acquainted with it and with its origin. Gesenius (Mon. Phœn., lib. iv. sec. 6, Morris; Erschen and Grubii, Encyclop., art. Phœnician) has collected with great care the differences between the Phœnician language and that of the Hebrew, and he finds that the Phœnician was an undoubted dialect of the Hebrew, leaning much to Aramian forms.

In Egypt itself (as we should expect, if the Phœnicians are Aramites) inscriptions have been found in the Phœnician characters written in the Aramian dialect.

This is surely more than evidence of mere contact; it is proof of actual relationship, proof of the Shemetic origin of both peoples.

Mr. Kenrick states that the early authorities are nearly unanimous in assigning to the Phœnicians the invention or early possession of an alphabet, and its communication to the Greeks.   Lucan (Phars. 3, 280) asserts that its possession and use amongst them was earlier than the use of the papyrus by the Egyptians; and Herodotus asserts that they gave the use of these letters to the Greeks; and undoubtedly the most ancient Greek characters, like the Hebrew and the Phœnician, run from right to left.

The ordinary Hebrew characters are known to be later in date than the Phœnician, and it is supposed that they were adopted by the Jewish nation on their return from the Babylonian captivity.   The Samaritan copy of the Pentateuch is not written in Hebrew but in Phœnician characters.   Scaliger had recourse to it to illustrate the connection between the Phœnician and the archaic Greek letters.

The derivation of the Greek alphabet from the Phœnicians is unquestionable. The oldest forms of Greek letters hitherto discovered are those of the inscriptions found in the islands of Thera and Milos (Franz Epege, p. 51), both of which were colonised by the Phœnicians; they are supposed to be of the age of Solon and Pisistratus. This at once shows the malice of Josephus, who asserts that the Greeks had no letters until long afterwards.

Layard (Nineveh, p. 346) proves that Phœnician characters were in use there, which shows an intercourse between the two nations, and tends to prove the Shemetic origin of the Phœnicians; but their community of knowledge is even a greater proof of relationship. It is impossible to suppose that they could have possessed language and learning in common and yet be of different races.

Pliny asserts that the Phœnicians were famed for the invention of letters, as well as for astronomical observations and naval and martial acts (Nat. Hist., lib. v. c. 12; so Curtius, lib. vi. c. 4; and Lucan, lib. iii. v. 220, 221).

Cherelaux speaks of a people who spoke Phœnician, and who dwelt in the Solymean mountains, and these Josephus takes for Jews; for Jews, he admits, spoke Phœnician in earlier times, as well as in his day. Aristotle speaks of Jews from Cele-Syria, who were derived from the Indian philosophers, and by them called Calami, and especially of one of them who came down from the upper country, and became, as he asserts, a Grecian, not only in his language, but in his soul, and imparted his philosophy to him. Pythagoras also emulated the doctrines of the Jews and Thracians, which appear to have been similar, and he took a great many of the laws of the Jews into his own philosophy.

The Greeks seem to be indebted as much to the Thracians as to the Pelasgians—who are believed to be the lost descendants of Peleg—for their philosophy and learning.

The Jews were a most prolific people, and Josephus relates that the Persians, who were their own kindred, carried away captive tens of thousands of them into Babylon, and many into Phœnicia. Josephus is evidently in the dark as to who were and who were not Jews even in his own country, and he takes this way of accounting for his ignorance.

Another strong proof of the relationship of the Israelites and the Phœnicians is in their common practice of circumcision, though, of course, Josephus denies that they had this custom; but even if they had not kept it up, it is no proof of their being a different race; for as they fell into idolatry, it may well be that they would neglect such a custom.

Theophrastus relates that the only people who were circumcised originally were the Colchians, the Egyptians, and the Ethiopians, and he asserts that the Phœnicians and those Syrians that are in Palestine confess that they learnt it from the Egyptians. Herodotus also asserts that the Syrians that are in Palestine are circumcised.

It is curious that the Egyptians should have adopted this custom, and it probably points to their subjugation under the Hyksos, and this may have been to them a badge of their servitude. They never surmised for themselves a foreign origin, but believed themselves to be natives of the soil. Nor, although their institutions are similar, have the Indians any tradition of having received or sent forth an Indian colony (Kenrick's Ancient Egypt, p. 105).

Mr. Palmer (History of the Jewish Nation), writing

of the Hyksos, states that they reigned over Egypt whilst Joseph was a captive, thus agreeing with Josephus; and this accounts, he asserts, for Joseph gaining such favour and marrying so highly. He thinks that the Hyksos were of Shemetic race, because Manetho and Eusebius both describe them as being Phœnicians; and he considers the statement in Genesis that there rose up a king who knew not Joseph to refer to their expulsion. To credit this theory it is not necessary to discard what has been written already, but only to accept Bunsen's view of the prolongation of the domination of the Hyksos.

# CHAPTER IX.

## THE LEARNING OF THE PHŒNICIANS.

UNFORTUNATELY we have but little literature left us upon which to form any opinion. Josephus, Theophilus, and Sanchoniatho, amongst the ancients, have preserved a few fragments.

Sanchoniatho, in the fragment preserved by Eusebius, tells us that the Phœnicians held that the two first mortals were Æon and Protagonus, and their children Genus and Genea, who inhabited Phœnicia ; and that when they were scorched with the heat they lifted up their hands to the sun, whom they believed to be the lord of heaven, and called him Baalsamen, the same whom the Greeks call Zeus. That Hysperiramus and his brother Ousous, Phœnician patriarchs, erected two pillars, the one to fire and the other to air and wind, and worshipped those pillars, pouring out to them libations of the blood of the wild beasts hunted down in the chase. As these early monuments were called Bathelea—a word probably derived from the Hebrew Bethel, which, just as Guthel is contracted to Gael, would contract to Bael—it is probable they had altars of loose stones, such as that which Jacob erected. As his was consecrated in honour of the true God, theirs were consecrated to the hosts of heaven ; and the form of consecration seems to have been the same, anointing the stone or pillar with oil. The ignorant worshippers supposed that by this consecration the intelligences by which the sun and planets were animated took possession of the consecrated pillars. Surely this is a more reasonable solution of the question of the purpose for which the Irish round towers were built than the supposition that they were only for the ringing and swinging of bells, or the reception and safe custody of hostages, for whom there is absolutely no room.

As they were dedicated to the host of heaven, they were usually erected on the tops of mountains. Even this is accurate to the letter of the round towers; some are and some are not on the hill-tops. Surely if they had been built for watch-towers—another absurd suggestion—they would always have been placed upon the highest point. But if they were built for the habitation of spirits, they are not only roomy enough, but absolutely perfectly adapted for such an idea; and their tapering form would seem to suggest the notion that they were intended to penetrate to the heavens.

The practice of building these pillars prevailed universally throughout the East, and the fact that they are not now to be met with does not militate against the theory; for Moses (Deut. xii. 2) requires the Iraelites to destroy the places on the mountains and hill-tops and under every green tree where the nations served their gods, and they were commanded to overthrow their altars and break their pillars and burn their groves.

After many generations came Chrysor, and he invented many things useful to civil life, for which after his decease he was worshipped as a god. Then flourished Ouranos (heaven) and his sister Ge (earth), who deified and offered sacrifices to their father Hypsestos when he had been torn in pieces by wild beasts. Afterwards Cronos (time) consecrated Muth, his son, and was himself consecrated by his subjects. In the reign of Cronos is said to have flourished a personage of great reputation for wisdom, who by the Egyptians was called Thoth, and by the Phœnicians Taautos, and by the Greeks Hermes. It was through him that religious worship was brought into order and method. He is said to have invented letters, arithmetic, geometry, astronomy, and hieroglyphics.

The gods of Greece and Rome were derived from Egypt and Phœnicia, and by following their order we obtain a clue to that of the latter. The first day of the week, Bel of the Phœnicians, Apollo's day of the Latins, was dedicated by the Scandinavians and the Gaels to the sun or Baal, the lord of the earth. The Romans early changed the name of the day to the Lord's day. Monday, Dies Lunæ; in Gaelic, Di Luain. Tuesday in Gaelic is Mart Di; Latin, Mars. Wednesday, Phœnician, Taautos, Hermes; Scandinavian, Woden (Mercury) ; Gaelic, do. Thursday, Thor, &c., the Thunderer (Jupiter) ; Gaelic, the same. Friday, Venus, Friga, Fria, Ashtoreth, Astore (Gaelic). Saturday, Seator, or Saturn; Chronos (Phœnician).

Of their civil laws we have no fragments, unless indeed, as they imparted to Greece the great gift of letters, we should find in her laws a reflex of those of Phœnicia.

But in the important matter of religion we have strong evidence of similarity; first, of course, in the worship of Baal, then Moloch, another name for the sun. Ashtoreth and Thaummez were of their gods.

Diodorus Siculus says that their chief deity was Chronos or Saturn. Jupiter was Belus, so was Apollo. Astarte or Ashtoreth was Venus or Juno.

There appears to be no proof that the horrible custom of

sacrificing children to Moloch (Saturn) was ever practised in Ireland, though it is clear that it was the practice of the Phœnicians, Carthaginians, Persians, Scythians, Laodiceans, Thracians, and those living on the river Borystheas, and the Grecians. It is a curious but dreadful fact that this practice is said to have been copied from the Jewish account of Abraham offering up Isaac at the command of the Almighty.

The Persians and Massagetæ, who were in direct communication with the Phœnicians, considered the mistletoe to be sacred, and this was a belief of the Druids.

St. Patrick is said to have come into conflict with the Druids on the subject of fire-worship. He offended them by lighting his fire contrary to the custom on Holy Saturday, a high day of the Phœnicians as well as of the Jews. (See Legends of St. Patrick, Aubrey de Vere, 1872, p. 26.) General Vallancy appears to deny that there were any Druids in Ireland.

But the chief point of similarity between the Phœnicians of Egypt and of Syria, and between them and the Chaldeans, is their knowledge of science and the arts, latterly debased by idolatry, but originally pure and holy. No nation of mere idolaters could unassisted attain such greatness.

Sanchoniatho attributes the invention of music and of the lyre to Sidon. The Sidonians were especially great in all manner of dyes, in glasswork and ivory carving, in the glyptic and plastic arts, in the manufacture of gold and silver drinking-vessels. Their skill in metallurgy and in all kinds of work is recorded in the correspondence of Hiram and Solomon, a correspondence which seems to indicate a close relationship between the parties. At any rate, the best workman was by birth half a Phœnician, half a Jew.

As merchants they engrossed the commerce of the Western world. They affected no empire but that of the seas. They seemed to aim at nothing but the peaceable enjoyment of their trade, which they extended to all the known parts of the world, and to many parts which were only known to themselves. Their merchants were indeed princes. Their country was the great warehouse of the world, their ships were the masters of the seas. They practised piracy in order to deter other nations from interfering with their trade; and they carried goods overland as well for Syria, Mesopotamia, Assyria, Babylon, Persia, Arabia, and India; indeed, they were the greatest importers, exporters, and transporters in the Old World. As navigators they were the boldest, the most experienced, and the greatest dis- coverers of ancient times. They had for many ages no rivals. They very early applied astronomy to navigation. They were great colonists, not for the sake of conquest, but in order to advance their commerce. It was a marvel in their day how they could colonise so largely without depopulating their own country. How completely these characteristics tally with our own is too obvious to point out; except that we do not practise piracy, every word might be written of ourselves; and we share with Ireland in their heritance and descent from this singular people. The share they took in erecting and decorating Solomon's Temple is fully recorded in the Scriptures. Their fame for taste, design, and ingenious invention was such, that whatever was elegant, great, or pleasing in apparel, vessels, or toys, was distinguished by the epithet Sidonian. They were addicted to philosophical exercises. Moschus taught the doctrine of atoms before the Trojan war. Abomenus of Tyre puzzled King Solomon with his questions.

And what was the language of Phœnicia, which Greek and Jew cherished and equally hated? It is lost, and but a few words remain, and these few words are inscriptions, and a short passage to be found in a Greek play by Plautus; and this language is found to be pure Keltic. General Vallancy was the first scholar who could give it a meaning. Here is a discovery: if Phœnician is Keltic, so is Etruscan; so is Sabine, the root of Latin, the mother of the Umbrian and other dialects; and that they are also Keltic is admitted. Professor Newman admits this. He writes (Regal Rome, p. 61), "The Sabines were Keltic, and Kelts nearer to the Gaelic or Erse than to the Welsh branch. They were formerly called Umbrian, thus proving that the English are a different branch of the Kelts from the Welsh." In the Sabine tongue the names of warlike and political things are native to Keltic, whilst very few of them bear marks of being native to Latin; so too the Etruscans were Keltic.

General Vallancy considers that the languages of both Italy and Greece are half-Keltic and half-Phœnician; and this is clear, that the Gallic or Keltic irruptions and invasions from the North cannot account for it. When the Cimbri invaded Italy in the time of Marius, a body of them called the Ambrones found to their surprise that they had a similar war-cry to the Ligurians who were opposed to them. Both of them were originally derived from Thrace, the one reaching Italy by sea, first settling in Sparta, and the other by way of Dacia, possibly having parted company more than a thousand years previously.

The question of the science of the Phœnicians, Carthaginians, Pelasgi, and the Greeks may best, in this day at least, be determined by a reference to architecture. There are two grand classes into which all the earliest specimens

must fall—the one called Promethean and the other Epimethean; or, as biblical scholars will more naturally term it,
Sethite and Canaanitish; or it may perhaps be more truly
described as Scythian as opposed to heathen.

The meaning of Promethean is science which is based
upon true principles of art, and in which the architect
calculates beforehand every step of his work.  By the
latter the reverse of this process is adopted, and the last
events determine the scope and form of the idea.  The
clearest and best example of both kinds is to be found in
the building of the pyramids of Egypt, which are supposed
to be the earliest specimens of architecture in the world.
The one known by the name of the Great Pyramid is an
epitome of all science.  The rest, which are mere imita-
tions of it by persons who had no conception of the Promethean views of its architect, are all built without design
or method, and the size and shape are determined very
much by the course of events.  It is enough to say of
them that they were probably built by different kings for
their own tombs.  In the first year of his reign the king
cut out a chamber in the rock, and covered it with a layer
of stone.  Each successive year he added to it, and at his
death his successor encased the heap with cut stones, the
size of which thus represented the number of years of the
monarch's reign—that is, it varied in size according to the
length of his life.  This is a fair specimen of the Canaanitish style.  On the other hand, the great pyramid was
designed upon a magnificent scale, proportioned to the
exact size of the earth and to its position in the planetary
system, and that not only of the solar system, but of the
greater system of which the sun itself, and the planetary
system which surrounds it, is but a unit.

Professor Piazza Smyth, Astronomer-Royal for Scotland,

has demonstrated mathematically, that word being used in the sense of absolute correctness, that the great pyramid, by reference to the grand astronomical phenomenon known as the precession of the equinoxes, which relates to a period of not less than 25,827 years, memorialises its own date of foundation, and fixes it at or close to the year 2170 B.C., or about 4048 years ago. No one has attempted to disprove this statement, and it may be taken to be strictly accurate; and this would indicate that it was built in the age of Shem, who died 2154 B.C. If we take the year 2170 as that of the completion of the building, we may conclude that it was designed by Noah himself, who lived 350 years after the Deluge, or down to about the year 2406 B.C.

To take only a selection from the results to be obtained from the measurements of the great pyramid, which prove that the building is purely scientific, and not the result of Epimethean architecture.

There is a small antechamber to the central king's chamber, deep in the interior of the great pyramid. It is 41·5 inches broad and 116·26 inches long, of which 103·033 are in granite, the rest being in limestone; and the same vertical measure of 103·033 appears in another part of the room; and the reason why these measures are made to the thousandth part of an inch was, that one of the 103·033 measures being vertical and the other horizontal, and both enclosing one rectangular corner, they typify the area of a square each side of which measures 103·033 inches in length.

The area of that square was precisely equal to the area of a circle having the length of the whole floor, or 116·26 inches for diameter, which satisfies the problem of squaring

I

the circle, a problem which has occupied the minds of men for fully 3000 years.

Again, if this same number 116·26 be multiplied by the quantity of the proportion of the length of the diameter to the length of the circumference of a circle, or 3·14159, &c., the result is 365·24, or the number of solar days and parts of a day contained in a solar tropical year, a proposition always missed by astronomers even 2000 years after the date of the great pyramid.

Again, it has been found that this antechamber floor stands on the fiftieth course of masonry forming the whole great pyramid from its base upwards, and if we multiply 116·26 inches by 50, we have for the result 5813·0 inches as the ancient vertical height of the great pyramid, as derived from the mean of all the direct measures of it.

And if 103·033 inches be multiplied by 50, we have 5151·5 inches, which is the length of a side of a square, which is exactly equal in area to a direct vertical section of the great pyramid, or again to a circle having the vertical height of the great pyramid for a diameter, exhibiting, in fact, another form of the problem of squaring the circle, and a form which is essential to the computation of the power of every steam-engine presently working in Great Britain.

Add to these curious facts that the great pyramid exhibits in addition a remarkable and immutably arranged system of weights and measures, which are actually founded harmoniously upon grand features of astronomical nature ; viz., on the size and weight of the earth, distance of the sun, length of the year and number of its days, and curiously fractional parts of a day, together with the enormous period of the precession of the equinoxes.

Professor Piazzi Smyth concludes that because, in the

great pyramid, astronomy, combined with mathematics and physics, guides and directs the whole fabric from its first base line to its last internal feature (its mere materials were put together in the Promethean or Sethite manner), it follows that it cannot but be the very primeval edifice of stone alluded to by Josephus as built by the sons of Seth, though in the Canaanitish land of Siriad, and it was the only one they erected there.

Mr. William Petrie in 1867 discovered that the great pyramid's first applied science or astronomical problem is the sun's mean distance from the earth accurately represented by its chief line of measure, i.e., its central vertical height when multiplied by the number which its shape typifies, viz., by 10 raised to the ninth power, i.e., 5·819 multiplied by 1,000,000,000 = 91,840,000 English miles. To verify this problem has recently occasioned not only Great Britain but several other countries vast expense and trouble, though with what result is not yet known; perhaps, with all the powers of science, the true measure can only be ascertained by means of this grandly designed building. This measure was never approached by several millions of miles until the last ten years, when it had by common consent been admitted to be very near the truth.

A peculiar relation exists between the sun's mean distance, the size of the earth, the number of days in the year, and the proportions of a $\pi$-shaped pyramid, such that the length of a side of the base at the great pyramid, and in that pyramid alone of all the pyramids of Egypt, does, when divided by well-known numbers of days and parts of a day in the year, namely, 365, 242, &c., yield a quantity which is not only a handy measuring-rod in itself, but, in the view of science, has the inestimably appropriate recommendation of being, as far as we can say, exactly

the ten-millionth of the straight distance from the earth's
centre to either pole, or of the same axis of the earth's
diurnal rotation in the course of its annual revolution
round the sun.

And, what is still more important to the subject in
hand, the measures still in use in Great Britain are the
pyramid measures. Piazzi Smyth calculates that after
4000 years we have only deviated a hair's-breadth, or $\frac{1}{1000}$
part of an inch, in our unit of measure, the pyramid inch
being 1·001 English inches; but it is difficult to conceive
where he can find a record of the English measure of such
extreme accuracy. Surely it is more rational to suppose
that there is a mistake somewhere, and that the two measures are exactly the same; certainly our quarter (corn
measure) is one-fourth of the contents of the coffer in the
great pyramid, which again, but on a smaller scale, exhibits the common measurements of the whole fabric. Is
not this quarter a clue to the meaning of the word
pyramid? Does it mean more than corn measure?

The king's chamber repeats the year-day multiplier of
the base and side length, in a form which, while it conceals
the standard more completely than ever from the ignorant,
yet proves it to the learned more undoubtedly by supplying, not merely an arithmetical repetition of the numbers, but a mathematical reason for their being there;
and Piazzi Smyth, guided by a similar discovery of
Captain Tracey's in the antechamber, found that pyramid
inches in the king's chamber stand for 25-inch cubits
outside the great pyramid.

The capacity contents of the coffer are 71·250 cubic
inches, precisely the same quantity which characterised
the capacity of the sacred Ark, of the Covenant constructed by Moses; this, as well as with the British

capacity, measures four quarters, and being divided into five 500 parts, produces a standard unit of pyramid capacity equal to the old British wine-pint, thus proving conclusively that the measure of each was the same, and that just as the Israelites used the pyramid measures, by some means they have been and are still our own.

The weight of the whole contents in water of the same coffer vessel forms the pyramid ton weight, which comes between the avoirdupois and our shipping ton, which, on being pyramidically divided by 5 × 500, gives the earth's commensurable and nearly British pound weight.

To any one who is acquainted with the modern measures of Europe, and especially with the French metric system, the importance of these measures will be fairly estimated, and it is also of importance to see what countries still possess the sacred cubit. It will be found that Greece and the Ionian Islands and Candia have preserved it as faithfully as any nation, and after them England and Italy, whilst it is still to be traced in Tunis, in Copenhagen, and Trieste.

These facts relating to the great pyramid are taken from several very able articles contributed by Professor Piazzi Smyth to the Bellringing Journal of Mr. Hine, verily pearls amidst something very different; and they establish more than the scientific problem referred to, for they are clearly evidence of the greater and more important truths resulting from its existence. Such problems are comparable to the miracles of our Blessed Lord in turning water into wine, in healing the sick, or in raising the dead; the act done taken *per se* is of small moment except to the individual the subject of the miracle, but as an exhibition of an unknown power or a manifestation of a secret intelligence, their significance is immense. What matters it that the earth is shown to be 91,840,000 miles distant from the sun ? the knowledge brings us no nearer to it, nor does it concern us largely to know that the problem of squaring the circle is at last effected; but the idea that this great silent mass of masonry, the largest building made by human hands that the world has ever seen, should relate these facts to us after they had been buried through the ignorance of men for four thousand years is wonderful indeed, for it proves to us the truth that the world has not yet regained all the science that it has lost, and that, learned and scientific as we think ourselves, the sages of antiquity were as gods in wisdom compared to ourselves; and they teach us also how rich an inheritance had the Jews, and how grand a people they might have been, and doubtless were before their great wickedness.

And from this one great fact we learn also that the Sethites did all their work according to principles of true and accurate science, and this one fact is a key to discover, not perhaps the people, but certainly those who came in contact with them, for whoever worked on Promethean principles must at any rate have acquired the knowledge from them. Apply this test to the Germans, and what is the result ? They have no proofs to exhibit of Promethean intelligence, no buildings, no works, no accomplishments of any kind. Apply it to the Cymri, to the Irish Kelts, and the result is very different; their architecture is a direct proof of it, and their musical compositions and instruments prove that they were possessed of the true principles of their art; that they worked on Promethean principles. Take the harp; it is of course a Jewish instrument, but it is also a purely Keltic one; we know that even Italy, the land of song, acknowledges her indebtedness to Ireland. Take the sister art—painting. Surely Irish MSS. prove abundantly that here also her artists worked upon true principles. Go to the Canaanitish kingdom, examine their work; sometimes it is very beautiful, but it is rarely in good taste, never good in design; it is more frequently tawdry and vulgar, always meaningless. Can there be a greater proof than this of the noble origin of the Kelt?

Take the test of poetry. From whence did English poets gain their power, their tender melancholy, their faculty of moving the passions and minds of men? The answer is, from the Keltic. Even their rhymes were borrowed from the Kelts. Neither the Greeks nor the Romans knew how to rhyme, and the English could not have done so had not they too been of Keltic blood. If we except the Jews, what people in the world except those of Keltic blood, those descended from or taught by the Phœnicians or Carthaginians, have ever breathed out their souls in poetry? Italy; yes, but Italy is the land of the Gael. Here the Gael from the North met in a stern embrace him who had come there by sea. In Liguria both contending hosts raised the shout of Ambrones, because they were akin.

It must not be forgotten that Professor Piazzi Smyth, and all who value the results obtained by the pyramid measurements, are immensely indebted to the French for their splendid services in measuring the great pyramid.

# CHAPTER X.

## THE PHŒNICIAN COLONIES.

As it has been observed, the colonisation by Phœnicia of all the coasts of the Mediterranean has become matter of history, and the same can be asserted of the islands. Indeed, it is not too much to assert that out of Phœnicia issued a vast number of tribes who peopled the whole earth. The first perhaps in importance, as well as in point of date, were the Isles of Greece. It would be intrenching too much upon Grecian history to do more than slightly glance at the fact, as will be proved presently, that the Aramian race, after colonising the whole extent of territory between the Caspian and the Euxine, using for the purpose the mighty river Euphrates with its numerous tributaries, overspread the heart of Europe, and settled permanently amidst the mountains of Thrace.

Greece had a dual system of colonisation, just as Sparta had a dual system of royalty; and it is a fact in Grecian history that swarms of colonists from Thrace encountered in her midst the settlers from the coasts of Palestine and Egypt. Amongst others, the Spartans were undoubted Thracians, retaining the peculiar laws and customs of their mother country. It is probable that the Pelasgian element entered into the composition of Greece so early as the expulsion of the Shepherd kings from Egypt. It has been asserted that this event occurred even earlier;

but dates are not of much consequence, or rather are not very much to be relied upon at that period. The coincidence of the expulsion from Egypt and a settlement in Greece of a people of the same name, and of precisely similar habits and customs, is, however, too curious to be without connection; and there can be little doubt that the Shepherd kings peopled Greece on their departure from Egypt, and this would account for the Grecian tradition that they derived their learning from that country.

Sir Isaac Newton asserts that Pelasgus was one of the Shepherd kings or leaders, although he dates the event of their occupation from the wars of Joshua. Without, however, giving any proof or any reason for his belief, he dogmatically asserts that the Shepherd kings were the Canaanites who fled before Joshua, and that they were driven out of Abaris 1070 B.C.

The Spartans in the North can claim an almost equal antiquity. Lykourgos is removed from the period of genuine history by a gulf of centuries. He belongs rather to the age of Prometheus, and may be identical with Noah. Herodotus shows that not merely did Sparta regard herself as the first city of Hellas, but that in the Hellenic states there were not a few who were disposed to look up to her as such (G. W. Cox, Greece, p. 94).

It is difficult to guess at the early events of Grecian history, and this perhaps arises from the conflicting parties having the same origin, or rather from two branches of the same people meeting after a long separation, just as in England the Gaelic and the Cymric met after a separation of many centuries.

The Greeks have no tradition of any writing anterior to that of the Thracian bards, but these bards used the Pelasgic letters (Dio. Sic., lib. iii.; Dion, Hist., lib. iv.).

Professor F. W. Newman (Regal Rome, p. 7) asserts that certain Pelasgic tribes near Thrace spoke a language the Greeks did not understand. They were closely akin to the Trojans. He also asserts that the Ionians, Æolians, Uelli, Hellenes, Dorians, Thessalians, Siculians, Austrians, and Latins were all Pelasgi, and that the Pelasgic tribes were all marked by the epithet Tyrrhene, which means Etruscan.

The following interesting account of the Pelasgi is from the pen of the Very Rev. Canon Ulich J. Bourke:—

" The Pelasgi, the real aborigines of Greece, the authors of those gigantic walls and constructions which are known in Italy by the name of Cyclopean and in Greece by that of Pelasgic, and some of which still exist, besides several others that existed in the Peloponnesus, and which are mentioned by the ancients, these aborigines, or this primitive race of people, occur in many countries under the same or at least very similar traits. To them we must ascribe those monuments of architecture we have just spoken of. A certain knowledge of metals, some rude religious rites without any mythology, which was clearly of later origin, nay, without any names of specific divinities, human sacrifices, manners and customs, if not actually savage, still very rude and barbarous, and a constant restlessness and disposition to roam. Deucalion alone is to be considered as the ancestor of the Hellenes, as all the noble families of kings and heroes derived their descent from him; and the later tribes of Greece, the Æolians, the Dorians, and Ionians, took their names from his sons. According to every indication, the people would appear to be a Caucasian race of Asiatics of India, or at least of a cognate origin."

Thomas Aske asserts that the Pelasgi derived their

letters from the Phœnicians, and he asserts positively that
they were of Phœnician origin, and particularly that they
settled at Samothrace, Lemnos, Imbius, and Scyros, in
Attica, Thessaly, all the old Hellas, Argolis, and all over
the Peloponnesus; and several colonies of them, particularly from Lydia, Lemnos, Imbius, Thessaly, and Arcadia,
settled in Italy. Solysius Polyhistor relates that the
Greek colonists who settled in Asia were aborigines,
Aurunci, Pelasgi, Arcades, Siculi. Pliny (Nat. Hist., lib.
3, c. 5) adds the Rotuli, Osci, Volscii, and Ausones. All
these colonists, like the Thracians and Phœnicians, wrote
from right to left till the reign of Tarquinius Priscus. The
Samnites continued to write in this manner till 230 B.C.

The Etruscans were Pelasgi direct from Phœnicia. The
Pelasgian language and characters are preserved in the
monuments which are called Etruscan, and everything
relating to the religious, civil, military, and naval estab-
lishments among the Romans was derived from the
Etruscans and other descendants of the Pelasgi who
settled in different parts of Italy.

The following account of the Etruscans is extracted
from Professor Newman's "Regal Rome" (p. 98):—

"The Etruscans in all civilising arts were exceedingly
in advance of the other nations of Italy. They belong
indeed to the era of Phœnicia and of Egypt rather than of
Greece, although in the later period they borrowed largely
from the plastic skill of Corinth. Their tombs and their
magnificent walls still testify to their luxury and industrial powers; their fleets commanded the seas, and their
heavy-armed infantry were unmatched on the land before
Rome existed as a city; their nobles were priests, as often
in Asia Minor; the ecclesiastical system was ancient and
very peculiar, and the use of letters familiar to them in

very early times. Their alphabet was a modification of the Phœnician, and, what deserves remark, like all the people of Western Asia, they wrote from right to left."

The Etruscans called themselves Rhasena, but foreigners called them Tarsh, probably from their having been a colony from Tarshish. "If," says Professor Newman, "we were at liberty to assume that the Etruscans, like the Solymi of Lycia, spoke a language of Shemetic relationship, we might conjecture that Rhas meant head, and that *ena* was a mark of place, as in Arabic in use." Surely this assumption is fully warranted; both spoke the purest Keltic.

The Sabines in all probability came from Sabana in the south of Arabia. There is tolerable proof, contrary to the ordinary assumption, that Dedan and Sheba, coupled with Tarshish, if they did not relate to the sons of Abraham, did not refer to the sons of Cush. The Greeks confounded the two names together, and called the people of Seba and Sheba promiscuously Sabæans. They were, like the Phœnicians, sun-worshippers. Sale, in his introduction to the Koran, thus speaks of them: "They believe in the existence of one God, though they also pay an adoration to the stars, or the angels and intelligences which they suppose reside in them and govern the world under the supreme deity; they endeavour to perfect themselves in the four intellectual virtues, and believe the souls of wicked men will be punished for 7000 ages, but will afterwards be received to mercy. They are obliged to pray three times a day, before sunrise, before noon, and before sunset, and in praying they turn their faces as some say to the north, according to others to the south, to Mecca, or to the star to which they pay their devotion. They have three fasts in the year; the first lasts thirty days, the second nine days, and the last seven. They offer many sacrifices, of which they eat no part but wholly burn them ; they abstain from beans, garlic, and some other vegetables. In all this is very observable the remains of the ancient Jewish faith."

In this people may or may not be found the origin of the Sabines of Italy, the progenitors of the several nations, amongst them the Umbrians, who certainly had the same language as the Carthaginians, as we learn from Plautus. The Very Rev. Canon Bourke (p. 471) positively asserts that the Sabines of Italy used a vocabulary which was akin to Gaelic, and gives a list of some Sabine words which are pure Gaelic.

Dr. Dyer (History of the City of Rome, p. 27) writes, " The importance of the Sabine element at Rome has not perhaps been sufficiently considered." The late M. Ampere has discussed the subject with great learning and ability in his interesting work " L'Histoire Romaine à Rome." He remarks that "not only did the Romans borrow from the Sabines almost all their religious and much of their political and social organisation, their customs, ceremonies, arms, &c., but also that the greater part of the primitive population of Rome were of Sabine extraction, and that what is called the Latin tongue contains a strong infusion of Sabine element."

It is curious how many writers, treating separately of the different portions of a nation, are apt to attribute to the subject of their discussion the sole possession of certain qualifications and qualities. Just as Dr. Dyer attributes to the Sabines all that was valuable in the constitution of the Roman Empire, other writers would give the credit of it to the Etruscans, others perhaps to different nationalities. Each writer seems to forget that several apparently distinct nationalities may have had the same origin, or may have come into contact with the same people, and so have acquired the same elements of learning. If this were borne in mind, many conflicting and apparently contradictory statements would be avoided.

In the Scilly Islands we have probably a trace of the Siculian nation, who, according to Francis W. Newman (Regal Rome, 1852), must have been akin to the Gaelic race. Assuredly the Sabines had a tongue allied to the Keltic; indeed the whole of the Umbrian race sided with the Latin and Gaelic, whilst the Oscan agreed with the Greek and Welsh.

Canon Bourke (Aryan Origin of the Gaelic Race, p. 113) says, " A thousand years anterior to the days of Homer and before the Greek was matured, in Southern Europe and on the coast of Ionia the second sprout of the Greco - Italo - Keltic branch was planted in the Italian peninsula, and there, like the grain of mustard-seed, grew into a large tree the branches of which ultimately filled the whole earth. The Keltic branch took root for a time in Northern Italy; it bore fruit, and, like the oak, scattered its seed to the west in Iberia or Spain, to the northward in Keltic Gaul along the banks of the Garonne, the Loire, and the Seine. The best part was wafted to our noble island, Inis Alga, where it sprang up and formed the luxuriant tree of Irish Gaelic, which at this very day presents all the features that mark the primeval speech of the Aryan race and country."

Josephus (Adv. Apion, s. 6) proves that the Phœnicians were mingled with the Greeks, and (sec. 12) he states that the Phœnicians who lived by the sea-shore by means of their love of lucre and trade (certainly not an anti-Jewish quality) mingled with the Greeks, and we read in Solomon how the Greeks traded with Tyre and Sidon.

. It is unnecessary to point out the connection between

the Greeks and the Romans; not of one race but of many. The Greeks, besides colonising and giving their name to Italy, colonised not only all the coasts and islands of the Mediterranean, but later beyond the Pillars of Hercules, the coasts of Spain and Ireland, and the British Isles also. The Locrians were regarded as Hellenes, and they were doubtless the affines of the Ligurians of the Gulf of Genoa and of Marseilles, as well as of the Llogri of Britain and Gaul.

It is to be presumed that several of the Italian nations, although they owed their civilisation to Phœnicia, did not obtain it through the Greeks, but direct from Phœnician settlements.

Carthage was the chief of the Mediterranean settlements of the Phœnicians, and the only one that did not eventually deny her parentage, and the relationship was always respected by the mother country. Kambyses proposed to the Phœnician sailors to join in the war against Carthage, but they refused to go against their kindred.

The Carthaginians, in their turn, as we have seen, sent out many colonies.

Corsica was conquered and colonised by the Carthaginians.

Pliny speaks of the Carthaginians as just, generous, valiant, and humane, their love of liberty being only equalled by their courage.

The Carthaginian tradition that Dido obtained from the Africans as much land as she could compass by the hide of a bull is foolishly claimed for Hengist. Verstegan, the father of our veracious Saxon history, relates with pious exultation how Hengist obtained from Vortigern leave to possess as much ground as he could compass about with a bull's hide, which the wily general split into thongs, and then called his place Thong Castle.

Diodorus Siculus and Justin relate that the principal support of the Carthaginians were the mines of Spain, in which country they had established themselves at a very early date; their first settlement there was probably Gades, now Cadiz, which they reached by sea; here, however, they had been preceded by Phœnician as well as by Hebrew colonies. Vetelpandus in his commentary on Ezekiel, after quoting Philo, Josephus, Seneca, and Cicero on the fact of the Hebrew colonisation of Spain, mentions that there was a stone at Saguntiam with Hebrew characters as follows:—"This is the tomb of Adoniram, servant of King Solomon, who came to collect tribute and died here." This person is mentioned 1 Kings iv. 6.

At the time of the first Punic war Carthage had extensive dominions in Africa, a great part of Spain, Corsica, Sardinia, and all the islands on the coast of Italy, with a great part of Sicily.

It is impossible within the compass of this book to do more than to indicate a name occasionally, but amongst the hundreds of names in Europe that may be traced to Asiatic origin two are curious. We find the name in France, the route by which some Aramites came to this country, of a town called Aramerat, some twenty miles from another called Uzeo, settlements probably from Aram, Damasene, or Dammesie. The Lydians are known to have colonised largely, and they were closely allied to the Lacedemonians.

The Ligurians are to be found in Italy side by side with the Umbrians; they occupied the province of North Italy, on the north coast of the Tyrrhean sea, from the frontiers of Gaul to those of Etruria. That the Keltic race were settled there earlier than the Gallic invasion of Italy is manifest from the fact which philology teaches, for Keltic is proved to be the foundation of many of the Italian dialects, notably the tongues emanating from the Sabine; and probably also the ancient tongue of Etruria had a Keltic base. And the fact above related, that in the Cimbric invasion both sides found, to their surprise, that Ambrones was a common war-cry, proves that the connection was of so ancient a date that there was no remembrance of it.

But it is under the name of Gaul or Gael that we shall best trace the Phœnicians in their own country, and under that name we find them still in the British Isles.

How then can it be accounted for except on the hypothesis that the Phœnician settlers were of Gaelic race? And there is little difficulty in showing this to have been the case, for the country of Tyre and Sidon was anciently called Galilee, the country of the Gael of the sea-coast, and the sea itself was called the Sea of Galilee. Curious that the same land should have so many names—Galilee, Phœnicia, Palestina, Cœlo-Syria, Idumea, and, above all. Canaan.

There is little doubt that here is the cradle of the Gael, for, amongst other divisions, it contained an Upper and a Lower Galilee, and a Gaulonitis; and above, to the north, is Galatia. Here, too, is to be found Gadeses, probably the original of that form of the name Gadhelion, so well known amongst us. Galilee is a country distinguished by its natural beauty and fertility; it is unquestionably the finest part of all Palestine; the true abode of the Pali or Shepherds. Above it rises Mount Tabor in a conical form, with a plain at the top commanding a most delightful prospect. The Lake of Tiberias or Genesareth is surrounded by lofty and picturesque hills, the sides of which were once covered by towns, but are now almost deserted.

K

The Galileans, as may be inferred from the fact of their giving their name to the sea, were the most bold and skilful maritime people of Asia Minor; *i.e.*, they were Phœnicians.

That the Gallic or Gaelic is a dialect of the primary language of Asia, has received the sanction of that celebrated philologist, the late Professor Murray, and in his prospectus of the "Philosophy of Language" he states "that the Celts were the aborigines of Europe, and their language the aboriginal one." Hence it is that it is found to underlie all the civilised languages of Europe, and, in fact, to be the basis of the dominant languages of the world. Like the country from which it comes, it is at the same time Gael and Punic, Pelasgian and Etruscan, Latin and Greek, and, as we shall presently show, it is also Cymric, Gothic, and English.

But is there no means of bridging over the gulf which separates Galilee from the British Isles?—nothing to show by which route the Gael arrived? Certainly by careful attention every step of the way may be indicated by the names of places along the route—that is, of one route, for the Gael came by land as well as by sea. He came along the Mediterranean round to Genoa and Marseilles, and then across France by the Loire and the Garonne, till he reached the English Channel, and was quickly transported over to the Land of Tin; and he undoubtedly entered Ireland through England, as unquestionably he also reached Ireland by sea—that is, through the Straits of Hercules and from Cadiz—and overflowed again into Britain through Scotland, meeting once more in the heart of Britain, as his kindred branch, the Cymric, met in the heart of Italy.

# CHAPTER XI.

IT is a curious and important question how and from what direction Britain and Gaul were peopled. That they were anciently stocked by the same people there is no doubt, and the same may be said of Ireland. This is quite certain as respects the period of five or six centuries before the invasion of Cæsar.

In Britain the Gallic wave was known as the Llogrian or Ligurian. In that country it was the second race, the brachydolicho people, as in Ireland it was the first. There can be no doubt of the direction of the current round by the Mediterranean, at any rate, to Gadiz, and across the south of France by the Garonne and the Liger. Whether the Phœnicians took the sea course to England or not is immaterial, though it is difficult to say why it should be more hazardous to sail from Gadiz, coasting along to the mouth of the Liger (as we know did both the Phœnicians and Carthaginians), than to sail to England and Ireland direct from that port. By one or other, and probably by both, of these courses the Gael of Syria found his way to Gaul and the British Isles, and peopled them both. But in England he found an occupant who had been there from a much earlier period—the ancient Cymry. How did the Cymry reach this country? That question can be readily answered, for they have left their names as signposts to direct us along the route by which they travelled.

That their port of debarkation was Hamburg may be inferred from the name of that city coinciding with the name of the country from which the Triads state them to have been derived; and a glance at the map will make it apparent that this was the best point of debarkation for a people coasting round Gaul and coming downwards from the north-east. The Germans state that Hamburg was originally Heimburg, and so it may have been—*heim*, from whence "home." This name is a curious confirmation of the statement of the Triads, lying as it does in the very road of the Cymry, for their next great station on their way from the East is the Crimea, the country lying close to the mouth of the Dneiper, the great water-way by which they made their way to the Baltic. It is curious to find that great rivers invariably connect the stations by which the tribes first move forward. This is naturally the case when they are designedly seeking new countries; when they are simply pushing forward by force of increase of population, they progress without reference to water-ways; not so when they are manifestly seeking altogether new homes.

The British Triads prove that they left the land of Ham to avoid strife and contention. Hu Gadarn would not have lands by fighting and contention, but of equity and in peace; hence the Cymry outstripped the Gauls, who crossed Europe more slowly, probably just as they increased and multiplied, and according to their law of borough English, which Dr. Mackay's " Gaelic Dictionary" indicates to mean the Gaelic system of settling the youngest sons in the homestead, while the elders pushed on in search of new ones. The literal meaning of *burgh*, as used in this sense, is "diggings"—a curious instance of the revival of ancient Keltic in modern slang.

That the Cymry and Cimmerians are the same people is proved conclusively by the route taken by the Cymry on their way between Hamburg and the Crimea, and is probably indicated by the curious fact that the ancient Cymric, a British language, was to be found in the time of Tacitus on the shores of the Baltic, being the speech of a tribe who were famous for collecting amber, and who were called Estones or Estmanni.

The fact of the intercourse between the Estones and the British is abundantly proved, not only by the name of the Estmanni, who are found both on the east coast and in Ireland and Scotland, but by the abundant evidence adduced by Canon Greenfield from the earliest British barrows, a frequent find being amber beads. Amber is found only in one place, like tin, and just as that commodity proves intercommunication between Britain and Phœnicia, amber proves it between Britain and the inhabitants of Estonia. Amber has been found in Wiltshire, at Cressingham, Norfolk, Proc. Soc. of Antiq., 2d. sec., vol. 4, p. 456; at Mold, Flintshire, Archæ., vol. 26, p. 422; Proc. Soc. of Antiq., vol. 4, p. 132; at Llanwith, Anglesea, Archæ. Camb., 3d series, vol. 12, p. 110; Hanley Earth, Orkney, Proc. Soc. of Antiq. of Scot., 3d vol., pp. 183, 295; see also Evan's "Stone Implements," p. 413 et seq.; at Hove, Brighton, Suss. Arch. Coll., vol. 9, p. 120; at Kettlethorp, near Driffield, Derby Arch., vol. 34, p. 255; at Gunton, East Riding of York; at Dartmoor, Devonshire, and Tan Hill, North Wilts; Canon Greenwell's "British Barrows," pp. 178, 207, 297. These authorities are given to show the extent of country covered by people who had dealings with the Estonians.

Dr. R. G. Latham seems (unlike his great penetration)
to have lost sight of this important link in the chain of
evidence binding the British to their Eastern home, for
he endeavours to explain away the distinct statement of
Tacitus by suggesting that for British, as the speech of
this people, we should read a word which would represent
Prussian, which would undoubtedly be very nearly like
it.   But why explain it away when it is the most natural
thing, and just what we should expect to find ?   Besides,
although the word in Tacitus might be an error, yet he
clearly intended it to imply that the language was different
from Prussian, for that is represented by the Lett of Cour-
land ; and Tacitus distinctly asserts that the language of
these districts was dissimilar.

It is a misfortune that the languages of this district are
only known as they now exist, the earlier stages being
unknown.   The fact, however, is admitted that archaic
words are only to be found in poetry, which, it may be,
taken without this fact, is likely to be the oldest form of
speech.   We must therefore rest content with a single
other fact, but that of the highest importance.   The people
of the amber coast were known to Tacitus by the name of
Gothones, which, as we shall presently see, is the same as
Scythian—the name by which, unquestionably, their ancestors the Cimmerians were known to the Greeks.

The Gothones left their name indelibly fixed on the
opposite coast of Sweden, and through Gothland over
Norway was their probable route into Denmark.   But in
England they had another name, which they carried with
them into Ireland—the Ostmanni—at best a translation of
Estonia, and again of the Esedones of Thrace, for they are
the same people, and the latter word is used to show the
derivation of Ostman from Estonia, for Esdoni is clearly

Gaelic for East-duhn or East-man. It may be asked how it is that East-men are found not in the east but in the west of Europe. They are, of course, East-men as regards the population of the British Isles, but they are West-men to their eastern neighbours on the Continent, thus clearly showing the route and the country from which they came. It may be mentioned that, in confirmation of the idea that the Cymry came to Britain direct from Hamburg, the Triads relate that they did come over the Mawr Tawch, which is literally (probably) the North Sea; for the Coritani, who we know were resident on the east coast of England, are said by these same Triads to have dwelt about the river Humber, a name which may be derived from Umbria, or it may be from Hamburg, to which port it lies exactly opposite, and in all probability it would be the route by which the Cymry came. The route, then, of the Cymry being clearly indicated by these facts, it would seem that they would invade Britain without ever encroaching upon Gallia, though in after ages, as their hordes increased, they were compelled to do so. But the Triads seem to indicate that, after reaching Britain, they entered France by way of Brittany. The Triads assert that after passing the Mawr Tawch they passed into Britain and to Llydaw, where they remained. Llydaw or Letavia or Lexovia anciently covered not only Brittany but the whole coast of Gallia.

The fact that the stream of emigration was kept flowing from the earliest period of history is tolerably clearly indicated by many writers. That it was flowing before the time of Cæsar is evident from his account of the intercommunication between the two countries, and, above all, from the fact that the Gauls admitted that their religion and civilisation came from Britain, for they sent

their sons to be educated in her academic groves long
prior to this period; and writers, subsequently to the
period of the Roman occupation of Britain, testify to the
fact that the Britons poured into France to escape the
Roman tyranny, and even subsequently, we learn from
Gildas and Bede, that they continued their emigration to
escape contact with the third great wave of British immigration, the Saxon or Gothic.

And in later times the Cymric stream, fed doubtless
by the same route from Asia, increased so abundantly that
the receiving powers of the British Islands became ex-
hausted, and then they encroached upon the Gauls, and,
streaming through their country, once more returned to
the Summer country, as the Triads called the sunny
South, covering not only Italy, Thrace, and Greece in
their career, but actually crossing the Euxine, and, under
the name of Galatians, invading the very cradle of their
race, the beautiful and prolific Asia Minor; but not as they
left it, peaceably, and in order to avoid war and confusion,
but driven by necessity, by the strong arm of might, by
the very means to avoid which they had left it.

We have few dates to aid us in tracing the limits and
time when the stream first welled up and turned southwards,
but we can trace the people with tolerable accuracy by a
description of their apparel.   The stream of people which
broke off at the ancient route from Hamburg, and took a
southwardly direction, were distinguished by the dress they
appear to have adopted in Asia, and which must have
been remarkable to have attracted such attention, by the
Romans called Braccatæ, and by the Goths Volcæ or Belgæ.
General Vallancy asserts that the Greek word corresponding to Belgæ is Scuthæ.   That the ancient Gauls, like the
Romans and the North Britons of to-day, did not all wear

breeches is a fact in history, for the Romans divided them into Gallia Braccata, or Transalpine Gauls; and Gallia Togata, or Romanised Cisalpine Gauls.   We know that some of the most ancient Britons wore the toga.   That the Gauls in France became wearers of the trews is possibly due to the encroachment of the Cymry or Saxons upon their ranks.   The first in history who are known to have worn this dress are the Sacæ, who dwelt about the Araxes, and they are the people who poured into Europe through Scandinavia, and who in Italy are called the Gesetæ.   The Braccatæ or Belgæ occupied presently the whole of the north of France, which, under the Romans, was known as Belgic Gaul.   They then invaded the south coast of England, driving up before them the Ligurians, in the rear of whom were the Hedui of Somerset and Wilts, and gradually encroaching upon the Irish, by whom they were known, and by whose description we recognise them, as the Firbolgs.

This is the second wave which passed over England into Ireland, or the reverse way, or possibly which passed probably nearly at the same time into both countries, and from the same direction.   The first, the brachycephalic race, who were the Gauls, the Keltæ of Ireland, and the Ligurians of England; and the second, the Firbolgs of Ireland, as their barrows show, a dolichocephalic race answering to the Belgæ of the south of England, who, like their neighbours of the Continent, spoke the Cymric and not the Gallic speech.

Irish historians claim, with the sanction of modern Welshmen, to have peopled England, because the Welsh admit that the names of rivers, towns, mountains, and places in general, as well as the names of people and races in England, are not Cymric but Keltic; and this claim may be

correctly made, but who shall say which was first peopled?
and whether or not they were not both peopled, either
simultaneously or successively, it matters not which, from
the parent race of Gaul? It may be well here to pause
to ascertain whether the names of tribes in both countries
will not throw some light upon the inquiry.

# CHAPTER XII.

## THE SECOND COLONISATION OF BRITAIN.

WE find in Mid-England two great waves of people, who, according to the Triads, successively spread over Britain after the Cymry had been led here by Hu Gudarn, the first of which were the Llogri, and the second were called by the Britons the Belgæ. These tribes were said to have come peaceably.

The first named, the Ligurians, were of such importance that they gave their name to the whole of England, and to this day in Wales it is still called Llogria.

They seem to have been a purely Gallic race, and to have embarked for this country from the mouth of the Loire or Liger. It is not difficult to follow the course this people must have taken round the Alps from the coast of Genoa down to Marseilles, from their leaving their place-names along the whole road to the sea-coast of the west; and to prove their Gallic race we can easily trace them from Italy back to their Grecian homes, and then in Lacedemonia we find them, or their successors it may be, as Spartans, but, whether so or not, in direct communication with Galilee of the Gentiles.

But perhaps the most important of all the Gallic tribes were the Ædui or Hedui. Cæsar, B. G., p. 143, states, "Docebat etiam ut omni tempore totius Galliæ principatum Ædui tenuissant;" and this tribe is to be found still in the wake of the Llogrians, occupying a broad belt crossing

Gloucester, Somerset, and Wilts; and no doubt at an earlier period they had occupied the greater part of the south-east of England   Divitiacus, their prince, who was also king of the Suessones in Cæsar's time, not only held chief sway throughout Gaul, but he governed the Belgic provinces of England and probably was chief monarch of the whole range of country from Kent to Cornwall   It is not probable, however, that his dominion extended much higher up than the counties which now or lately formed the Western Circuit.

Cæsar relates the fact that the tribes on the south coast of England corresponded in their names with those of the Belgic races of Gallia; and it would seem that the Damnonii, whose name probably indicates a close connection with the Lacedemonians, subdued the Carnabii of West Cornwall, and the Cimbri of North Cornwall and South Somerset, and the whole of Devonshire, the Duro-triges occupying Dorset, whilst the Belgæ proper conquered the Hedui of South-West Gloucestershire north of Somer-set and north of Wilts, and the Segontiaci of Hampshire. The Regni seized Sussex and part of West Anglia.

The Trinovantes, who had formerly occupied Middlesex, Essex, Sussex, and Kent, were replaced in the first country by the Suessones or Soissons of Belgium, and on the east by the Cantii, who gave their name to Kent, and had Canterbury for their chief town.

The Welsh Triads agree that the Belgæ, who are called by them the Britons, because they came from Lesser Britain, were sprung from the primordial line of the Cymry, and it was long supposed that they were of German and not of Keltic race, but modern research has clearly established the truth of the Welsh tradition. Besides this, we learn from Cæsar that they, as well as the inhabitants of the Loire, sent aid to their kinsmen the Gauls when he was attacking them—direct proof, if we had no other, not only of their ancient but of their continuing connection. That the Belgæ sent colonies into Ireland is clear from their being called Firbolg, like their Continental and English kinsmen, because they wore braccatæ; but besides this generic name, we can still trace the names of some of the tribes. The Damnonii, the Caucii, and the Menapii all found settlements on the east coast, and other tribes have names so nearly similar that there can be little doubt of their identity also; but these are sufficient to indicate the stream of emigration.

The Voluntii of Cumberland found a settlement on the east coast of Ireland, whilst the Iceni, clearly a Cymric race, under the name of Veniceni, sailed round Scotland and landed on the west. The Brigantes, one of the greatest tribes of all England, who occupied the whole of the northern counties, are found in the south of Ireland; both came from Belgium, as the names of their chief tribes, Parisi and Gabrantaici, indicate; probably they found their way direct to Ireland from Belgium.

The Cotti or Scotti of England are also found in the Scoti of the centre of Ireland; so that it is clear that in both countries are to be found a large number of inhabitants bearing the same tribal names, and the similarity of family names is so great as to constitute an absolute identity of race.

In Scotland, too, are to be found many of the great English tribes, the Brigantes, the Cautæ or Caucii, the Carnabii (extending from Somerset to Cornwall), the Atta-Coti, the Damnii from Devonshire, the Novantes or Trinovantes from Kent, and many others. And an iden-

tity of names and tribes can also be established between
Scotland and Ireland ; in fact, all three countries possessed
probably large divisions of every tribe of the other, and
certainly of all the leading branches of the nation.

It is remarkable that although this identity exists with
reference to the older tribes, that still the same thing can
be said of every other wave of people who successively
settled in the islands.

The Triads, after speaking of the three original tribes
of Britain, after their manner refer not only to three others
who came by consent peaceably, but also to three tribes
who came in a hostile manner.   It would hardly seem
that the subjects of these invasions differed very much
from their predecessors or from each other, and no tribal
name is given for the last batch ; for the names Caledonian,
Gwyddelian, and Galedin probably mean the same word,
Gaul, so that nothing very decisive can be stated about
them, except that unquestionably the Gallic race are
especially largely represented in Ireland and in Scotland.
This class of invaders are probably designed to account
for the inhabitants of Scotland and Ireland, who are
known to be Gaels, and whose presence in these countries
could not otherwise be accounted for.

The Triad is of the greatest importance, for it deals
with events well within the range of history, especially
when it states that three usurping tribes came into the
isle of Britain and never departed from it.

The first of these were the Coranied, who came from
the land of the Pwyl; the second were the Gwyddelian
Fichti, who came into Alban over the sea of Llychlyn;
and the third were the Saxons.

The first were Northmen or Estones, those who followed the first race of the Cymry through Hamburg and

the Humber; the second, the Picts; and the third, the Saxons—all of them of Scythian origin, all of the great Cimbric family—the Cimmerian or Scythians of Asia. The Coranied are the people of the east of England, quite distinct from the old inhabitants, the Coritani, the Corii, the Cortani, the Cotti, the Atta-Cotti, and the Scoti; they were the precursors of the Belgic invasion from the south, and they drove on the ancient Ligurian or Gallic population westward and intermixed with them; they were, in fact, of the same Kelto-Scythian race, but they had travelled northwards, and had become estranged in their speech and habits.

It is conjectured by Davies that the *Cor* in their name signified shepherd, *cor* being a sheep in Gaelic. They were closely allied to the Brigantes, the Iceni, Cenomani or Tigeni, Trinovantes, Cattii, and Cattechlani. And both in Scotland and in Ireland these tribes are to be found, and Britain may have the honour of establishing them upon the land of Erin. The Triads assert that they came from Pwyl, which Davies tells us is the land of pools or Holland, or, it may seem, of Denmark also.

The Gwyddelian Fichti are the Goths or Jutes, or Whites, or Fights, or Fichti, or Pichti; they too are of Scythian race, and came through Denmark. They are of Gallic or Keltic origin, and in Ireland—for they too wandered there—they are called Galloway Picts, and in Scotland simply Picts. John of Hexham writes, " Picti qui vulgo Galweiensis dicunter Gallowegensis terra Pictorum." The Saxons are the Kelto-Scythians of the country south of the Cymbric Chersonesus, and they too settled in Ireland and Scotland.

No dates are given in the Welsh Triads, for the very excellent reason that none were known; it was only known

for certain that an intrusive tribe of the same kiu had at
some date or other invaded the kingdom ; but as their invasion had been going on for some two thousand years, supposing the Triads to be one thousand years old, it was then
simply impossible to give dates or accurately to describe
events ; hence we can rely only upon the Triads for giving
us divisions of races, and for this they are most valuable.

The date of 350 B.C. is given as that of the invasion of
the Belgæ, but looking at Irish records, it would seem
that it should have been fixed much earlier ; and certainly that cannot be too early a date, for that of the
eastern settlements probably is many centuries too late ;
but it is sufficient to establish the falsity of the date
usually assigned for these invasions—that of the Saxons
in 442, and of the Danes two or three hundred years
later ; probably the Danes were much the earliest settlers, and most certainly the Saxons or the Belgæ had
settled long before the time of Cæsar; and during the
Roman occupation we have evidence of their still encroaching, for a Count of the Saxon shore was appointed,
which could not have been done had the Saxons only
intruded after their occupation.

Professor Freeman has done good service in the cause
of truth by exposing the inaccuracy of the statement of
the Saxon Chronicle, which is in fact copied from Bede,
that the Saxons first landed in Britain after the Roman
occupation, though he has fallen into a greater error in
supposing that this invasion only occurred during the
second or third century after Christ.   Still in destroying
the false date of the Saxon Chronicle he has done good
service, and in giving the other he has done no harm, for
he has not offered the shadow of a proof or even a suggestion in aid of it.

One good reason why positive dates of these invasions cannot be expected is that they occurred too frequently and by too small degrees, except in a few instances, such as the first entry of the Cymry, the invasion of the Ligurians and of the Belgæ, all great events, and the latter only attended by war and bloodshed. The Triads assert that, just as they came into England to avoid war and oppression, the Ligurians settled peacefully amongst them, and this is probable from the fact of the peaceful character of the Cymry when unopposed, and there being ample room for their brethren, for it is admitted they were of the same race originally. And the fact that the Belgæ were fiercely opposed is to be inferred from the want of room, being probably the cause why they changed their route and took a southward direction through Gaul.

Except on these great occasions, and always succeeding them, the probability is that the stream was as continuous and regular as it flows in our own day towards our own colonies, and it was probably flowing contemporaneously from each quarter; hence the impossibility of assigning dates for these invasions. Irish as well as English historians fall into the error of distinguishing these tribes ethnologically and then arbitrarily assigning special dates for their entry, whereas all we can hope to do is to separate them and then to indicate a probable date for their successive entries. When we come to follow the progress of the waves of invasion upon the Continent, we do indeed get something like satisfactory dates, for the Cymric and Belgic waves came into contact with people not more civilised, nor perhaps so highly civilised, as the British and Irish, but who have had the good fortune to have had their language and literature made the especial study by the Irish and English, to the utter and shame-

L

ful neglect of their own.    If matters had been reversed, and if, instead of ourselves studying the Roman and Grecian literature, the Romans and Grecians had studied ours, we should indeed at this day be able to state something much more definite regarding our origin; but unfortunately it was but of slight interest to them; and besides, whilst we have remained, they have decayed; and whilst our language is still living, and exerting even a greater influence upon mankind, theirs is politely called dead, although in truth the Greek and Latin races and languages of to-day are quite as near to the Greek and Latin in study and lore as our own speech of to-day is similar to the language of our ancestors who were contemporaneous with the Greeks and Romans, whose languages we cherish.    It is possible that by reference to the dates of the successive waves of Northern emigration which the classics, as we call these dead languages, afford us, we may approximately date our own invasions, and therefore it is well perhaps to look at the facts which we can glean from them.

## CHAPTER XIII.

THE INVASIONS OF THE CYMRY IN SOUTHERN EUROPE.

THE first account that we possess of the invasion of the Northern hordes is the incursion into Italy under Bellovesus, A.A.C. 622, when the Gauls, as they were then called, seized Lombardy and Piedmont—Little Piedmont, which in our own day has followed the Gaelic course by annexing to itself the whole of Italy; in other words, the island of Sardinia led Italy to the front, just as Corsica, in the person of the great Napoleon, once more restored the Gauls of France to their foremost place in history. The second Northern expedition was that of the Cenomani under Eletones, a Cimbric race, who settled in those parts since called Bresciano, Canovenese, Mantua, Carniola, and Venetia. In the third incursion two other Gaelic nations settled on both sides the Po, and in the fourth the Boii and Lingones settled in the country between Ravenna and Bologna. A fifth expedition was undertaken by the Senones some two hundred years after the first-named expedition had taken place. How many expeditions had occurred earlier it is now impossible to say, but looking at the imperfect nature of the materials we possess for arriving at a solution of the question, it is highly probable that earlier incursions had been made from the same quarter. However, this is amply sufficient to establish the fact of a current in this direction.

Then we have evidence of the presence of a Gaelic element in Spain, the inhabitants of which have the characteristics of their French brethren. Mighty in war and in the chase, and famous for their poetry and song. the Galicians are accounted the first poets of Spain, and it is said they composed and sang verses before the descent of the Romans; but, as we have seen, the Galicians are a wave flowing from the East.

Again, expeditions were sent out against the Greeks in A.A.C. 279. The Gauls, finding themselves greatly overstocked with inhabitants at home, sent out these great colonies to conquer new countries. It is tolerably clear that just as the Phœnicians, who probably learnt the practice from the Israelites, the men so sent out were chosen by lot. One of their expeditions marched into Pannonia or Hungary; the second, Thrace; and the third, into Illyricum and Macedonia; and not content with sweeping the whole of Europe, they penetrated into Asia Minor, and seizing the upper part of Phrygia, they gave it their own name of Galatia. In the east various tribes crossed the Rhine, and established themselves in that wild and barren country which was left uninhabited, or was sparsely peopled by tribes of Germans or Goths. In fact, in every quarter but the north there was a constant and powerful overflow from the earliest times of which we have any knowledge of their habits.

If the history of the successive waves of this great family of nations be traced, it will probably be found that the enormous inroads of Asiatics from the north country and through Scandinavia caused the constant succession of emigration from those parts, making the country to overflow in every other direction. Now the name by which they were known to their neighbours is of importance.

They were styled usually Gauls by the Latins, and Celtæ by the Greeks, as well as Galatai and Keltai; and in the northern provinces which bordered on Scythia they were styled Celto-Scythians. This fact we learn from Plutarch, that when, in the great immigration into Italy, the Cimbri and Teutones left their ancient homes vacant, they were at once filled by Scythians. It would seem that this was the course of the stream, and that therefore Scythia, and not the smaller and colder countries of Sweden and Norway, produced these wondrous hordes; and this too follows, that as the stream was constant, the older inhabitants were being displaced by the new, and yet no change of language occurred. The Scythians, from whose ranks they were recruited, must have spoken the same language, and must, in fact, have been the same people, meeting here the descendants of the tribes from whom they had branched off some two thousand years previously.

# CHAPTER XIV.

BEFORE proceeding with the task of attempting to prove who were the progenitors of the English and Irish races settled in these islands, it may be as well to take a glance at the popular view of the subject.

It is not extravagant to state generally that Irish history, like that of the early British, is dispensed with as wholly visionary and unreliable.  It is not pretended that there was any change of inhabitants either by the Romans or by any tribes of Saxons—Germans, of course—who succeeded them; but that " all scholars know " (that is the favourite expression) that there is nothing in their history or in their language worth study.  With regard to the English the case is different.  The ancient British, it is now allowed, may have been an interesting race, but there is no trace of them left.  We English have nothing to do with them. Cæsar either exaggerated the numbers of the people he found here, or they all passed over the seas into Brittany, or they were exterminated.  History does not exactly state the way in which they were disposed of, but that is immaterial.  It suits the views of Sir Edward Creasy or Professor Freeman, Mr. Stubbs or Mr. Green, to dispose of them, and accordingly they are disposed of; and a fair field and some favour is open to their German successors, the Anglo-Saxons,—so called, it is said, from Angeln in

Denmark, or the Angli, a tribe mentioned by Tacitus, it does not matter which; and Saxon from our Saxon cousins of the Continent, the modern inhabitants of German Saxony.

The one great tenet of the Oxford school is that everything Keltic and Roman in this country has been wiped out—extirpated, exterminated—laws, literature, language, and people; and this was probably done, it is thought, during the century after the departure of the Roman eagles. Professor Freeman is a practical philosopher. He not only believes that this was done in England in old times, when locomotion was a difficulty, but that it is easy and possible to be done to-day in Turkey. In this he is at any rate consistent.

The following information is gleaned from one of Mr. Joseph Boult's very able tracts on our early history (unfortunately they are only known to a few; it is to be regretted that they are not published more extensively).

Professor Stubbs, with charming simplicity and with great powers of imagination (for he adduces no kind of evidence in support of his statements), has described how these Saxons came into England, but his mind is too gentle, or he is too humane, to tell us how they got rid of the Kelts. As to that trifling difficulty we are left in the dark; but as to their successors he writes:—" The invaders came in families and kindreds and in the full organisation of their tribes; the three ranks of men—the noble, the freeman, and the serf; even the slaves are not left behind." (How can he tell that they did not use the Kelts as slaves?) "The cattle of their native land are imported too" (Is it possible that they stole the British cattle?) "The store they set by their peculiar breeds is proved by the researches into the grave-places of the nation" (vol. i. p. 64).

"The tribe was as complete when it had removed to Kent as when it stayed in Jutland; and when they found a new home, the Angles, at least, left a desert behind them; for in the days of Bede, the Angelus, the land between the Continental Saxons and Jutes, whence the Angles came, still lay without inhabitants, testifying to the truth of the tradition that they had gone forth, old and young, noble, gentle, and simple, free and slave, their flocks and herds with them."

There is a delicious simplicity in this creed, though perhaps a logician might be tempted to quarrel with it for its inconsequence. It, however, sums up fairly enough the creed of the otherwise sceptical Oxford school of history.

One can understand from the fact of the Angelus—by the way, the Professor omits to tell us how he derives that word from Angeln—being still, as it was in Bede's time, and probably from all time, a desert, that the noble, gentle, and simple, if they ever lived there, would be rather glad to leave it behind them in exchange for the fair pastures of the unfortunate Brittanni; but it is difficult to see how the fact of the place itself being barren is any proof that the gentle and simple ever lived there; and if they did, the wonder grows how these same three ranks, with or without their slaves and favourite cattle, could manage to exist upon it: looking at the nature of the soil, it would certainly require a miracle for such a purpose. Although the Angles were only one of three tribes, yet as Kent held the Goths (one of them), and the three small counties of Essex, Middlesex, and Sussex the others, and the Angles spread at once over the whole of the rest of England and gave the country their name, they must have been a very extensive or a very powerful people; and, indeed, there can be no doubt of the fact when it is remembered that

the Brittanni even in Cæsar's time were very numerous,
and after the Roman occupation they must have greatly
increased, for we know that they were not cannibals
under the Romans, and the Romans planted many colonies
amongst them.

How the Angles existed in Angeln is quite as mysterious
as the cause which brought them there, or whether they
were indigenous, or, if not, from whence they came; and
if they were so numerous, how could they be transported
to Britain?  Professor Freeman throws some light upon
the matter in an early work, wherein he tells us that they
came from one of the Alpine mountains, and in proof of
the fact he found a trace of something similar to one of
their laws.   This account is nearly as miraculous; for
how could all these three ranks, with their favourite
cattle and institutions (Professor Freeman does trace
their institutions to this spot), be sustained on a barren
hill-top?

Surely, when they were strong enough to exterminate
the Brittanni, they must have held a large country somewhere; and this would lead us to the conclusion that they
had another name, for none of the ancient writers mention
the Angles.  The first writer who mentions any people of
that name is Tacitus; but he only records that an unimportant tribe of the Swevi was called the Angli, which is
not quite like the word, and he does not even state the
locality in which these Angles dwelt.

The term Swevi itself is no guide to us, for it was
applied to those living in the country now called Germany
who were not of German blood.  The Longobardi were a
tribe of the Swevi; but Paulus Diaconus, who was one of
them, tells us that they were Scandinavians, and their true
name the Virili, and they were called Longobardi not from

their beards, but from their having dwelt upon plains.
This is a derivation of Dr. Mackay's, although Verstegan,
the father of English history, says that this people were
so called from their long beards (?).

Dr. R. G. Latham, who is not only one of the most able,
but one of the most honest writers of the day, frankly
admits that the bare mention of their tribal name of Angli
by Tacitus is no proof of any connection with the English—
it is a name and nothing more; and he objects "that the
doctrine that the Saxons came from three small islands
and a fraction of Holstein, and the Angles from a few
thousand acres on the wrong side of the peninsula, is beset
with objections, and intrinsically improbable." And this,
surely, must be sound reasoning; for if the Angli of Tacitus occupied so unimportant a post amongst the tribes of
Europe that they had not even a known locality, they
could not possibly be the great people who were about to
exterminate the Brittanni. They must, if they existed in
Germany in his time, have gone by another name; and if
so, there is an end to the story of Hengist and Horsa and
their three ships.

Ptolemy is the next writer who refers to the Angli, and
he does give them a locality; and he relates the fact that
they were the greatest tribe then resident in the interior
of Germany, extending farther east than the Longobardi,
and to the north as far as the river Albis, from which it
might be argued that they gave the name of Albion to this
country, except that the fact that it was so called a few
centuries previously might not fit in with this theory.

Ptolemy says that the Angli were a tribe of the Swevi,
that is, of probable Scandinavian blood, and certainly
not of German, i.e., Sarmatian. This would seem to indicate a connection with the old Norse tribes; but that

does not further the views of the Oxford school. For there is an undoubted connection between the Gauls of Italy and those of France; but that does not prove that France was peopled by Italy. It may well be that both peoples came from the same and quite another country—the one branching off into France, the other pouring into Italy.

And there is, again, no proof that the Angli of Ptolemy and Tacitus had any connection with Angeln of Denmark. German writers have arrived at the contrary conclusion (see the Allgem. Archiv für die Geschichte de Preuss. Staats, c. xiii. p. 75).

Dr. R. G. Latham, who is a giant amongst the literati of our day, in his calm, incisive manner has written a few truths which must be very unpalatable to the Oxford school, and the more so that they cannot and do not attempt to refute them. He writes, referring to the English, which, in deference to the Oxford school, he designates the Saxon language (Germania, p. v.), " The Saxon language is extinct in Germany, being supplanted by the Platt-Deutsch."

And again, " Throughout the whole length and breadth of Continental Germany, there is not only no dialect that can be called English, but there is no dialect which can be said to have originated in the same source, no descendant of the Angle form of speech (p. x.). The same applies to the allied dialects of the old Saxons when that was once spoken. Platt-Deutsch and High German are now the exclusive idioms; no descendants from anything Saxon, but descendants from proper German groups. What applies to the Anglo-Saxon and the old Saxon applies to the Mæso-Gothic also."

No one than Dr. Latham knows better that language is

no absolute test of race, that it may be merely evidence of contact; but he shelters himself under no such plea, but applies his strictures as well to the race as to the language itself.

At page xxv. he writes, " Of all the populations east of the Elbe, which Tacitus in the second century calls German, no single vestige appears in the tenth."

He is evidently puzzled by the discovery, although he recognises its great import, for he writes—

"There is no want of natural strongholds in Germany. The Saxon Switzerland, the Bohemian range, the forests of Lithuania, might well have been to the Germans of Tacitus what Snowdon was to the Britons of Agricola, or the Pyrenees to the old Iberians, in which case the present Germans of those countries would be the oldest inhabitants of them, not the newest, as they are."

And in his Epilegomena, c. xvii. (Germania), he tells us who these Saxons were. " The conquerors of the Slavonic country at present called Saxony, the ancestors of the Saxons of Dresden and Leipsic, were by no means Saxons as the people of Sussex were. They were not even Saxon as the speakers of the language of the high and the old Saxon were; they were rather Platt-Deutsch or High-German Germans, most probably a mixture of both; yet they were called Saxons because they conquered the Saxony of the nineteenth century from a country which was called Saxony in the seventh or eighth, but which probably was not so called in the fourth or fifth, and which was certainly not so called in the second or third."

Although Dr. Latham knows well enough who were the Saxons who' gave their name to that country, or, at any rate, the name of the inhabitants, in the second and third centuries, he does not mention it, but leaves it to be inferred that on the departure of the Saxons in the seventh or eighth century their places were taken by a Slavonic race who took their name as well.

In giving the date of the fourth or fifth century as that of the date when this region was first called Saxony, Dr. Latham has unconsciously done remarkable service, for it indicates that Saxon was not the native name by which the tribe who occupied it called themselves, but the foreign name which was applied to them by their neighbours.

The importance of this question will best appear by recurring to the second and third centuries, when the learned Doctor informs us that this country was certainly not called Saxony. The name by which it was then known was Scythia, and the name by which the neighbouring tribes, whom the Doctor truly calls a Slavonic race, were known was Sarmatian. It will be presently shown that the terms Scythian and Saxon are identical. Here it is sufficient to point out that this corruption had not taken place, at least universally, in the second and third centuries, and that it had probably only originated after the departure of this people by those who succeeded them and adopted their corrupted name.

The history of Europe, which is tolerably clear and accurate for several hundred years prior to this date, at any rate from the time of Herodotus, shows that the whole of the country of Thrace, modern Hungary, and Germany, except perhaps the eastern portion, was peopled by the Scythians, who held the territory in a broad belt down to their Asiatic homes in Armenia and Assyria, and pressing upon them the whole length of their line were the Sarmatians. What, then, can be more natural than that upon the departure of the Kelto-Scythians or Cimbri from this district, the Sarmatians, the ancestors of the modern Germans,

should step in and supply their places? The Kelto-Scythians were a nomadic race, living in tents and building
no towns; and this, we learn from Cæsar, was the character of the inhabitants of this district in his day. That
they were true Kelts there cannot be a shadow of a doubt,
and why they were called, as some of them were by Tacitus, " Germans," it is impossible to say, unless upon the
hypothesis that he used that word as synonymous with
Gothic. Enough that it is clear that the Sarmatian
invaders took the name with the neglected and vacant
locality, and with it some of the language. That this was
the case is not remarkable, seeing that the Sarmatians
were of an inferior race to the Kelto-Scythian tribes, and
far behind them in all matters of civilisation. The probability is that few of the old inhabitants remained behind;
but that some did so is obvious from the number of Keltic
words which the German still retains, to the wonder-
ment and puzzle of philologists. Probably it was the
remnant of the old Scythæ who caused the old names,
or rather a corruption of them, to be retained. And what
became of the original inhabitants? Vast numbers of them
left the country under the name of Goths and invaded the
states of Southern Europe. Some, doubtless, at the same
time removed into England, where they would find a kindred race, and probably but very few remained to be
incorporated with the Sarmatians, the progenitors of the
present German nation.

It will doubtless horrify the admirers of the Germans
to be told that they are of Sarmatian race, and some may
doubt it; but it will be seen by inquiry into the language
of the Prussians, the leading race of Germany, that they
at any rate are of pure Slavonic race, and, as Dr. R. G.
Latham points out, a Lithuanic race, with the fullest contact with the Fin and the Sanscrit (Latham, Comparative

Philology, p. 623). The present German is a language quite foreign to the Prussian. It is a compound of many tongues, and so properly called German, or all tongues, the base of it perhaps being Gothic, the language of the Scythians or Goths, who formerly inhabited the country. The dialects of Germany are very dissimilar, so much so that Dr. Latham asserts that they are mutually unintelligible. The present German was fixed—it may be said invented—by Luther, and it was long contemptuously styled by the natives Luther's Misnian, although it is wholly unlike that dialect. It is a clumsy contrivance, and its structure difficult of application; in fact, like all made or invented languages, it does not work easily. Literary men endeavour to polish it in vain; the only result is a continuous coinage of new words. Even Pinkerton, who endeavoured to prove that the German nation was Gothic, that is, identical with its Keltic predecessor, was compelled to admit that, in its harshness and inflexible thickness of sound, the German language resembled the untutored languages of Asia.

No one has been able to surmise which of the ancient languages of Asia is the groundwork upon which the Gothic was engrafted; but it is a well-known fact in philology that a nation which changes its language for another will preserve still its old forms, idioms, inflections, and merely change some of the words. This accounts for the fact that, although so many words in German and English are alike, both being Gothic, the construction of the tongues are so different. We do not possess any specimens of the real old Saxon, unless the so-called Mæso-Gothic Gospel of Ulphilas of the fourth century be a fair representation; so that we have no means of judging what was the language of the early inhabitants of the Cimbric Chersonesus.

( 176 )

## CHAPTER XV.

THE LANGUAGE OF GERMANY.

PERHAPS the greatest objection to Max Müller's Aryanic theory is his intrusion of the German language.  The very term German is a misnomer, unless we acknowledge as a fact that the German of to-day is a different thing from the German of two thousand years ago.

German in the days of Tacitus usually meant Gothic, which, as Dr. R. G. Latham has conclusively pointed out, is a very different word at this date.  Strabo, in writing of German tribes, intended to describe the Galatai as those who were of genuine Gaulish origin; so those who lived immediately beyond the Rhine, and are asserted by Tacitus to be indubitably native Germans (and he asserted the same of the Belgæ, who were clearly Gauls), are expressly denominated Galatai or Gauls by Diodorus, and by Dio are asserted to have been distinguished by the equivalent appellation of Celtæ from the earliest period; and Dr. Whittaker asserts that the broad line of nations which extended along the ocean and reached to the borders of Scythia were all known to the learned in the days of Diodorus by the same significant appellation of Galatai or Gauls.  In the early period of Gallic history the Celtæ of Gaul crossed the Rhine in considerable numbers, and planted various colonies in the region beyond it.  The Volce Tectosages settled on one side of the Hercyean forest and along the banks of the Neckar; the Helvetii upon the other and along the Rhine and Maine; the Boii beyond both, and the Senones in the heart of Germany. So the Treviri, the Nervii, the Suevi, the Marcommanni, the Quadi, the Venedi, are all Gaulish tribes, and they covered the chief part of modern Germany; but as a body they did not remain there, but were ultimately displaced by the savage Sarmatian tribes which hung on the skirts of the Celtæ.

Dr. R. G. Latham has stated his views on this point very clearly, p. 663 of "Comparative Philology." Writing of the German languages, he states: "The blood and language in this family coincide but slightly, the range of the latter being the widest. Before the spread of the German, Scandinavia was Ugrian, and possibly to some extent Prussian or Lithuanic; Denmark, whether Ugrian or Sarmatian, other than German; all the parts beyond the Elbe, and possibly beyond the Teutoberger Wald, Sclavonic; all the parts to the south of the Maine, the same. Hence the original area of the Germans is included by the Teutoberger Wald, the Elbe and Saale, the Maine and the Rhine. It should be added, however, that these limitations are by no means currently admitted, least of all in Germany itself; and they are incompatible with two current doctrines—(1) that all the populations mentioned in the 'Germania' of Tacitus were German, and (2) that the name Goth indicates a German population. The Germans were Goths just as the English are Britons, i.e., they took the name when they settled in a country originally Gothic."

Tacitus asserts that the Goths were not Germans. He writes, "Gothinos Gallica, Osos Pannonica lingua coarguit non esse Germanos." And Plutarch proves this conclu-

M

sively; for he states that the term Cimbri, which certainly was applied to them a hundred years B.C., was applied by Germans to plunderers,—a clear proof of the difference and hostility between the two races. Doubtless, as the Germans pressed upon them, they occasionally met with harsh treatment at their hands; hence the name had become in the mouths of Germans at the period a term of reproach. No better evidence could be desired to prove the difference of race.

True it is that the ancient Germans of Tacitus did not remain; iu process of time the fierce and determined Sarmatians drove them westward and settled down in their territories. That some of the Gallic people stayed behind and incorporated themselves in the ranks of their invaders is clear from the fact that so large a portion of Gothic remains in the German language of to-day and in the names of places; but the structure of the German language is Sarmatian, not Gothic; hence it is improper and unscientific to rank it with Gothic and Gaelic languages.

The immense confusion which prevails amongst historians and philologists is chiefly owing to their disregard of these two facts: that in the early history of the world the whole population (especially when, as in the case of the Gallic race, they were nomads) changed; the successors, though of very different blood, frequently adopted the name, and perhaps even the language, of their predecessors. This confusion is especially manifest in the history of the Goths or Scythians and the Sarmatians. They were confounded together in the earliest times; but a little attention will enable us perfectly to separate them; and in order to understand the histories of each it is absolutely necessary to bear this in mind.

This is especially the case with regard to the Sarmatians, or, as they are now called, the Germans, and the
Gallic and English. Dr. Latham, with all his lights,
writes confusingly upon the subject. In one page he
asserts that the English language is German; in another
(Germania His., p. x.), "Throughout the whole length and
breadth.of Continental Germany there is not only no
dialect that can be called English, but there is no dialect
that can be said to have originated in the same source—
no descendant of the Angle form of speech." It would,
indeed, be remarkable if there were; for though unquestionably the Saxon tribes of England passed through Germany on their way hither from the East, they did not
return to it, and there they learned the language called
English; when they left Germany, as Dr. Latham admits,
the Saxon language became extinct, and was supplanted
by the Platt-Deutsch. At page xxv he writes, "The same
applies to the allied dialects of the old Saxons."

The Germans are fond of appealing to an early fragment
of the Mæso-Gothic as belonging to them. Dr. Latham
ruthlessly cuts the ground from under them by informing
them that Mæso-Gothic is only another name for the form
of speech of the Goths who conquered Mæsia, and that
Germans have no claim to Mæso-Gothic either.

Nor have the Germans, as they pretend, an exclusive
right to the term Teutonic, which bewilders and confuses
so many writers. There are Teutons and Teutons; and
inasmuch as some may so call themselves from the worship of the Egyptian Thoth, the acknowledged god of the
Sarmatian race, and even of Germany, they may have a
right to it, but it is too frequently confounded with the
term meaning Northmen. The Teutones, who united
with the Ambrones or Saxons, who were cut to pieces by

Marius, were Old Norse or Scandinavians, a Celtic or Cymric people quite distinct from Sarmatians or modern Germans.

How the Asiatic language of the Germans, with its harshness and inflexible thickness of sound, ever coalesced with the Gothic, is difficult to account for. That the German language would have been better without it is clear, from the great superiority of the best Sclavonic languages. The Gothic, as the last wave of the Keltic, and as the one chiefly in contact with the Sarmatian along the whole line of march northwards, is from that cause the most debased of any of its congeners. Still it was infinitely superior to the Sarmatian when those races intruded upon Germany, and its few survivors proved their superiority by making it dominant. But the mixture of the two is anything but successful, and nothing can ever render the German speech beautiful or true. By its complex mode of expression and its habit of compounding words it proves its debased origin and its incapacity for improvement. Like all savage languages, as distinguished from pure and cultivated tongues, it is confused and complex. Though it incorporates some good Gothic words, it cannot be simple.

Luther's Bible has fixed it, and upon a wretched basis. At his date there was an immense variety of languages as well as of dialects throughout Germany, and even at this day the difference of pronunciation is so great that a native of North Germany is understood with difficulty by a Bavarian, although both readily read the same language. We do not know much about the language the Prussians spoke at Luther's date, for though an intelligent people, they were rude and unlettered, and it is practically extinct. We know that, like most of the so-called German tongues, it was not a German language at all, and it would be perfectly unintelligible to a German of to-day. It is a member, according to Dr. Latham, of the Lithuanic division of the Sarmatian, of which the Russian is the chief, the Sclavonic division comprising the Servian, Illyrian, Slovak, Tshek, Lusatian, and Polish, the Kossack and Livonian. This is the classification adopted by Dr. Latham; and those who remember how thoroughly subservient Prussia was to Russia before she acquired the chiefship of Germany, will not be surprised to learn that it was a natural and filial obedience.

The Lithuanian had a high philological importance, and, like its relative the Russian, is of infinite superiority to the modern German, but unfortunately we know almost as little of it as of ancient Phœnician.

There is only one Lithuanian author who has any pretension to the rank of even a minor classic, and little of the language we have is older than 1745, the date of the publication of that work. Hence there are no stages in the Lithuanian languages. Of all the Sarmatian languages it is in the fullest concord with the Fin.

Yet now Prussia having, by the aid of Field-Marshal Moltke—from his name a pure Sclavonian—become the head of the German Empire, utterly ignores her true tongue, the Pryttisc, and out-Germans the German. Here is a clear case of language being entirely foreign to the people who use it; for ethnologically the Prussian is no German, but a Sarmatian—a grim comment upon the German creed of including within the Fatherland all German-speaking peoples; in other words, the true meaning of that doctrine is to include within the Empire as many peoples as · by the sword or by guile can be brought within it.

The modern German Empire comprises a great number of peoples of quite distinct nationality; doubtless many

Gauls amongst them still; for the Rhine population is chiefly Gaulish, and so attached are they to their natural laws, that in a large portion of Rhenish Prussia, not including Alsace and Lorraine, which are purely Gallic in blood, but in some of those provinces which were annexed by the great Napoleon, and which were afterwards returned to Prussia, the people, who felt the value of being governed by the Code Napoleon, rather than by the stupid German laws, actually retained it, and still retain it under Prussian and German administration—a great compliment to the wisdom of Napoleon, and at the same time a proof that his Code, which was in fact founded upon and was in perfect accordance with the principles of Gallic law and the feeling of the Gallic people, was appreciated by those Prussians who are of Gallic blood.

Modern German, in spite of the high-flown compliments which it is fashionable to pay to it, is crude, coarse, and barbarous, like its author, Luther.    Literary men who write in German, and some of the rarest and finest intellects of the Sclavonic races, of the Jews, and of the Gauls, who enjoy its benefits, have exercised themselves to polish it, but in vain.    It is a splutter and a clatter, and it will always so remain.    Nor is the common ground between the two languages of England and Germany any proof whatever of affinity.

The Rev. J. H. Sayce, "as a philologist," maintains "that language cannot be held to be a test of race; it is a test only of social contact;" and he asks, "How are we to reconcile the assumption of Germanic origin of English with the daily experience of learners of German—not excepting Greek?—it is precisely the most difficult for English students.    The number of words reconcilable without the dictionary are extraordinarily few.    The involved com-

plication of inflectional categories not only bewilders these
supposititious children of the Teuton, but are a confessed
burden to the Teuton himself."

Mr. Cockburn Muir has summed up the argument in a
masterly manner. He says : "The true tests, however, of
close affinity in language are grammatic structure and
idiomatic texture. It may be sufficient to direct attention
to a comparison in these respects between our own and
that Germanic tongue which we are told was its progeni-
trix. Knowing a handful of languages in particular and
something of language in general, I confess it becomes
for me increasingly difficult to understand how these two
languages have come to be accepted, except from mere
habit, as belonging to the same ethnic category. It would
be difficult to cite any two which are more dissimilar in
grammar and idiom ; as, for example, in these characteristics
of the German :—

" 1st, The position of the verb in the sentence, and its
inverted form.

" 2d, The conjugation of the verbs, particularly of *sein*,
to be.

" 3d, The apparently arbitrary distribution of gender.

" 4th, The declension of the noun by terminal inflection.

" 5th, The declension of the adjective as a noun.

" 6th, The declension by inflection of the demonstrative
pronoun and definite article.

" 7th, In idiom the circumlocution often necessary to
express the simplest proposition.

" These characteristics are for the most part typical of
the older Aryan tongues, but not of the Shemetic, particularly the Chaldee and Hebrew ; and the general aspect
of the English tongue, to my mind of the English language,
is that of a Shemetic tongue which has been for a long

period in contact with Aryan tongues, and suffered a long transfusion of verbal roots and dialectic forms, while it has preserved with tenacity the primitive basis of its grammatical and idiomatic structure."

The English of the time of the Conquest differed surprisingly little from the vernacular broad Scotch of the present day, and is easily readable by a Scotchman, who instinctively sees through its quaint spelling the indications of those Doric euphonies which are his delight. Nor can any comfort be derived by resorting to the earliest specimens of our language, for it has been justly observed, "The sober truth is, that Anglo-Saxon is available for etymologic purposes in studying the English language, but not half so available as German, Swedish, Danish, Dutch, old English, Scottish, Greek, and Latin. The reason is obvious. Such was the illiterateness of even the Saxon literati, that they knew not how to depict to the eye their own barbarous sounds; hence the caprices of Saxon orthography, as they are leniently termed by the candid and enlightened author of Saxon history. To have a true idea of these caprices (more properly rude essays at spelling), we have only to compare them with the literary attempts of our most unlettered mechanics, or labourers who can barely read and write; their orthography and spelling and that of the Saxons will be found remarkably similar." (The editor of the article "Grammar" in the "London Encyclopædia.")

The great defect in the reasoning of the Oxford school is that it is too conservative. It takes for granted that the world was much more stationary than it really was. The state of Europe some 2000 years ago was very different from what it now is; it was peopled for the most part by nomadic tribes, and the descendants of these tribes did not cease to wander until Europe became too thickly populated to allow of migratory movements. The terrible account of the attempted migration of the Helvetii is instructing. They are said to have been the last of the Keltic tribes who wandered in Europe. There were irruptions of Danes afterwards, but they were hardly of the same character. They partook more of the character of the military conquests of the great Napoleon. Dynasties changed hands, but the people remained in their homes; besides, the Normans were not a purely nomad race. They were great builders, and certainly the only people who built in England after the departure of the Romans; for the few remains which scholars in these days call Saxon architecture probably date back to their time — another proof that the Brittanni were a Gallic race. This fact proves how erroneous and misleading is the modern nomenclature of the Oxford school, which adopts the term Aryan from the German. Aryan means those who are not of nomad habits, and therefore the Celtic races should be excepted from this nomenclature. It is curious that all should agree to adopt the title when nearly every other writer assigns a different meaning to it, the views of Max Müller, its inventor, being opposed by such scholars as M. Pictet and the Very Rev. Canon Bourke of Tuam, whilst Dr. Mackay produces an entirely different meaning. In fact, it is an invented term, and means nothing or anything. It is time it was exploded.

## CHAPTER XVI.

### THE RISE OF THE OXFORD SCHOOL OF HISTORY.

THE Oxford school of history is not of a very old date; probably they date their beginning from some time since the Reformation. After the dissolution of the monasteries and the destruction of their libraries, learning rapidly decayed. This was felt so early as the reign of Edward VI., not half a generation after the date when the sovereign of England became head of its Church—the spiritual head, less like the Pope than the Pope-king of Russia—and the ministers of Edward endeavoured to stem the tide of ignorance that had set in with deadly malevolence by the institution of grammar-schools; but they were too few and too small to be of much service; and during the reign of Elizabeth, though education was still cherished amongst the upper classes, the middle and lower sank into crass ignorance, and consequently into the most brutal vice, the reaction against which produced the reformation of the Puritans, and with it, on the utter collapse of that movement, the degenerate morals and manners which disgraced the seventeenth century. Archbishop Parker was one of the first to see the approaching evil, and by going upon the wrong track he did much towards producing the present state of affairs. He was not unversed in the study of our early records, but he fell into error by drawing a sharp line across the period of their commencement, and this he termed the Norman conquest, as does Professor Freeman. Subsequent to that period everything was supposed to be Norman, whilst prior thereto he called it Saxon. The study of Keltic or Gaelic, from which everything Saxon in this country is borrowed, was simply ignored. He did not know that both prior and subsequent to that period everything was first of all English. He felt the want of a history of the so-called Saxon period, and he himself assisted to invent one by interpolating in a poor Life of King Alfred of West Anglia a number of passages from a chronicle of no value, but which tended to prove the importance of the individual. This is no invention; there exists the MS. at this moment at Oxford, with the interpolated passages written by Parker himself in his own hand. No doubt he acted honestly enough, as the fact of his leaving the proofs of his act behind him abundantly proves, but he acted most unwarrantably, for the book from which he took these facts is proved by clear and unmistakable evidence to have been a book of comparatively modern origin, and in any case he had no right to interpolate these extracts without avowal. There is, however, no difficulty in pointing out at once, as the author has indicated in his book upon Early English History, what passages are interpolated, for in every instance they are marked by the use of the term "Anglo-Saxon," the shibboleth of the Oxford school, and the invention probably of Archbishop Parker himself.

But Archbishop Parker did not utterly destroy all true knowledge of history, and it was reserved for a very able and learned man, Richard Verstegan, to accomplish it, and he founded what may be termed the Oxford school of our time. Verstegan was possibly acquainted with Parker,

though he published his book thirty years after his death;
but he was probably then a very old man, for he relates
that his father, a native of Gueldres, was born in the reign
of Henry VII.  He, however, followed in the Archbishop's
steps, and wrote his "Restitution of Decayed Intelligence
in Antiquities concerning the most Noble and Renowned
English Nation," which he dedicated to that "learned and
judicially-sighted monarch, James I.," in 1605, who, just
as Parker had dubbed King Alfred the Great, he so styled
this sapient monarch.  Verstegan, in some dedicatory verses
to the "Renowned English Nation," thus writes :—

> "Live and increase in honour and renowne,
>   Under *Jacobus Magnus*, now thy king,'
>   Whose greatnesse to thy glory doth redowne
>   As does the sun's reflection brightness bring."

No one, after that, can accuse Verstegan of being a
flatterer, although, perhaps, posterity has given up the
"magnus" as applied to Jamie, and also the appellation
of Apollo.  What a rise had this king from the petty
kingdom of Scotland to the crown of England, and to be
called the Sun, when his predecessor, Queen Elizabeth,
according to the Prayer-Book, was only a "bright occi-
dental star"!

It would seem from his preface that Verstegan hardly
anticipated the wondrous success he has in this age attained,
for our learned professors vie with each other how they
shall best Germanise the English people.  In Verstegan's
day it was the fashion to regard the English as British,
and he very severely castigates several authors who had
confused these terms, or rather had treated them as relating
to the same people; he impales one author as being
guilty of an absurdity in commencing his epistle to a huge
volume with "Constantine, the great and mighty emperor,

the sonne of Helen, an English woman," &c.; "whereas," writes Verstegan, "in truth, St. Helen, the mother of Constantine, was no English woman, but a British woman, and, in all likelihood, never knew what English meant, for that she died more than a hundred years before the English Saxons came into Britain."

It is noteworthy that Verstegan, although he was a contemporary of the author of the term "Anglo-Saxon," prefers the equally erroneous one of "English Saxon," and thus almost invariably writes of the English. Perhaps this arises from the fact that Parker wrote in Latin, and it was reserved for the folly of our own day to invent such terms as "Anglo-Saxon," "Anglo-Catholic," &c. Verstegan violates the rule that it is not safe to identify a people with the soil, and asserts that the ancestors of the English Saxons must have been Germans because they came from thence, forgetting that they may have been part of the Scythian or Scottish races which preceded the modern Germans and swept over Europe centuries before any of the Sclavonians or Sarmatians were resident in Germany.

Verstegan knew well how deeply rooted the idea was in his day that the English were of the ancient race of the Brittanni, for he writes deprecatingly of the censures he anticipated; he little thought that within half-a-century of the publication of his book the family of the Magnus James would be swept away and a German family be called to the throne, whose followers, whether native or sycophant, would adopt and propound his views to the utmost extent. Yet so it happened; and after Dutch William's reign the advent of the Georges necessarily led · to the more complete adoption of the Germanic theory of the origin of the English, and the complacent Oxford school of the present day industriously attempts to keep up the delusion, and this in the teeth of the fact that the royal family of England are not more German than ourselves, but are in very truth of our own British race, at least of the Gothic branch of it, which is admitted to be of Cymric blood.   Indeed, it is a well-known fact that the progenitors of the house of D'Este, the patronymic of the royal family of England, are of Gallic blood. A Gaul from Italy married the heiress of the Guelf family, and founded the family which in the male line ascended the throne of Great Britain in the person of George I.; and the Guelfs themselves were not of German, but of Scandinavian or Gothic origin.   And the same fact is equally true of the family of the late Prince Albert, the consort of our Queen.   In the male line the house of Saxe-Coburg-Gotha are not German at all, but old Norse of the purest race, allied to the Jutish kings of Kent, who were Jutish simply because they dwelt in the Cimbric Chersonesus, then called Jutland; and the present royal family, therefore, are of precisely the same blood as the majority of the English people.

It is a curious fact that nearly if not quite all the royal and noble families of the Germanic kingdoms and duchies are not of the same blood as the people; they are truly Germans or Goths, and not Sarmatians or Sclavs. We know that this country of Germany in early times was almost a desert, the land poor and almost uncultivated, the climate raw and inhospitable, and so poor that it escaped the rapacity of the Romans, not being worth the trouble of conquest, as not producing a race of people · capable of paying tribute; but as the Cimbri and Gauls pressed downwards from the north, they crowded over the Rhine and peopled its best provinces, and their issue remain, and are now, like the Prussians, considered to be

Germans.  The leaders of these people, as the superior race, soon became the rulers of the whole of Germany, and this singular phenomenon is the result, that the rulers are of Gallic and Scandinavian blood, quite distinct from their subjects; and the conduct of these princes has been in accordance with this fact, for they have governed the land for their own special convenience; and there is even at this day a wide difference between the servile and noble classes of Germany; they do not intermarry or interfere with each other, except under special circumstances.  There is, in truth, as distinct a difference between the noble and plebeian classes of Germany, both in race and in habits, as exists between the black and the white populations of America.

## CHAPTER XVII.

THE SAXON MYTHS.

IT is, of course, difficult to account for the legend of the landing of Hengist and Horsa, or even to suggest an origin, but that hinted at in " The Hide of Land," one of a very useful series of papers read by Mr. Joseph Boult of Liverpool before the Historic Society of Lancashire and Cheshire, 2d November 1871, is very valuable and suggestive. He writes (p. 14) : " It is not impossible that the legend may prove to be another Teutonic version of the actions of the Dioskouroi. The names are suspiciously eponymic, both signifying horses, and thus in singular parallel to Romulus and Remus." So too the legend of the Saxon slaughter of the British at the feast given to Vortigern is but a clumsy imitation of the true story of the slaughter of the Massagetæ by the Persians. Remembering that Bede is the author of the stories, or perhaps it may be that his work has been made the vehicle for disseminating it, and remembering also that Marianus Scotus in composing the Saxon chronicle implicitly trusted to the statements of Bede, so that practically it rests on his sole authority, and remembering too that Bede's evidence is avowedly chiefly derived from a hearsay source, and not from chronicles and documents, and considering the time at which he wrote, some 300 years after the alleged event, it may well be that the English of his day had re-

ceived a confused account of the foundation of Rome by
Romulus and Remus, and in their ignorance applied it to
their own country in the time of the Romans. It would
be the common property of all who regarded the Roman
Empire as their own. That it was adapted to England by
the narrators is obvious by the addition to the story of
ships, but the very details prove its falsehood, and that
the narrators were ignorant of the history of the period
they affected to relate. The story of the three tribes, each
being subdivided into three ranks of people, all coming
over in three ships, has a very Welsh appearance, or rather
of an imitation of the Triads, and this is increased when it
is seen that by the addition of Ella there were three leaders,
and that Ella had three sons. In fact, the number three
figures rather too conspicuously in the composition. Again,
it is clear that the narrator who stated that the three tribes
came over in three ships has drawn upon his imagination.
We can hardly suppose that in the days of the decline of
the Roman Empire, when civilisation had a sharp fight for
very existence, that the art of shipbuilding would increase,
and yet to transport those tribes who were strong enough
to conquer the Brittanni they must have been very large.
The Carthaginian ships could scarcely carry a thousand
men each, so that these ships must have been equal in
size to the great Leviathan mentioned in Scripture, which
a Dorsetshire parish clerk, whenever he came across
it, always indicated as that "Great Leveret." If, as
Professor Stubbs asserts, they brought their families,
slaves, and cattle with them, they must have constructed
a bridge across the Channel, and this is more credible
than the supposition that they were all crammed into
three ships. Cæsar had to employ ninety-three vessels
to convey over an army that did not conquer us; and to

N

cap the absurdity of the Triad theory, we read in the
veracious Saxon Chronicle that this invasion was followed
by three others.   Now it is curious to read the names
of the leaders of these expeditions; they are nearly all of
them purely Keltic.   The leader of the last expedition was
Port, who landed at Portsmouth, and probably on the
same hypothesis at several other places, for there are
several Portsmouths in England, just as many indeed as
there are rivers of the name, a purely Keltic one, and well
known here before the Roman invasion, a fact of which
the inventor of the story was probably unaware; but the
detection of an imposture of this sort shows the sort of
stuff out of which the story is composed.   As Mr. Boult
suggests, it is possibly the old story of Romulus and
Remus in a British dress, and as such of course absolutely
worthless.

It is a curious fact, pointed out by Mr. Coote, that
Paulus Diaconus (Warnifred), writing in the seventh century, asserts that the leader of this expedition was not
Hengist or Horsa, but Vortigern himself.   It may well be
that he was compelled to fly the country, and did return
the leader of an expedition, and as Hengist means the
Hereman or leader of an expedition, he may have been that
leader.   But what does that prove ?   Only that, as under
the Romans, the Scandinavians were still invading England, or the expelled British might be the invaders.

It has been asserted, with a great show of reason, by Mr.
Stevenson, the editor of Bede's History (for the English
Historical Society), that the accounts which Bede gives of
the arrival of the Teutonic tribes and their settlement in
Britain is purely fabulous, being, in fact, not the history,
but the tradition, of the Jutish kingdom of Kent.   The
name (Trinovantes) of the Kentish people seems to con-

firm the idea. This may or may not be the case; all stories of invasion, broadly told, are pretty much alike, and if we eliminate the purely inventive circumstances, there is nothing very remarkable in the narrative.

Historians seem to forget that there never was a time when the populations of Europe were not upon the move, wave after wave following each other, the last comers overcoming or pushing their predecessors before them. That one tide always flowed westward is not curious; it would have been remarkable had it been otherwise. Another set in from the west, and whilst England was pouring her surplus population into Brittany and Ireland, she was continually recruiting it from the Saxon coast; and even the Irish returned the compliment, for as the British drove them northwards they returned in large numbers through Scotland, and as Picts and Scots ravaged the country which had once belonged to their ancestors.

And it was the same upon the Continent; whilst the northern hordes were pressing southwards others were coming up, some from England *vid* Brittany, others from Scythia and Germany, and a seething mass of various tribes from all parts of the Continent.

No theory, therefore, can be more fallacious than to identify any tribe with any particular place; the Celtic tribes, we know well, were always on the move; the Damnonii are a well-known case. This in Keltic seems to mean pastoral people, *i.e.*, people who possessed cattle, nomad races, *i.e.*, not of the Aryan class. The Virili is another instance; they came from Scandinavia and settled down in Germany by the Rhine, and finally they deposited themselves in Italy. In every place where they sojourned they probably left people, laws, and customs, and of course words, behind them; hence their successors, be they Sarmatians or any other race, would annex these benefits, so far as they were able, with the land; hence their existence is a puzzle to the historian. In some cases, where the people left behind of the tribe who departed were numerous, their conquerors would even take their language. So little dependence is to be placed upon language as a test of race, for it may be only a test of contact.

The compiler of the Saxon Chronicle, though generally he has followed Bede, has contradicted him in one important particular. The whole period between 459 and 596, that which ensued immediately after the alleged Saxon invasion, is occupied by the recital of wars between the Saxons, Angles, Jutes, and Britons, when, as Bede asserts, there was some respite from foreign, but not from civil war — statements which cannot be reconciled unless upon the supposition pointed out by Mr. Boult, that they were all of them native Brittanni, and this would be an accurate statement if they were the same people and all of them long resident in the island.

The fact that up to the birth of Christ or thereabout the inhabitants of Europe were still unsettled, still nomad in their habits, speaks volumes for the youth of the world; for if it had been as old as some writers assert, it had all been parcelled out and appropriated long before this event; but the world was yet young, or nomad habits could not have existed; and this is another reason why we should not hastily arrive at the conclusion indicated by the Saxon Chronicle.

# CHAPTER XVIII.

## THE ANGLO-SAXONS.

BEDE himself disposes of the story of there being three tribes in England, for he unquestionably states that the Angles were the same people as the Saxons. He invariably styles them Angli sive Saxoni, and in this he follows Gildas; and to show that both of them used the same language, he omits all mention of the Saxons in enumerating the different languages of Britain. This is very remarkable, for he enumerates the Scots and Picts as different nations having separate languages, when it is clear that they were of the same race, although the one was Gaelic and the other Cymric, and only differed dialectically in their language; so that if the Angles and Saxons had only a dialectical difference, they would both of them have been enumerated.

On this point Dr. R. G. Latham gives valuable evidence, for he too asserts that practically the Angles and the Saxons were the same people, although of the two the word Angle, he thinks, was most extensive.

Professor Freeman has given valuable evidence upon this point (Norman Conquest, App. A, vol. i. p. 598). He writes, "The word Saxon is never used in the native tongue to express either the whole nation or any part of it which was not strictly Saxon." That is to say, only the Belgic colonies of the Soissons who colonised that part of

the country of the Trinovantes called Essex, Midsex,
and Sussex, the only parts of England which were
called Saxon. "On the other hand," writes Professor
Freeman, "Angle and Anglecyn are constantly used to
express not only the whole nation, but particular parts of
it which were not strictly Anglian. Engle, in short, in
native speech is the name of the whole nation of which
Seaxe are a part." But it is only just to Professor Freeman
to remark that, after stating his views so clearly and in
such language that a writer is only thankful to borrow
such an illustration, he almost immediately, and in the
same page, relapses into the Verstegan school, and, apparently without seeing it, adopts the contradictory theory of
Sir Francis Palgrave, who would divide our history into the
well-known division of Norman and Saxon, and who writes
deprecatingly of the term Anglo-Saxon as not only being
unhistorical but conventional, and as conveying a most
false idea of our civil history; and he adopts the idea,
which is the true one according to this writer, that
England was Angle and Saxon by turns. This could be
only true of those parts which were colonised by the Soissons of Belgium, but not strictly true of them, for even their
kings styled themselves kings of the English. In fact,
there never was a monarch in this country who did not
do so. It is lamentable to find a writer holding so distinguished a position as Professor Freeman publishing his
ideas upon a matter upon which he has not made up his
own mind. He cannot really hold his own as well as Sir
Francis Palgrave's views, and it is to be regretted that he
cannot discriminate between them.

Professor Freeman has, however, entirely lost sight of
the true distinction and meaning of the words Angle
and Saxon. They are not properly to be used in suc-

cession, as Sir Francis Palgrave would use them, or as pertaining to separate parts of the Empire. Whether the inhabitants of that part of England seized by the Belgic Soissons asserted their name of Saxons we have no proof, but the true difference between the names is that Angle is the native name, whilst Saxon is the name by which the Angles were known to their neighbours. A very cursory glance at the Irish, Welsh, Scotch, Flemish, and German dictionaries will prove this fact. Of course the French understand this word in the same way as the English. The word Angle is now admitted to be An Gael, or the Gael. The author first broached this idea in his "Introduction to the Study of Early English History," citing as an authority Dr. Whitaker, whose learning is unhappily almost lost in this generation. Since then Dr. Mackay, in his great work the Gaelic Etymology of the English language, has fully assented to the principle, and it has been endorsed by Irish Keltic scholars, and expressly by the Very Rev. Canon Ulick J. Bourke.

The identity of the word Angle with that of An Gael does not rest on a mere fancied similarity of sound, but upon the fact which the author some years since discovered and embodied in the " History of the Common Law of Great Britain and Gaul," that the common law of England, which is also the common law of France, dates back to the time and is derived from the Gallic or Keltic system, which was also common to the Scythians; and this is evident from the purely Keltic custom of appointing a Hereman or Pendragon of all the kings confederated together, and who thus ruled them all by a common law. It was not, as all legal historical writers upon the English law have asserted, of Saxon origin—Saxon meaning German —but was of Keltic or Gallic institution. This idea can be proved to demonstration, and some day, when the legal profession is sufficiently interested in the subject to relieve the author of all risk of publication, he hopes to do so. Meanwhile, and without at all attempting to shift the burden of proof from himself, yet to show how clear it is, he refers to Dr. Mackay's Gaelic Dictionary. There are sufficient points in that book to prove the soundness of the idea. To take only a few of the English law terms: attorney is in Gaelic one who fights for another; bailiff, a town's officer; barrister is from barra, a court of justice; brief from breiw, the data on which a judgment is founded; counter, the old term for pleader, is from counteur, an orator; court, from coir, a circle, referring to the Druidical circles, the first courts in Britain; client, from cliunte, one who has been heard; coiff, a serjeant's wig, from kiaff, the hair; code, from coda, law; fealty, from fial, generous, liberal, bountiful; feudal, from feudail, cattle (our Saxon etymologists had derived it from the Roman emphytifsys); folk, from fo-luck, the under people; hanaper, from anabar, excess, superfluity; hue and cry, from eubb (b silent), to cry; jail, jeal, a setting apart; jeofail, jeoval, loss, damage; law, lagh; manor, mainoir, a fold for cattle; mayer, from mæor, an officiating justice; parchment, pathach, dried up; panel, pannal, a band of men; plea, ple, to beg; pleddair, to cajole; scrivener, sgriebhamner (pronounced scrivaner), a clerk, a writer; seal, saoil, a seal; shire (county); tir, earth or land (pronounced tsher); socage, soc, a coulter or plough; tail (estate), taile; term, tearman, claiming protection of the law; tort, teort, a mischance, a wrong; utter (barrister), uachdar, the top, the extreme height. The accuracy of the whole of these etymologies is not vouched for, but some of them are so surprisingly and ridiculously similar, that the conclusion is irresistible that our common law is Keltic. Of course this violates the principle laid down by Max Müller, that when you meet with two words in the Sanscrit, and the Greek, Latin, or English exactly alike, you may be quite sure that the true meaning is very different, but it also exposes the utter folly of that rule. The Welsh, Irish, and English have many words in common exactly alike, many nearly similar, simply because, although they have dialectical differences, they are all branches of the same form of speech; but it may be true that they have no words having the same sound and meaning as the Sanscrit, and that words of the same sound which they both possess have a different meaning, and this is simply true because they are perfectly different languages. The test of common sense applied to this rule demonstrates its absurdity, and yet English scholars have suffered it to live and flourish amongst them to their confusion for nearly twenty years.

The author arrived at the conclusion that our common law was Keltic and not Saxon, in the sense of modern German, from a comparison of the law and not of the language, but the same rule holds good with both; and astonishment is aroused by seeing how many English words Dr. Mackay has shown have a genuine Keltic root, the meaning of the law term "burgh" in English, which is incomprehensible unless English means Gaulish, is clear and precise when viewed by that light; and so in numerous instances it is clear that the English common law is purely Gallic or Gaelic.

This being so, it follows almost as a matter of course that the people who owned this Gallic or Keltic common law must themselves have been a Gallic or Keltic race. Hence the theory of the Gallic origin of the British people, a theory the argument of which is capped, and indeed proved, by the derivation of Angle from An Geal.

Mr. Joseph Boult, in a very able paper entitled "The Angles, Jutes, and Saxons," read before the Historic Society of Lancashire and Cheshire, November 28, 1872, has anticipated the author in his derivation by suggesting the same thing. Mr. Boult resolves the word Angle into three Keltic words: An-geill-eis, men of a very wooded country, *geil* signifying a wood or wooded country, *eis* a man, and *an* being merely an intensitive particle. This, no doubt, is correctly stating the true meaning of Angle or Gael, for Gael is a contraction of Gathel or Gadheil, which means one who dwells in woods or houses made of boughs; in other words, a wanderer, as distinguished from an Aryan, who dwelt in houses. And this is the true meaning of Scot or Scythian, as is apparent from that form of the word Scuit which is engraved on the Lia Fail or Coronation Stone. Now, as the words Lia Fail are clearly Hebrew, or perhaps also Phœnician, *Lia* meaning stone, and *phail* shepherd, we shall not be surprised that this Hebrew-named stone had another Hebrew word upon it, Scuit, which is only a form of the Greek word Skuthes, and the Hebrew Succothes, dwellers in booths, wanderers, a term applied to the Israelites, to remind them of their wanderings in the wilderness, and naturally enough borrowed by their kinsmen of the Shemetic race to describe their own wanderings. Justin and Herodotus tell us that the Scythians were but wanderers. Justin describes them as ignorant of all the arts of civil life, for they occupied their land in common and cultivated none of it. A remnant of this custom, by the way, is traceable in Galway leases, the Gaels of which country take leases in a sort of partnership, and agree amongst themselves how to hold it in common. The ancient Scythians had no houses nor settled habitations, but wandered with their cattle from desert to desert, just as neither the Irish nor British after the departure of the Romans, nor for many centuries prior to their advent, built any permanent dwellings.

They were without laws, or codes of law, but were governed by the dictates of natural equity; that is, just as by our common law we are governed without a code by the decrees of equity. So that Mr. Boult is strictly accurate in his definition, only he has gone back to the primary meaning of the word.

Of this, then, there is no doubt, that Angle and Saxon are convertible terms; this is actually capable of proof. Bede proves it by invariably interposing the word *seu* or *sive* between the two names; just the contrary of the course followed by Archbishop Parker and the Oxford school. Nennius does the same, and so do Gildas and some of the writers subsequent to that date. Dr. R. G. Latham himself admits the truth of this; so, practically, does Professor Freeman. Every Saxon charter, whatever weight may attach to these documents, proves it, for in them the king or duke of the Saxons is always called the king or chief of the Angles.

And finally, the Irish, Scotch, and Welsh have no word in their tongue for England and the English (as it is their own name), but they have the words Saxon and Sassenach which they apply to the English. It is needless to prove that the Irish have the word Gallic amongst them. Keltic is admittedly the general term for the same people, and so of the Gael; and even Verstegan admits that the word Wales is simply Gaulish, as the French, by calling the Prince of Wales the Prince of the Gauls, clearly prove; and Cornwall, of course, is simply the kin or family of the Welsh, *i.e.*, *Cynne wealh*, so the words Kelt, Gaul, Saxon, English, and Welsh are synonymous.

Dr. Johnson, who was profoundly ignorant of everything Keltic, gives as the derivation of Wales the word foreigner, and in this, like Mr. Boult, he has not gone to the primary meaning, for there is no doubt but that Welsh means foreigner, stranger, wanderer. The Irish to this day call such a person a Gall, which is just the same thing as a Gael; and so Dr. Johnson and his latest editor are not positively wrong, although they have both missed the proper etymology of the word.

It is an undoubted fact that the Romans drove before them into Cornwall, Wales, and Scotland a great part of the English or Gaelic people of England. It is not, therefore, very surprising that each of these provinces took the name of the people who flocked into it; and that the people who remained behind, when once freed from the Roman provincial names, reverted to their own native name, with an intensive article prefixed. If this is not the meaning of it, from whence does it come? If, therefore, as it is alleged, 'Angle' simply means the Gael, and Angle and Saxon are convertible terms, it is clear that they both mean Scythian, as both the Gauls and the Saxons are of Scythian origin; and curiously enough, just as the word Gael is found encrusted in Angle, the word Scythian is equivalent to that of Saxon.

This idea first flashed upon the author in reading a passage from Verstegan, page 21, in which he asserts that in his day a Scythe was called in Netherlandish a Saison, the very word by which that people call a Saxon. If this be so, the words Saison, Sassen, Scythian, mean the same thing.

Verily there is nothing new under the sun. This idea was published so long ago as 1818 by Mr. Thomas Heming of Magdalen Hall, Oxford, in his " Complete Survey of Scripture Geography." At page 29 of the preface, referring to people of Asia, and citing Megasthenes as to the great populousness of the Eastern territory, he states :— " Herodotus, lib. i., iii., iv., Siculus, lib. ii., Strabo, lib. xi., plainly evince that the nation of the Scythians, from whom all the European people descended, were Indians or Persic Indians, called Sacæ; afterwards in other districts Sasones and Saxons." And he adds—" In addition to these and many other ancient writers, our own eminent historians and antiquaries, Stukely, Heylin, and Raleigh, with others of high celebrity, have judged that the original seminary of mankind was in the east of Persia." Nor has this view entirely escaped the author (Dr. Latham) of the article on Scythia in Dr. William Smith's Geographical Dictionary. After stating very fairly the different views upon the subject, he says that " the Indo-European hypothesis makes the Got in Massagetæ Goth=German. The extreme form of this hypothesis is Sacæ = Saxons, and the Yuche of the Chinese the Goths."

It is, however, of little use to throw out these suggestions unless they are followed up to their logical conclusion, but this neither writer referred to attempts to do; on the contrary, both of them follow the well-beaten path of the Oxford school upon the subject. It will be the object of the following pages to show that this is the true view of the question, and whether or not the word Saxon is derived etymologically from the word Scythian, that Sacæ is a common term between them, and that all three are identical if not coextensive in their meaning and application.

With regard to the etymology of the word, its history is as follows:—The Persians used the terms Sacæ and Scythian as convertible, whether from a corrupt rendering of one from the other, or because the Sacæ, a great tribe of Scythians bordering upon them, were so called from a tribal name (a great question which Persian scholars must determine). Of the fact of the identity of the Sacæ and Scythians there is not the shadow of a doubt, and it is clear that these people called their country Sacasena.

It is equally clear that the Saxons of England were Scythians or Celto-Scythians. Their geographical position in Europe is accurately described by Plutarch, Tacitus, Ptolemy, and many other authors.

The Saxons of England were called Saison by the Welsh, Sasun by the Scotch, Saison by the Irish, Sasse or Sachse by the German, Saisen by the Netherlander, Saisson by the Sclav or Prussian.

The same nations gave the same name to a scythe, and even in Devonshire to this day a reaping-hook is called a sasin. The ancient Netherlander called it saisen, the modern Flemish seysene, the Dutch zeissen. The modern Gaelic (see Dr. Charles Mackay's Dictionary) is from sgud, to mow or lop, and sguids is to thrash, swish, whilst Scythian or Scot, which is the same word, is said to be derived from Sguit, a wanderer.

It has been asserted by Verstegan that the German word scheitan is from the old verb scytan, to shoot, because the Scythians were great shooters. One would think that shooting was so called because it was a great art of the Scythians; so the· scythe is the implement, sword, or scythe of the same people.

The word sickle, a little scythe, is a proof how readily

a *k* may be added to the sound, so Saxon may possibly be derived from Scythian.

All German writers, after their manner of putting the cart before the horse, assert that the Saxons were so called from using the saxe; so the axe, from the Axions, the same people.

Englehusus has a couplet to this effect—

> " Quippe brevis gladius apud illos saxa vocatur,
> Unde sibe saxo nomen traxisse putatur."

The *th* in the word Scythian is of course dropped by the Germans, who cannot pronounce it, and becomes Syssan in their mouths, just as Gathel, by elision, becomes Gael; Cather, a fort, Caer; Argathel, Argyle, &c.

These suggestions are offered with the greatest hesitation, for it is felt that philology is a most dangerous guide, and that although laws by the score may be laid down, cases will be found outside of them, and again words which fall clearly within them may not be changed as we imagine; nor is this inquiry of great importance to the argument of this book, for it is sufficient to prove that Saxon and Scythian are in this case convertible terms, whatever may have been their separate roots, or whether or not they are both of them derived from the same root.

## CHAPTER XIX.

### THE CHANGES IN THE NAMES OF THE TRIBES WHO PEOPLED BRITAIN.

BUT if the derivation of one word from another is a difficult matter to determine, there are some changes which may be attested by witnesses of such a character that we cannot well dispute their authority; and in endeavouring to trace the tribes who settled in England from the north-east, or rather from the north and east, to their original homes in Asia, it will be necessary to show the changes which have been made in their names—changes which arise sometimes from their advent into a new country, and sometimes, perhaps, by the mere lapse of time.

Thus we find that the Galli or Gael, who kept the name of Gaul in France, retains the Latin name Gael in Scotland only, assumes the Greek form Kelt in Ireland, Welsh and Cornish in the west of England, and Angle in middle and east England.

The Jute or Goth of England went through no fewer nor less important changes, and we must trace him in turn through the varieties, Jute, Goth, Getæ, Massagetæ, Gothones, Guthes, Skuthes, Scythæ. This is obviously, therefore, a generic, and not a tribal name. So, again, by a tribal name of these same Goths, Dannan in Ireland, Dani in Scandinavia and England, and also in Ireland Daci,

Thraci, Scythæ. And again, Dani, Doni, Donian, Cale-
donian, Macedonian, Dones, Tones, Teutones, &c. So
Cymry in Wales to Cimbri in Scandinavia, Cambri and
Sicambri, Cimmerii, and, like Daci, to Thraci and Scythæ.
So Sassen, Saxon, Axon, Ambrones, Sassones, Sacæ,
Scythæ. So Scythæ to Scotæ.

So the Goths became Jutes, Whites, Fights, Ficti, Picti
each in their turn. Perhaps it will be best to reverse the
order and trace these names from the Scythians, the name
by which they were called before we knew them.

First, then, to prove that the Scythians and Goths, or
Getæ, are identical. Herodotus, writing 450 B.C., at a time
when the change had not been so far distant but that
the truth might be known distinctly, avers that the
Goths or Getæ are the Scythians. Strabo, Pliny,
Ptolemy all rank the Getæ as Scythians. Thucydides
(ii. 96) mentions the Scythians in connection with the
Getæ in Greece. Trogus, who flourished fifty years B.C.,
says Tannas, king of the most ancient Scythæ, fought
with Vexores, king of Egypt. Valerius Flaccus (lib. v.)
calls this first-named king, King of the Getæ.

Trebellius Pollio, " in Galliem Scythæ autem id est pars
Gothorum Asiam vastabant id a Claudio Gothico Scytharum
diverse populi Pincini Truhengi Austro-Gothis prædæ."

Dexipus (who Grotius asserts wrote in the reign of
Gallienus) entitled his work the " History of the Wars between the Romans and the Gotho-Scythic Nations."

Priscus uses the words as if synonymous.

Goropius called the Goths whom Valens placed in Mæsia
Scythians; they were afterwards called Mæso-Goths, or
Massagetæ.

Procopius (temp. Justinian) writes "of all the other Gothic
nations, who were also called Scythians in ancient times."

o

Anastatius in Hist. Chronograph., "When many Scythians, who are called Goths, had passed the river Ister in the time of Decius, they wasted the Roman Empire."

Ammianus Marcellinus (lib. xxxi.), recording the death of Decius, calls the Goths "Scythæ."

Theophanes, writing A.D. 300, "For that the Scythians in their own tongue are called Goths."

Trajanus Patricius states the same thing in his history of his own time.

Georgius Symmachus: "The Scythians are also called Goths in their own language."

Jornandes speaks of the Goths, Getæ, and Scythians as the same people.

Isidorus, in his chronicle of the Goths in Spain, thus writes :—"Gothorum antiquissimum esse regnum certum ut quod ex regno Scytharum est exortum."

Procopius (lib. i. c. 2) says the whole Scythæ were anciently called Getic nations; and he calls the Fœderati, so well known in the Lower Empire, Goths; Suidas calls them Scythæ.

Most if not all of these authorities are taken from the valuable work of Pinkerton, which contains a mine of wealth upon the subject. That writer is little noticed now, but nearly every historian has utilised his labours, which were immense, and his work is logically correct though his deductions are absurd. His great object was to prove that the modern Germans were identical with the Goths. He only proved the identity of the ancient Germans, of which there can be no doubt, for all historians unite in asserting that the so-called German tribes were Galatæ or Keltæ. Modern research, and especially Dr. R. G. Latham, has proved that the modern Germans are not relatives in blood to their predecessors of the same name, but are of Sarmatian origin. With all his learning and powers of discrimination, Pinkerton fails to understand this fact, hence his labours were useless for the object he had in view.

That the Goths and Getæ are identical many writers combine to prove. So clearly is it established that there can be no rational doubt about it.

Suidas, a Greek writer of the tenth or eleventh century, states that Dio, writing 230 A.D., called his history of the Goths "Geticon."

Spartianus (writing about A.D. 300), Vita Caracalla, "Gothi Getæ dicerentur," Hist. Ang. Scrip., p. 419 ; and in his life of Aristum Gela (p. 427) he writes, "Geticus quasi Gothicus."

Claudian, in his poem on the Gothic war, calls it "De Bello Getico."

Sidonius Apollinaris in the fifth century calls the Goths Getæ, and the Ostrogoths Massagetæ.

Ausonius (Idyl. 8) speaks of the Getis.

Orosius (lib. i. c. 6), "Getæ qui et nunc Gothi."

St. Jerome (Epis. ad Galat.) says the Goths were anciently called Getæ.

Eunodius, in his panegyric to Theodoricus, king of the Goths, calls his people Getici.

Procopius, temp. Justinian, says that the Goths are a Getic race.

Jornandes entitled his history "De Getarum sive Gothorum."

Isidore Origines (lib. xx. c. 2) says the Getæ and the Goths are the same.

That the Getæ were Thracians. Dr. R. G. Latham asserts this to be the case.

Voconius, Ovid, and Strabo all assert that the Thracians and the Getæ spoke the same language. Ihre proves that the Getæ and the Thracians were known by each other's

names.   Of course this may be taken with the limit that
the Getæ were only a portion of the Thracians.

Strabo (lib. vii. c. 3, s. 2), "The Greeks consider the
Getæ to be Thracians."

Herodotus (iv. 93), "The Getæ are the most valiant
and just of the Thracians."

Menander writes, "All the Thracians truly, and especially above all the Getæ (for I myself glory in being
descended from the race)," &c.

The Getæ were living side by side with the Daci, not
only in Thrace but along the whole course of the Danube,
and even in Scandinavia.    Strabo asserts that they spoke
the same language in Thrace (lib. vii. c. 3, s. 12) as undoubtedly they did in Denmark, and that they were the
same people.   That the Daci and the Dani are the same
people is clear from Denmark having been anciently called
Dacia.   Dacia is, in fact, Thrace, so called by people who
were unable to pronounce the theta.

Sir Isaac Newton (Chron., p. 1125) writes, "The ancient
inhabitants of Dacia (Transylvania, Moldavia, and Wal-
lachia) were called Getæ by the Greeks, Daci by the
Latins, and Goths by themselves."

There can be no doubt that the Daci or Dani, as well as
the Getæ or Gothi, were all of the race called Cimbri.   The
Cimbri were also Cimmerii, and so of Thracian origin also,
or the Thracians were Cimmerians, it matters not which.

The Thracians were the widely extended race called the
Pelasgi, a name which it is asserted is taken from the
Stork, and means, like Scythian, a wandering nomadic
race.   It is clear from Homer that active communications
were established between the Thracians and the Trojans,
who were probably of Pelasgic race.   The Thracians were
anciently called Peske and Aria, which would intimate an
Asiatic origin connected with those districts.

In the Trojans, Mysians, Maconians, Mygdonians, Dolco-nians, Daci, Bibrice, Scordisci, Edones, Estæ, Cicones, and other Thracian races, may readily be traced tribes con-nected with the Cimbri and with Britain.

The Cicones, who were also Galai and Briantes (British tribes had the same name), fought with Ulysses after the fall of Troy; and it is asserted that the Cimmerian Briges of Thrace went into Asia Minor and became the Phrygians. They were the Brigantes of Britain.

The chief part of European Scythia, which includes Thrace, had been possessed by the Cimmerians.   They possessed all the land on the south of ancient Scythia, about the Tyra and the Danube.   On the banks of the Tyra lay the monuments of the Cimmerii who had fallen in the great conflict with the Scythians.

That the Cimbri were the same as the Cimmerii is asserted by Plutarch, who states that it is related that the Cimbri and the Cimmerii were the same people (Vita C. Marius).   He also affirms that the Teutones, Cimbri, and other nations who were banded together were all called Celto-Scythian.

Strabo (lib. vii. c. 2, s. 2) states that the Greeks called the Cimbri Cimmerii.

Herodotus (iv. 13) cites Aristeas the Preconosian, who lived before Homer, in proof that the Cimmerii lived on the South Sea till pushed forward by the Scythæ, and he states that they were in Europe before the Scythians, who subsequently occupied their territory.   The whole of the nations north of the Greeks were at one time called by them Thracians, including the Cimmerii, and the Cimbric Chersonesus was at one time called the Taurica or Thracian Chersonese.   That portion of the Cimmerii who lived near the Palus Mæotis invaded Asia Minor, 1284 B.C., and in 624 B.C. they seized the kingdom of Cyaxares, but after being masters of it for twenty-eight years they were driven back by Alyattes, king of Lydia. About 665 B.C. they were driven out of the Crimea by Scythian hordes, in all probability the ancestors of the Saxons, then called the Sacæ. It was then called the Chersonesus Scythica. Soon or after this date the Cimmerii disappear from history, probably to emerge again as the Cimbri of Scandinavia. In 629 B.C. they took the city of Sardis.

That the Cimmerii or Cimbri were Kelts is proved by the fact that Homer places them where other writers place the Kelts. Apion, a celebrated historian, born in Egypt in the reign of Trajan, distinctly calls them Kelts (De Bello Civ., lib. i. p. 265), and again (in Illyr., p. 1196) he writes of "those Kelts who are called Cimbri." Dion Cassius speaks of them as Gauls. Plutarch and Lucan call the slave who was ordered to slay Marius both a Gaul and a Cimbrian. This, of course, was after their journey through Gaul. Posidonius, Strabo, and Plutarch assert that the Cimbri or Cimmerii came from the German Ocean to the Euxine.

Sallust and Cicero point to Gaul as the home of the Cimbri. Cæsar fixes them south of the Marne and the Seine (Bello Gall., lib. i. 1, lib. ii. 4).

Diodorus Siculus deals with them as a Gaulish people (s. 32). Strabo, who only wrote from hearsay, places them between the Rhine and the Elbe. Velleius Paterculus had learnt something more; he calls them Gallic, and puts them beyond the Rhine. Ptolemy pushes them northwards; and Pliny, whose knowledge was more extended (iv. s. 28), states that they were as far northwards as Norway.

Appian states that the Teutones, as well as the Ambrones who accompanied the Cimbri, were also Kelts.

Plutarch relates that the war-cry of the Ambrones was similar to that of the Ligurians, as both found to their surprise; and the Ligurians were undoubtedly a Keltic race.

·Dr. Latham considers them of the Gaulish rather than the Gothic branch.

Ariovisti spoke Gallic to the Romans, who understood it.

Mallet writes, "Les Celts ont été connus anciennement sous le nom général de Scythes."

Aristotle calls the British tin Celtic.

Niebuhr attributes to Johannes Müller considerable credit for having proved the Cimbri to be Celts (Lecture on Ancient Ethnography, 1853, ii. 326).

Mr. H. L. Long considers the Cymry as the first wave in the tide of the human race, which, rolling continuously from Asia and the East, reached eventually the coast of Britain.

Zeuss proves that the language of the Gauls and the ancient Britons, or the Cymry, was identical, with only dialectical differences; and philologists generally agree in attributing the Cymric language to the Belgæ. That this was akin to the Gaelic branch is admitted by the Irish Kelts, who allege that all the people who invaded Ireland spoke the same language (Canon U. J. Bourke).

We see from the accumulated testimony of Homer, Appian, Posidonius, Strabo, Plutarch, Sallust, Cicero, Cæsar, Diodorus Siculus, Velleius Paterculus, Ptolemy, Pliny, Dion Cassius, and Lucan, that the Cimbri who descended upon Italy about 100 B.C. came through Gaul, and the country they possessed above Gaul is bounded by Cæsar southward of the Marne and the Seine, by Strabo westward of the Elbe, and by successive writers, as their acquaintance grew, up to Norway on the

north. In fact, each writer places them as far north as
he knows anything of the Northern country, thus undoubtedly identifying them with Scandinavia and the
Norsemen; and they concur in stating they came down
to Italy from the north.

Ihre remarks that the ancients comprised all the
people in the oblique ascent from the Caspian to the
farthest point of Scandinavia under the general name of
Scythians; and our own Bede calls Scandinavia Scythia.
Their own traditions prove that they originally came
from the south. According to the Gothic annals, the first
migration came to Scandinavia in the time of Serug,
great-grandfather of Abraham, under their king, Eric. The
Welsh records relate that they came from the summer
country. The chronicles of the Swedish kings commence with a people on the banks of the Tannersquil,
Dannerstrom, or Danube, who were governed by Odin.
The Icelandic Eddas and Sagas state that Odin, the
great god of the Scandinavian Goths, led his people into
Scandinavia from Scythia on the Dannerstrom.

Herodotus, who lived some four hundred years before
the Cimbric invasion of Italy, places the Getæ on the south
of the Danube, and the Scythæ on the other side; the
Tyssa Getæ north of the Euxine (lib. iv. s. 121), and in
the heart of Scythia (s. 11); the Massagetæ, on the north
and east of the Caspian; Pliny and Strabo all over the
west of the Euxine; and the latter through half of Germany, thus fully corroborating the native traditions.

It may be asked how it is that a nation is known at one
time as the Cimbri, at another as the Scythians, at others
as the Getæ, the Keltæ, the Galli, the Daci, the Dani, the
Gothi, the Sacæ, the Saxoni, Scandinavian, Norsemen,
Teutones. It would seem that there are two reasons

which can be given.  Although this people (call them
Kelts if you will) have that general appellation, yet they
are a confederation of many tribes, each of which has
a distinct name of its own; and that many of these
names are variations of one and the same, whilst others
differ because, perhaps, as it was a Keltic custom in time
of war to choose one leader over all, his name, or rather
the name of his tribe, became for the time the name of
the whole clan.   So at one time they are Cimbri, at
another Ambrones or Saxones; now Scythæ or Skuthes
to the Greeks, and Goths or Getæ to the Latins.  The mode
is explained by Salmasius (De Lege Helenes, p. 368).
Skuthes, Sguthes; dropping the *s*, Guthes, Gethes, Gothes,
are the same words, *s* in Greek being but a servile letter,
and may be omitted at pleasure, as Skimbri for Kimbri ; .
so that Goths, Getæ, Scythæ, Sacæ, Saxones, &c. are all
one and the same name.

# CHAPTER XX.

## THE SCYTHIANS.

THE question who were the Scythians has been mooted time out of mind, and with a wonderful variety of response. It may appear presumptuous to endeavour to answer it, but taking a wide view of it, and remembering the part played in ancient history by those bearing the name, it is not so difficult to arrive at an approximate determination. Professor Newman has remarked that the term Scythian has been used with infinite license. It has been calculated that at least fifty nations have at one time or other been so called; nor is this remarkable when we remember that the Scythian people were distinguished for their knowledge as well as power, and that nations under tribute to them, just as those conquered by the Greeks, the Romans, or the British, would delight in taking the name of their conquerors.

It is difficult to arrive at the true meaning of the term. The older writers, assuming that the Scythæ and the Scoti were identical, as they probably were, have produced a story of one Gathulus, the mythic leader of the Gaels —who, be it remembered, was also called Gathel—inter-marrying with a daughter of Pharaoh whose name was Scotæ, and in her honour directing his followers to call themselves Scots. This legend is either mythic or absurd according to the taste of the objector. It can hardly be relied upon as a solution of the difficulty. Verstegan, of course, is equally ready with a derivation; and of course, in accordance with the principles of his mania, with a German one. The Scythians were so called because they were great shooters, and the Germans had an old verb *scytan*, which means "to shoot." Possibly the German word is derived from the name Scythian, but certainly the Scythians did not go to Germany to obtain their name. It is simply ridiculous to suppose the converse to be true, for the Scythians were known by this name to numerous people who never heard either of the great German people or of their great verb *scytan*, or its more modern form of *schitessan*. Besides, we have notices of the Scythians for at least a thousand years before the first German was heard of. But this argument is disposed of by the fact that in Greek the word does not signify either a shooter or to shoot, and the Greeks knew the word long before the Germans had it. It is said that the term was not originally indicative of any particular nationality, but of a habit, and the habit was described by the name, the meaning of which is usually given as wanderer, or as designating one of nomad race, and unquestionably the Scythians were of this race, and were not of Aryanic origin, if Aryan means one not of nomad habits.

There is another meaning, which seems even more probable, and is certainly very apt. It is also a designation which was applied to many different peoples, not on account of their nationality, but of their habits. The Scits or Scythes in religion were followers of Seth, as opposed to the Canaanites, the leading principle of the one being Promethean, and of the other Epimethean; and the Eastern world, from which it is acknowledged the Scythians sprang, was in the earliest ages divided into these two great classes so described. The Irish have a word, seth-fhior, the latter being plural of fear, a man; the former, Vallancy asserts, has no meaning in Irish, and he would refer it to the Egyptian word seth, strong, able.

It must be remembered that the nations would remain Promethean although they lapsed into idolatry—the worship of the Canaanites—for we know that the Israelites themselves at times lapsed into the worship of Baal and Astaroth.

But it is submitted with great confidence that the name, although it may have come to denote a meaning as above mentioned, yet originally is corrupted from Gether, the father of the Getæ or Goths, and it is not difficult to trace the steps by which it may have been transformed. Goths or Gothes, S'Gothes, Skuthes, which is the Greek form of it. The probability of this derivation is heightened by the fact that the Scythians proper, or Royal Scythians, were undoubtedly a Getic race.

On the other hand, some of the earliest facts of history are of Scythic origin. The Greeks owed their knowledge of the arts and sciences directly, no doubt, to the Phœnicians, but indirectly to the Scythians, from whom they obtained it. The ancient Grecian mythology is founded upon events recorded in Scythian history. The Greek gods are Scythian heroes. Deucalion himself is said to have been a Scythian. Amraphel, king of Shinar, Arioch, king of Ellasar, Chedorlaomer, king of Elam, and Tidal, king of nations, mentioned in the 14th chaper of Genesis, and contemporary with Abraham, on the authority of Eupolemous are said to have been Armenians, while Symmachus styles them Scythæ (Eusebius, de Præp. Evang., p. 418). They would seem to have been a great confederacy of Shemetic people. The king of Ellasar was king of

Armenia proper, or at any rate of a portion of that country. The Elamites are known as the Persians, who were Armenians (De Herbelot, p. 212). They of the Vale of Shinar were Assyrians, and "the nations" were the nations of Gilgal or Galilee of the Nations, the descendants probably of Chul, who resided by the Sea of Galilee, that is, the Galls of the sea—the whole of the four kings thus occupying a territory of great extent and importance. Why Abraham should have fought against his own race in favour of the king of Sodom is a puzzle, except that the kings had turned their arms upon his kinsman.

Villanuava, p. 54, doubtingly asserts that the term "Scythian" is derived from the Phœnicians. He writes: "Mihi probabilius est ne dicam indubiam 'Scythus' a Phœnicibus hoc nomen sortitus ex quo illis admixti sunt magnum Syriæ partem occupantes et illos sic vocasse quoniam eorum tribulis viderunt ad id tempus per agros et silvas discurrentes et per incultas solitudines et asperos montes errare solitus verum Phœniciis 'Shitin' sunt 'circuentes' 'discurrentes' ob 'ambulantes' a 'Shit' ire 'circuire discurrere' a via divertere vel quia maxime principium terrore suum imperium subactes valides, copiis expandereat 'Shitah' expandere 'deletari' 'extendere' sed a Armenia regio 'Saca' vel 'Sacasena' quæ ab ipsis nomen traxit e Phœniciæ linguæ 'fortibus' videtur appellata in qua Sacæ significat 'jugeri' 'discurrere' 'ambulare' et 'Sacati' 'tegumentum' 'Fagarum' Fortassi si justitium gentes respicians Saca eos appellatio crederis a 'Zaca' 'justus' imprehensibilis quæ omnia paucis Chæritus in Xerxes Drabar corruptus est 'inquiens' Zaca etiam Phœnicibus erat 'superare' 'vincere' quod bellica Scytharum virtute et victoriis apprimi congruit."

It is curious that Villanuava in the one word simply

shows that the nomad habits of the Scythes were called
after them, and in the second that their attributes or
Sethite qualities were the foundation for the name.

Vallancy asserts that the true derivation of Scythian, *i.e.*,
of Scuthai and Sacæ, is shipman, navigator, or swimmer,
again mistaking a habit of a part of the Scythians for the
origin of their name.

No doubt there were Scythian sailors as well as lands-
men. The Southern Scythians were most famous for commerce and navigation, in other words, were Phœnicians or
traders; whilst the Northern or inland Scythians carried
on no trade, but excelled in the arts of the chase and in
all the peaceable arts.

Homer and Hesiod, the first Greek writers, both mention that they knew them as Nomads, not as Scythians;
and Homer's description of them is very important. He
calls them Hippomolgi and Galachelphali and Abii,
and speaks of them as the illustrious Hippomolgi, milk-
nourished, simple in living, and most just men (Iliad, xiii.
5), and as being "blest with length of days"—a clear
description of the patriarchs. Anarcharsis, a Scythian,
was one of the seven sages of antiquity. Hesiod speaks
of the Ethiopians, the Ligurians, and the Scythians as
milkers of mares. This is perhaps the first mention of
the similarity of habits between the Gauls and the Goths.
Æschylus spoke of the Scythians as being governed by
good laws, and feeding on cheese of mares' milk.

And their character for justice remained to them.
Ephorus, writing A.A.C. 350, contrasts their manner of life
with that of the cannibal Sarmatians, stating of the
Scythians that they exceed all men in their justice.

One of the earliest notices we have of the connection
between the Ligurians and the Scythians, which proves,

at any rate, that there was contact between them, is to be found in Hesiod, who mentions them together. This is a curious confirmation of the idea that the Gael was a Scythian also.

It is curious how this term Scythian has been abused. Professor Newman may well speak of the "infinite license" with which it has been treated—scarcely an exaggerating phrase, for at some time or other nearly every nation of antiquity has been called Scythian. The Cimmerii were anciently called Scythians (Eresthal in Diog., s. 167). Newton and Appian assert that all Europe had been peopled by Cimmerians and Scythians. Anarcharsis, the Scythian philosopher (apud Clem., lib. i. p. 364), pronounced the Greeks Scythæ. St. Jerome states that the Greeks had spread themselves over the whole of Europe. Strabo asserts that the ancient Greeks comprehended two-thirds of Europe under the name of Celto-Scythians and Scythians. In fact, the two words, Cimmerian and Scythian, seem convertible terms; so the words Greek and Scythian; so Greek and Keltæ; so Keltæ and Scythæ, and Keltæ and Galatæ, we know, are the same, and so of many others; the probability being that the whole of these words have the same derivation, and are simple translations or corruptions from each other. It is curious to see how different writers, each taking the history of one of these names, makes it the generic name of the whole, and makes its equivalents merely species. Dr. Borlase has actually written that the Celts anciently comprised the Scythians, Celto-Scythians, Getæ, Galatians, Gallo - Grecians, Celti - Berians, Teutones, Germans, and Gauls. Others assert that the Scythians comprehended the whole of these, and this would appear to be a more rational classification.

Herodotus and Pliny assert that Sacæ was a general

name given by the Persians to the Scythians, and that the Sacæ and Massagetæ were the generic names for the Asiatic Scythians on the east of the Caspian, who were called the Scythæ intra Imaum.

Dr. Latham (Germania, p. v.) states that the Mæso-Gothic tribes were the Goths who conquered Mæsia.

Cheritus writes, " The sheep-feeding Sacæ, a people of Scythia."

Strabo (lib. xi. c. 8, s. 4), "The Sacæ occupied Bactriana, and got possession of the most fertile tract in Armenia, which was called after their own name, Sæsene"—a word very nearly like Saxon, especially the old form of the name, Sæasena, which Verstegan assures us is the oldest form of that name.

Herodotus (c. 7, s. 64) positively asserts that the Sacæ are Scythians.

Cheritus, speaking of the Sacæ as inhabiting wheat-producing Asia (the Gallic race were famous in England for their red wheat), says truly they were a colony of nomads, a righteous race; and describing the expedition of Alexander the Great, thus mentions the Sacæ—

> " Next marched the Sacæ, fond of pastoral life,
> Sprung from the Scythic Nomads, who lived
> Upon the plains of Asia, rich in grain.
> They from the Shepherd race deduce their source,
> Those shepherds who in ancient times were deemed
> The justest of mankind."

The Basques of Spain are said to have been so named by the Tyrians, because they were Bua Sacæ, or the western navigators, an idea which is strengthened by an anonymous writer in French of a small tract upon the comparisons by Vallancy of the Punic and Irish languages, who points out that it had been previously supposed that Irish had been compounded of Celtic and Basque.

Herodotus, in relating the account of the expedition of Darius, joins the Bactrians and Sacæ together (lib. v. 133); and describing the costume of the latter, he says (lib. vii. s. 64) :—

"The Sacæ, who are Scythians, had on their heads caps which came to a point and stood erect; they also wore loose trousers, and carried bows peculiar to their country, and daggers, and also battle-axes, called Sagares. These, although they are Amygrian-Scythians, they called Sacæ, for the Persians call all the Scythians Sacæ. Hystaspes son of Darius, and Alossa, daughter of Cyrus, commanded the Bactrians and the Sacæ.

"Cyrus, when he wished to conquer the Massagetæ, pretended to woo their queen, Tomyris.

"The Massagetæ resemble the Scythians in their dress and mode of living. They have both horse and foot bowmen and javelin-men, who are accustomed to carry battle-axes. They use gold and brass for everything; for whatever concerns spears and arrow-points and battle-axes they use brass, but for the head and belt and shoulder-pieces, they are ornamented with gold; in like manner, with regard to the chests of their horses, they put on breastplates of brass, but the bridle, bit, and cheek-pieces are ornamented with gold."

Herodotus acquits the Scythians from the charge of polyandry, but he charges the Mæso-Goths with it—a thing hardly likely to be true, since adultery was with them a capital crime, and Horace commended them for the chastity of their women. They live on cattle and milk, worship the sun only of all the gods, and live in tents, building no houses.

Hesiod: "The Delians say that sacred things were brought from the Hyperboreans, and came to the Scythians, and from the Scythians each contiguous nation received them in

P

succession." IV. s. 46: "The Scythians have learned men
amongst them; they are equestrian archers, living not
from the cultivation of the earth, but from cattle, and their
dwellings waggons." (This accounts for the migration of
the Cimbri, which Strabo says only occurred by degrees.)
"They divine by the use of willow rods." S. 93: "The Getæ
are the most valiant and the most just of the Thracians."

Appollinaris Sidonius says that the Scythians were
shod with high shoes made of hair and reaching up to
their ankles; their knees, thighs, and legs are without
any covering, their garments, of various colours, scarcely
reaching to the knee; their sleeves only cover the top of
their arms; they wear green cassocks with a red border,
their belts hanging on their shoulders; their ears are
covered with twisted locks; they use hooked lances and
missile weapons.

Dio asserts that they encouraged the study of philosophy
above all other foreign nations, and often chose chiefs
from amongst their philosophers. They were celebrated
for their kindness and hospitality.

Strabo bears honourable testimony to their uprightness.
He says they had few commercial or monetary transac-
tions, and, except their swords and drinking-cups, possessed all things in common, living not in houses but in
waggons. Strabo speaks highly of their bravery and
disregard of life, if unaccompanied by honour; and in
respect of their valour and cruelty and brutal madness,
he places the Kelts, Thracians, and Scythians in the
same category; and he relates that the women of all
these people were equally brave and careless of life.
And with regard to their extent of territory, Strabo asserts
that the Sacæ, a portion of the Scythians, occupied Bactria,
and had possession of the most fertile tract of Armenia,

which was called Sacasene after them ; and beyond Bactria they occupied a much larger territory bounded by the Northern Ocean ; and he adds, "Here they dwell, though to be sure theirs is a nomad life" (lib. ii. c. 1, s. 17).

"Most of the Scythians, beginning from the Caspian Sea, are called Dakæ-Scythiæ, and those situated more towards the east, Massagetæ and Sacæ. The rest have the common appellation of Scythian, but each special tribe has its peculiar name. All are nomads."

"The tribes are the Asii, Pasiani, Tochari, Sacaranti, Aparni, Xanblii, Pissuri (lib. xi. c. 8, s. 6)."

"The Massagetæ regard no other deity but the sun. They use bows, swords, breastplates, and sagares of brass, and wear golden belts and turbans. Their horses have bits of gold and golden breastplates."

"They press out and drink the juice of the fruit of certain trees."

"They dye their clothes and use sealskins."

"Though they possess land they do not cultivate it, but derive their substance from their flocks and from fish, after the manner of the Nomads and Scythians. Their burial-places and their manners are alike, and their whole manner of living is independent, but rude, savage, and hostile ; but in their compacts, however, they are simple and without deceit (s. 7)."

"Ptolemy and Strabo (lib. ii.) state that the Sacæ and Massagetæ amongst the Persians were the same as the Scythæ and Getæ of the Greeks."

A region at the fountain of Oxus is still called Sakila, and Scythia extra Imaums was called Getæ and its people Getes at the time of Tamerlain, as appears from his life written in Persian.

The present Persian, though mixed with some Arabic,

is a dialect of the Gothic, as Scaliger, Lipsius, Benholm,
and Barton have shown.  It has auxiliary verbs and other
radical marks of a Gothic origin.  But what still more
clearly demonstrates the connection between the Saxons
and the localities of Scythia, extra and intra Imaum, is
the names of tribes.  Among them are to be found Chatti
(Catti), Sassones (Saxones), Syebi (Swevi), Tectosaces (Tectosages), Iotæ (Jutæ), and a town called Menapia; a combination of names of such importance as to constitute almost
absolute proof of the identity of the Sacæ and Saxons.

The Scoloti of Little Tartary, the Scythians, were neigh-
bours of the Essedones, who are to be found in Thrace
under the name of Edones, and by the Baltic as Estonians.
They, too, may be identified by the use of war chariots,
not only in Asia and Europe, but in Britain (Step.
Byzant. de Urbe).  Archbishop Usher (In Veterum Epis.
Hebr. Recensione) identifies the Estiæ or Estonii of the
Baltic with the Ostioi and Ostones of the Greeks, the Æstii
of Egenhard (Life of Charlemagne), the Estones of Saxo-
Grammaticus, Æstii of Tacitus, with the Ostmanni and
Easterlings of the Irish.

So little is known of the Sacæ of Asia, and their identity
with our own Saxons is so evident, that the views of any
writer who has studied their character and habits are of
interest.  No writer has paid them greater honour than
Mons. D'Ancarville, from whose valuable work on the
"Origin of Greek Art" the following extracts are taken.
They are given *verbatim et literatim*, because it is little
known, and perhaps few readers will have access to his
works at the British Museum Library.  It is catalogued
under the name of Huguet.

Mons. D'Hancarville, in fact, endorses the view, whether
it be the true derivation of the word Scythian or not, that

it was a religious distinction, and his account of the people would be an accurate account of the patriarchs, the Pali or Shepherds of Palestine. He translates the word Sacæ into the French word Sacques, just as the article so called is in that language described.

"Les Sacques, ces peuples nomades s'etendaient dans ces terrains les plus élevés du Caucase où fût autrefois la Nyse des Scythes. C'est de la que vint l'emblème du bœuf et le nom de Dionysius que lui donnèrent les Grecs. Cet Dieu il y a plus de 5400 ans ; ils l'attribuerent ensuite à l'être secondaire que la superstition leur fit confondre avec l'être suprême, plus défiguré encore depuis ; il est à present ce qu'ils appelent l'Erlich Kan ; ils en font le Dieu qui juge les hommes et les punit après leur mort ; mais ils le peignent toujours avec l'attribus du Dieu de la vie, et lui donnent des titres que expriment sa domination sur toutes choses car son nom signifie le Seigneur Roi.

" Les Sacques pouvoient se vanter de ne tirer leur origine d'aucun autre peuple possesseur du terrain que les Scythes dèsirent avoir été le premiér habitable ; ils gardèrent toujours les mœurs des premiérs habitans de la terre et continuèrent, à mener la vie de nomades ou de pasteurs.

" C'est de ces terres habitus par les plus anciens peuples connus que l'on voit descendre le culte transporté dans toutes les parties de notre continent" (vol. i. p. 149).

The vast country (Mid-Asia) was called Sakai as well as Kathai or Katha, and La Syrie also had the name, and its inhabitants seem to have been regarded as descendants of the Sakai.

"Abraham est moderne en comparaison des Sacques; c'est chez eux qu'il peut chercher les antiquités les plus reculés et leur histoire seroit la plus ancienne de toutes les histoires (p. 155); on trouve donc chez les Sacques l'origin des Scythes

nous apprenons de cet auteur (Herodotus) que le Roi Scythe
dont les Scythes prirent le nom portoit chez eux celui de
Scolotes aussi ils s'appelèrent eux-mêmes Scolotes et non pas
Scythes; cette dernière dénomination est absolument grecque;
le nom de Scolote est antérieur á celui de Scythe, et celui
de Sacque a du précèder celui de Scolotes, puisque le Prince
qui le porta naquit chez les Sacques le nom sî ancien de
son peuple n'a jamais changé " (p. 156).

Sac, Saceus, in Latin, belongs to a great number of
languages, ancient and modern.

" Les Sacques furent à la fois Pasteurs et conquerants; on
leur attribue l'invention du bouclier; cette arme défensive
portait le nom de Sacos chez les Grecs, qui en attribuaient
l'invention aux Sacques (Izit. ch. xii. v. 894); le peuple
etoit si belliqueux que les femmes mêmes accompagnoient
leurs maris á la guerre et combatoient à cheval. Le mot
Sakos scutum bouclier se tourna chez les Grecs dans celui
de Sage d'voi vint le mot Sagma par lequel ils expriment
la Sac fait pour enveloper le bouclier. Je trouve que les
Sacques, Sacæ, furent aussi appeles Sagæ et de l'habille-
ment très court qu'ils portoient à la guerre vint le nom
d'où vint de Sagos, Sagum, que l'on donna aux habits
militaires de diverses nations (Plut. vid. Cicero Philipp. 8).
C'est la Saye ou le Sayon des Gaulois et des autres peuples
Celtes chez qui le mot Sach exprime une sorte de robe à
l'usage des femmes. Les termes Sagitta, flêche, Sagatti, fer,
Sagittarius, archer, viennent de la même source, et ce fut
par ceci que les Scolotes ou les descendans des Sacques
étoient repules pour leur adresse a tirer l'arc et qu'on leur
donna le nom de Scythes, on prétend même que Scythes né
comme on l'a vu chez les Sacques fut le premier qui trouva
l'usage de l'arc et des flêches. Plin. lib. vii. c. 156: Scythes
qui primum arcus Sagittarum que usam invenesse dicitur.

"Si les Sacques comme guerriers paroissent avoir inventé des armes et des habits propres à la guerre comme pasteurs ils semblent avoir inventé la panetière ou le sac dans lequel les bergers portaient leurs provisions car on l'appeloit Lagis Pera, et comme la musique est un art dont l'invention paroit due au loisir des bergers on voit chez les Grecs un instrument de musique auquel ils donnaient le nom de Sakadion.

"C'est ainsi que les Saxons distinguèrent par les noms de l'est ou de l'ouest, les pays qu'il avoient conquis des Bretons. Cette coutume etait celle des Sacques qu'on appellait Scythes orientaux pour les distinguer de ceux qui demeroient vers l'occident et des hyperboreans qui habitaient le septentrion.

"Les Sacques de qui descendaient les Agathyrses et les Massagetæs, p. i. 93, Ancarville.

"Les Alains qui accompanaient Attila etoient les Sacques, les Huns aussi avoient une commun origine avec eux.

"Les Sacques portoient des cuissarts.

"Les Saxons et les Angleos en faisoient usage et les appellaient Sahs; ce nom indique l'épée inventée par les Sacques.

"Les Sacques passaient pour un peuple très sage et très modéré; ils n'imposèrent a l'Asie conquise par eux qu'un large tribut c'étoit plutôt une redevance propre à marquer leur domaine qu'une imposition dont ils chargeoient des peuples soumis par la force de leurs armes, p. 96. C'est le premier état governé pendant de longs siècles par cette espèce de constitution dans laquel le on peut reconnaitre l'origine du droit feudal apporté en Europe par les descendans des Sacques.

"Les Cimmeriens etaient de la même origine que

les Scythes issus de la branche d'Agathyese. Ces fêtes des femmes Bretonnes et des femmes indiennes ressembloient encore a celles que les Scythes de la Thrace célébraoient en l'honneur de Cotys et de Bendis; les Syriens changerent le nom du Tho en celui de Thor qui chez eux signifie un bœuf. Boch. Phaleg. lib. i. c. 5. p. 271. Les Getes qui comme les Masagetes furent une branche des Agathyrses etoient suivant Procope les mêmes que les Goths (Proco. Goth., lib. i. c. 24, p. 372), getices gentes assent Gothes esse." Borough English, a purely nomad custom, taken from the Scythes. See Herod, lib. iv. s. 10, p. 228.

This is quite sufficient evidence to show that the Scythians were a very remarkable people; and from the fact that even those who abuse them admit that they were righteous, just, law-abiding, and honourable, it is simply impossible to believe the calumnies which are rife amongst the Greeks. It is related of the Scythians, just as it was stated of the early Britons, who were of precisely the same habits and manners, that they practised polyandry. However, Herodotus acquits them generally of this conduct, but endeavours to fasten it upon the Mæso-Goths, who, as we have seen, were only a branch of the same people. Then, as if this charge would not lie, it was asserted that promiscuous intercourse took place between them, married or single, without shame. Against this, it is proved that each man had one wife, and that the punishment of adultery amongst them was death, without any chance of remission. The charge becomes absurd. No doubt, in later times, according to the evidence of Menander, they practised polygamy, but this may have been a remnant of the patriarchal age. Equally inconsistent with the charge of brutal and savage conduct is the admission made by many writers that they were kind and hospitable. So of all the other charges it may be said that they were utterly inconsistent with well-known facts.

This may fairly be said of them, that their lives were not like those of their neighbours, and that they disliked being intruded upon. To their reticence may possibly be ascribed the malicious things that were said of them; and it may safely be asserted that during the whole period of Grecian history, nearly 1000 B.C., they were known as a God-fearing people, just and honourable, living pure and simple lives; indeed, we find their lives are fairly described by Moses in speaking of the patriarchs; and when we consider that the period of which we have some proof covers half the time to the date of Abraham himself, we may well believe that, whatever their race may have been, they were a people who followed Sethite principles.

But their history extends even farther back, for the very few writers besides Moses who treat of this epoch of history seem to deal with them as the greatest people of antiquity. Although we cannot rely upon their chronology, we may glean these facts: that somewhere about 1480 B.C. they were a great people, holding sway not only in Asia but in Africa, and that about this time they lost power and position in both countries.

Trojus relates that the Scythians conquered Assyria and Egypt, and held both for 1500 years before the time when Ninus conquered Assyria; and Sesostris, in 1481 B.C., drove them out of Asia. There is, of course, a confusion of dates here.

That such a person as Sesostris did reign in Egypt, and drove out the Shepherd kings, is very probable, but there is at present a dearth of information upon the subject, and certainly no chronology to be relied upon; and, unfortunately, the works of Moses do not contain any information upon the subject, except a hint here and there which may support a possible hypothesis.

Diodorus Siculus relates that the Scythian Nomads were at first a small nation on the Araxes, whence they spread to the Caucasus and the Palus Meotis; that they invaded Egypt 3600 B.C., and again in 640 B.C.

Eusebius traces the Scythians up to Serug, and curiously the Gothic annals give his date as that of their departure from the East and entrance into Scandinavia.

Lucian, in tracing the descent of the Helenes, says that Helen was the son of Deucalion the Scythian, in whose time was the great flood (De Dia. Syra., p. 882, ed. Benedic., 1619).

Again, Deucalion is said to be the son of Prometheus (Apollon., iii. p. 1086), and Prometheus to be king of the Scythæ (Schol. Apollon. Argonaut., ii. p. 1252).

Now, as unquestionably Prometheus and Deucalion are but other names for Adam, the first man, and Noah, the man who repeopled the earth, we find that tradition assigns a Scythian character to each. Surely this must show that the term Scythian was originally applied to the patriarchs, who it is known led a nomad life. Homer indicates as much when he relates that they were blest with length of days; and their moral character for justice proves them to have been a righteous race. And especially do we learn that the progenitors of the Greeks are traditionally Scythæ. Besides Prometheus and Deucalion, Eusebius assigns to the Ionians a Scythian origin (p. 7. See also Chron. Pascale, p. 49).

Epiphanius adv. Horef., lib. i. p. 1, states that all the people south of the Hellespont were Scythians.

Thessaly was anciently part of Thrace, which, as we have seen, was clearly Scythian; and Strabo asserts that the Thracians colonised Attica.

Pausonius (lib. x. c. 5) shows that the oracle at Delphi was founded by the Scythæ Hyperborii, and ancient Greek poets call it Pelasgic; and there is a tradition that the Scythians first received the sacred things in wheaten straw from the Hyperboreans, and then in their turn delivered them to other nations.

Strabo asserts that all the Greeks were formerly called Pelasgi, even the Helenes (lib. v. p. 337, and lib. vii. p. 504); and Herodotus states the same thing, including the Argives, the Arcadians, the Ionians, and the Athenians.

Apolonius, Rhodius, Virgil, Statius, and other Latin poets, use the word Pelasgi as equivalent to Greek.

Dionysius reckons amongst the Scythians the whole nation of the kingdom of Pontus, the Bythinians, the Macyandini, the Rhœti, Paphlagonians, Chalybes, Tiburini, Mossonese, Peeleares, Macrones, Bectives, Byzeres, Chalcedonians. The Ligures and Pamphilians were branches of the Helenes.

The Spartans, the noblest people of Greece, were descended from the Thracians. They were called Helenes, and came from Pthiotis through Ossa and Olympus to Pindus, thence to Dryope, and thence to the Peloponnesus.

The gods of the Greek mythology are illustrious princes of the first Scythian empire. Herodotus states that the Greeks derived their religion from the Pelasgi.

Plato bears testimony to the fact that the Scythæ had letters. Eustatius notes that Linus, Sipheus, Musæus, Thanyris, Ernulphas are all Thracians.

In 647 B.C. the Scythians passed the Caspian, fell on the Medes, routed Cyaxares their king, crossed Mesopotamia, and as they passed it laid it waste, and they met with no resistance in Judæ. These were a sheepskin-clad people called Sagartii or Togarmah, a race of Scythians from the country lying between the Black and the Caspian Seas.

A Scythian custom was to carry an idol before them, and that idol was an imitation of the ox, which was to them an emblem of the generator of animal life. Bromley, in his "History of the Fine Arts," remarks upon this Phœnician custom, that the idea of having an idol to go before them was completely Scythian, for so the Scythians' acted in all their progress through Asia, with the difference that the idol was a living animal. The Israelites, who were neighbours to the Phœnicians, were greatly attached to this worship, and probably learned it from them, as also may have done the Egyptians; and this custom can be traced home to us in the name of John Bull. The British retain a distinct relic of the custom, and it is well known that the Cimbri carried an ox or bull of bronze before them in all their expeditions, again proving the pedigree to be as it is here surmised.

An interesting question arises as to how Greece was peopled. Amidst the chaos of Grecian history, no fact stands out more clearly than that there are two great waves, the Helenes and the Pelasgi, and both are of Scythian origin, the one coming down southward from Thrace, the other from the coast of the Mediterranean, from Egypt and from Syria. If the Scythians started on their course from the river Araxes, we should expect to find the one branch coming down through the Euphrates to the Erythrean Sea, and the other crossing the Euxine on going round it into Thrace. History only records two occupations of Egypt by the Shemetic race, that under the Shepherd kings, and that of the Israelites; and the fact that in Egypt inscriptions are found of a Shemetic character and in the Aramean dialect proves that there were two such occupations; for the Israelites of course would use the Hebrew dialect, and those who used the Aramean must have been Shemetic people of the race of Aram, who were settled in Armenia, Assyria, and Mesopotamia, or who were in contact with them; possibly those who were settled in the land of the Zummims.

Josephus admits that the four sons of Shem all settled in Asia, and became the heads of nations; that Elam was father of the Persian people, Assur the Blessed of the Asyrians, Lud of the Lydians, and Aram through Hul of the Armenians, through Gether of the Bactrians, through Uz of the Syrians (about Traconitis and Damascus, including, of course, the land of Ham), through Mesa of the Messanians. That is, we have the direct authority of Josephus for stating that the Scythians, who were lords of Assyria before Ninus conquered it, were Shemetic sons of Assur the Blessed; that the Bactrians, Sacæ, Mesogetæ, and other Scythæ, were all Shemetic, although he denies that their congeners in blood are of this race. It is, therefore, of little consequence to us from which of the sons of Shem the Shepherd kings descended, although it is most probable that either Aram or Assur was their progenitor. It is enough to show that the Shepherd kings were of Shemetic race.

We see that the Scythæ could, when they pleased, become a maritime people, and that they settled at the mouths and heads of great rivers, evidently determined to turn them to account; and no doubt from the Erythrean Sea they sailed round Arabia and invaded Egypt, and by the aid of the canal of Amram sailed into the Mediterranean.

Here happily they left a work which stands for all time as a memorial of their piety, their knowledge, and their grandeur and power as a lordly people—lordly though yet nomad in their habits; for a shepherd in their eyes was a king, and hence the title of Shepherd kings. This monument is the great pyramid of Gheza, itself a Hebrew name, and the word pyramid is probably Phœnician for corn measure. Pyra = corn, and mid = measure.

We here get a fixed date for the occupation of the Shepherd kings, and from this point all history depends; nay, it is not too much to say that all future history must be dictated by this proud monument of human grandeur, and all philosophy and science bow down to it.

Although it is probably otherwise, it is not necessary to assume that the great architect who designed it was an inspired man. Regarded as a scientific work, it is sufficient to indicate that it was the work of man's hands directed by human intellect, and that it is the epitome of man's knowledge, the embodiment of the chiefest of his latent powers of mind. It is a wonderful work. No building in the world can compete with it as to size or massiveness of construction. It appears to be the work of giants, yet it can readily be the work of ordinary men; and this magnificent structure is designed to show to man in all ages a little lesson, in itself a mere trifle—a just measure—a system of measurement adjusted according to the mensuration of the earth. It may have other lessons to teach, but this is its primary object. And for what purpose could this expense of time and money be sacrificed for such an end? Just this and no more: to meet the wicked act of the Canaanites, who, as Josephus records—and his testimony on this point is true—had set up false weights and measures in order to cheat the poor and to beguile mankind. The great pyramid was built to give an exposition to mankind, in a durable monument which should last till the end of time, of what truth was as opposed to falsehood. It was to establish for ever the grand difference of right and wrong.

Frederick von Schlegel, himself of Jewish origin, like his wife, the daughter of the celebrated Jewish philosopher, Mendelsohn, and who, like many of his countrymen, have shed lustre upon the German name to the literary loss of his own race (perhaps it is not too much to say that Germany owes her modern character for learning as well as her proficiency in the arts entirely to the Jewish nation), has set forth this view in language which is almost prophetic in its nature, so true is it, and so exactly fitted to meet the discoveries of this age of the true meaning of the great pyramid, a thing in this day, let it be remembered, utterly misunderstood.

In his second lecture on the philosophy of history, upon the disputes in primitive history and on the divisions of the human race he naturally takes a Jewish view of the question, and asserts that in the beginning mention is made but of one separation of mankind into two races or hostile classes—the Canaanite and the Sethite; and he shows that the sagas of other nations, notably the Greek and the Indian, corroborate it in a very remarkable degree. He writes: "Under these two different forms, therefore, doth tradition reveal to us the primitive world, or in other words, these are the two grand conditions of humanity which fill the records of primitive history. On the one hand we see a race lovers of peace, revering God, blessed with long life, which they spend in patriarchal simplicity and innocence, and still no strangers to deeper science, especially to all that relates to sacred tradition and inward contemplation, and transmitting these sciences to posterity in the old or symbolical writing—not in fragile volumes, but on durable monuments of stone. On the other hand, we behold a giant race of pretended demigods, proud, wicked, and violent, or, as they are called in the later sagas, the heaven-storming Titans.

" This opposition and this discord, this hostile struggle between the two great divisions of the human race, forms the whole tenure of primitive history. When the moral harmony of man had once been deranged and two opposite wills had sprung up within him, a divine will or a will seeking God, and a natural will or a will bent on sensible objects, passionate and ambitious, it is easy to conceive how mankind, from their very origin, must have diverged into two opposite paths.

" The struggle which divided the primitive world into two great parties arose far more from the opposition of feelings and of principles than from difference of extraction.

" Great as is the interval which separates those ages and that world from our own, we can easily comprehend how this first mighty contest of nations which history makes mention of was, in fact, a struggle between two religious parties, two hostile sects, though, indeed, under far other forms and in different relations from anything we witness in the present state of the world ; it was, in one word, a contest between religion and impiety, conducted, however, upon the mighty scale of the primitive world, and with all those gigantic powers which, according to ancient tradition, the first men possessed.

" According to sacred tradition, pre-eminence was conferred on the race of Seth. With the high powers which the father of mankind had preserved after his fall, or had a second time received, we may well suppose that after the crime and flight of Cain he would endeavour to retrieve his errors by the establishment of the better race of Seth, and by a consequent renovation of humanity. This is not a mere arbitrary supposition, for it is expressly said in Holy Writ that the first man ordained to be the father of the whole earth (as he is there called) became, on his reconciliation with his Maker, the wisest of all men, and, according to tradition, the greatest of prophets, who, in his far-seeing ken, foresaw the doctrines of all mankind in all successive ages down to the end of the world. All this must be taken in a strict historical sense, for the moral interpretation we abandon to others. The pre-eminence of the Sethites, chosen by God and entirely devoted to His service, must be received as an undoubted historical fact, to which we find many pointed allusions, even in the traditions of the other Asiatic nations. Nay, the hostility between the Sethites and Canaanites, and the mutual relations of those two races, form the chief clue to the history of the primitive world, and even of many particular nations of antiquity."

It is curious how completely these extracts illustrate the meaning of the builders of the pyramids and actually describe it. No other building in the world can answer to the description in so perfect a manner. It is unnecessary to add one word to this, but the remark may be conjectured that since the great characteristic of the Shepherd kings was their Sethite knowledge, may they not have been so termed Scythians ? in other words are not Scythite and Sethite similar in etymology as they are in meaning ? If this be so, and no etymology has ever been offered to contradict the idea, a grand clue to the discovery of the peoples of the Shemetic race is in our hands. We have only to find out what nations possessed Sethite knowledge, or, in other words, who are Scythians, to prove the relationship.

Q

Who shall say how the great pyramid was built, or who was the actual builder? Was it Assur the Blessed, or Sala, whose name seems to be found in the name of the first Shepherd king, and who may have lived long enough for the purpose? for we cannot trust implicitly to the chronology of the Bible, since it has clearly been corrupted, and probably by the enemies of Christianity. It is supposed, and not without reason, that Melchisedek was the builder, and it is related that Abraham paid tithes to him. One cannot conceive that a building so designed could be built by fraud or violence, or that slaves could be made to work upon it against their will; hence probably tithes would be collected to pay for the cost of it.

This date of 2170 B.C. is an important one for many purposes, and not the least is it important as showing that there was an occupation of Egypt by a Shemetic race prior to the sojourn of the Israelites. Manetho relates circumstantially that Israel was allowed to dwell upon a spot that had previously been occupied by the Shepherd kings, proving that they had then ceased to remain in the land. Probably their departure had been recent, for otherwise the land would have been reoccupied, and they probably would have been there when Abraham went down into Egypt to avoid the famine in Canaan. He was then dwelling in Phœnicia, and the Phœnicians were identified, at any rate by the Egyptians, as of the same race as the Shepherd kings. We have seen that there is the highest probability for believing that they were of the race of Aram.

This identity is curiously strengthened by the name given to Joseph by Pharaoh: he was called Zaphnath Phœnix. Surely this could only be because the country had been ruled by Phœnicia. Another curious coincidence, showing the double connection of the Phœnicians, Greeks, and the Shepherd kings, is to be found in the tradition that Tanaus or Danaus, king of the Scythians, resident in Egypt, left at the same time as the Israelites, and returned to or settled in Greece, becoming the father of the Danii. If there were such a king and such a people, the probability is that they left at the time of the overthrow of this power; but this is immaterial. The strength of the evidence consists in the fact that a tradition existed, and was, in fact, so clear as to be historical ; for we find in the Book of Maccabees that about 180 B.C. the king of the Lacedemonians wrote to the Jewish high priest claiming relationship with the Jews, which was acknowledged by the latter on many occasions (Maccabees, xii. 5–23).

We learn, too, from the Scriptures that Dan remained in ships, having united with the Phœnicians in trading to Greece and other places ; and we learn from the letter of King Hiram of Tyre to King Solomon that the Danites intermarried with the Phœnicians, a fact which shows them to have been closely connected. It has been objected to the Phœnician history that it is fabulous, chiefly because it is not a history of Phœnicia only, but a history of all mankind since the Deluge. If the hypothesis that the Phœnicians are a Shemetic race be correct, this is no objection, but the reverse; for if it is so, this is a confirmation of the fact. Eusebius states (Præp. Evan., lib. i. c. ix. p. 30) that Sanchoniatho of Berythes relates in his history the Jewish affairs with great veracity. He dedicated his work to King Abibulus, and his history was allowed by him, and by those appointed by him to examine it, to be true. He relates that Taut (or Tanaus), son of Miser, son of Hamyre, invented the first letters for writing, and sat on the throne of Egypt, and he and his

posterity ruled in Egypt and in Thebes for eighteen generations, thus identifying themselves with the Shepherd
kings.    Now, although the Phœnicians traded and settled
in towns, yet they had one strong characteristic of the
Scythian race; though they settled in Phœnicia they were
not of it.    They made no conquests of the soil, but out of
the country sent a vast number of colonists who settled in
all parts of the world, in Egypt, Asia, Cyprus, the isles
of the Mediterranean, Sicily, Sardinia, the African coast,
Spain, Britain, and several other countries.    This fact is
attested by Bochart and by a host of writers.

A great proof of Shemetic origin, though by no means
a positive one, is to be found in the language.    The
Phœnician is undoubtedly a dialect of the Hebrew, which
is clearly Scythian.

Salmasius, Junius, Meric, Causauban, and Ihre pronounce the Gothic and ´Greek languages to be dialects of
the same tongue, and both are dialects of the Phœnician.

The Waldenses of the Alps speak a perfect Irish Gaelic.
Sir William Betham, however, denies this, and asserts
that the MSS. which gave rise to this story were foreign
importations.

# CHAPTER XXI.

## THE TUATHA DE DANNANS.

THERE is one wave of population common to both England, Ireland, and Scotland in a minor degree (for the southern parts of Britain were chiefly affected by it) which deserves a separate notice.

Of all the tribes or clans which peopled the British Isles, the Tuatha de Dannans are the most remarkable, for unquestionably, from whatever source they sprang, this people possessed in the highest degree that knowledge of the arts and sciences which was the traditional inheritance of the patriarchs. This possession proves that they had a Shemetic origin.

It must not be supposed that the possession of a literature superior to that of the British of a later date, and of arts and sciences which we cannot directly prove that we possessed, is any proof that the Irish are of a different race from ourselves. The Roman occupation and the subsequent Irish invasions and other inroads upon English territory have deprived her of all records until a few were invented for her; but England has an equal claim to the treasures of Irish art and literature. They must have been hers also, since she possessed the same races of people, and she has only lost the memory of them. In Irish history, then, we must look for our origin, and in Irish literature for proof of it; but from our persistent ignorance of the Keltic tongue we are unable to decipher it, and Irish scholars are apparently too jealous of their treasures to impart a knowledge of them to us. What do we know of the Tuatha de Dannans except their other name, the Damnonians, but from Irish records ? We have lost our own altogether; we must go to the Irish for their account, and it is worth reading, for this race was certainly the most singular and the most intelligent of all the tribes who peopled these islands. From whence did they come? By way of one of the rivers of Dan probably, as the Dannan indicates, and from the north, as the prefix of Tuatha tells us. Tuatha is also the word for clan in Ireland, but this can hardly be the meaning in which it is here employed, for there are many clans in Ireland, and none of them but that of the Dannans retain the use of it in their name. And what is the meaning of the de? De is God in Irish, and signifies royalty also. Can these same Dannans be the Royal Scythians of Asia? Their similarity to the Spartan's other name, Lacedemonians, is striking, and this would indicate a Thracian or Parthian origin or connection. The Lacedemonians, we know from Maccabees, were of the stock of Abraham, and therefore they would be De Dannans, Royal Scythians.

And if we find that every tribe that peopled England found, either previously or subsequently, an asylum in the Emerald Isle, we shall not be surprised to find that the connection has been maintained, and is, in fact, the most natural alliance in the world. Within the memory of English history it has always been the case.

The following extract from the valuable work of Canon Ulick J. Bourke, " The Aryan Origin of the Gaelic Nations," shows that he is inclined to take this view of the question. After writing of the immigration of the

Firbolgs, a shepherd race, who were described by a Galway man (one Duald Mac Firbis, writing 200 years ago) as dark-haired, talkative, guileful, strolling, unsteady, disturbers of every council and assembly (surely this race is not yet extinct), he thus describes the so-called sixth migration of the Irish race :—

"The next immigration we hear of in the annals is that of the Tuatha de Dannans, a large, fair-complexioned, and very remarkable race, warlike, energetic, progressive, skilled in metal-work, musical, poetical, acquainted with the healing art, skilled in Druidism, and believed to be adepts in necromancy and magic (no doubt the result of the popular idea respecting their superior knowledge), especially in smelting and in the fabrication of tools, weapons, and ornaments. From these two races sprang the fairy mythology of Ireland.

"The Dannan spoke the same language as his predecessors the Firbolgs. They met and fought for the sovereignty; the men of metal conquered and drove a great part of the others into the islands on the coast, where it is said the Firbolg, or Belgic race so called, took their last stand. Eventually, however, under the influence of a power hostile to them, both these people coalesced, and have to a great extent done so to the present day. They are the true old Irish peasant and small farming class.

"Then, on the other hand, their physiognomy, their fair or reddish hair, their size, conjoined with other circumstances, incline one to believe that they came down from Scandinavian regions after they had passed up as far as they thought advisable into north-western Europe. If the word Dane was known at the time of their arrival here, it would account for the designation of many of our Irish monuments as applied by Molineux and others. Undoubtedly the Dannan tribe presented Scandinavian features, but did not bring anything but Grecian art.

"I believe that these Tuatha de Dannans, no matter from whence they came, were, in addition to their other acquirements, great masons, although not acquainted with the value of cementing materials.

"I think they were the builders of the great stone cahirs, duns, cashels, and caves in Ireland, while their predecessors constructed the earthen works, the walls, circles, and forts that diversify the fields of Erin. They certainly made the more lasting sepulchral monuments that exist in Ireland; such, for example, as New Grange, Louth, Howth, and Sheve na Cailleagh, and other great cemeteries within the interior, and around these tombs were carved on unhewn stones certain archaic markings, spires, volutes, convolutes, lozenge-shaped devices, straight, zigzag, and curved lines and incised indentations, and a variety of other insignia, which, although not expressing language, are symbolical, and had an occult meaning known only to the initiated."

The whole of these passages are given because they aptly describe as well the Tuatha de Dannans as the ancient inhabitants of Scandinavia. The archaic markings so aptly described are only runic signs which are peculiar to the Danish race; and the presence of the Danes in England and Scotland in later times can be traced by these same markings. In the county of Kent, which was almost purely Danish, they are most frequent.

The date of the arrival of the Tuatha de Dannans or Damnonii is said to be the year A.M. 2541, *i.e.* 1219 B.C.; much more likely it was 600 years or more later.

The Danes, as we have seen, are also Daci, or, as it is suggested, Thraci; and Dr. Latham has noted what he calls the mysterious fact that the Dani or Daci are to be found side by side with the Getæ on the Danube, and also in Scandinavia. Possibly these are the Royal Dani whom we find in Ireland preserving their names distinct amongst the Getæ or Scythians, because they were of the Royal race.

But perhaps it is in music that the Irish are first after the Jews among all the people upon the earth; not now, possibly, but in days gone by, although the names of Sullivan and Balfe in these days stand prominently forward.

If Sethite knowledge distinguishes pre-eminently the children of Shem, and separates them as completely from the sons of Japhet as their physical appearance separates them from the race of Ham, the practice of music in early times was itself a sign of a higher race and of a nobler people; and this alone is sufficient to indicate a Shemetic origin, for true music is unattainable by those of other races. Music means melody, and melody is hateful to the souls of those who are incapable of true refinement, just as in these days the Germans are proving their Sarmatian origin by endeavours to cultivate music without melody. The music of the future, as it is called, is not music at all—for this very reason, it has no melody in it; it is all sound and fury, a braying of brazen instruments—music of the Hametic sort.

In music the early Irish were pre-eminent, not only in the science displayed in musical compositions, but in the construction of musical instruments.

The books of Leccan and Ballymote assert that the Tuatha de Dannans brought the harp into Ireland 719 B.C. Indeed, no fact of Irish history seems better authenticated than that to this singular tribe they are indebted for their most precious gift and possession; nor have other nations denied their claims to such distinction.

Galileo, writing in the sixteenth century, asserts that the harp was brought from Ireland into Italy, as Dante testifies, where they are excellently made and have been in great repute for many ages.

It was said to have been introduced into Wales by Griffith, king of North Wales, who was born in Ireland about 1098 A.D. (Caradock, Chron. of Wales). Wharton says the Welsh received instruction from Ireland as late as the eleventh century.

It is in the construction of the Irish harp that the greatest stress is to be laid. It is constructed on true harmonic principles (see Beauford and Walker's "Irish Bards").

The Egyptian harp, according to Bruce, Denon, and Roscellini, was not nearly so scientifically constructed. The Irish harp has been tested by the application of the strictest mathematical principles, and it was not known to the Greeks, Romans, or Egyptians. They used the cythera, a harp of inferior curve, with some equal strings, and it was not till long afterwards that the Egyptians improved in the construction of their harp.

M. Guigene observes that several learned men are of opinion that Ireland is not indebted to the Egyptians for their harp, but to the North, and that they were indebted to the Saxons, and the Saxons were indebted to the Sacæ.

Fortunatus (lib. vii. carm. 8) mentions the harp as an instrument of the Goths.

Other writers think that it was brought to Ireland with the alphabet.

The only other people who are known to have possessed the harp at this early period, and who too are the only other musical people in the world besides the Kelts and Scythians, are the Jews and their Shemetic relations.

# CHAPTER XXII.

ALTHOUGH it by no means follows that the question of race can be absolutely determined by a reference to either its laws, literature, or language—or the present occupiers of German territory would be entitled to style themselves Gothic, since they in a measure enjoy a participation with the Goths in all these matters—yet, as a link in the chain of evidence, it is of the first importance. *Prima facie*, it may be taken that a nation uses its own laws and language rather than those of another; and it requires stronger proof to support the latter proposition than the former, since the instances of nations adopting the systems of their neighbours, or those in contact with them, are extremely rare, and it has only happened under very peculiar circumstances, such as the living in such close proximity to each other that intimate relations were a necessity, or the fact that one nation was subjected to the other by force of arms.

The insulated position of the British Isles prevents the idea of an intimate connection with any neighbouring state; and the traditions of the British themselves ignore the notion of any conquest, for they expressly state that the British took possession of the country peaceably, and in

order to avoid war with other peoples in distant lands,
leaving an inference to be drawn that the laws, language,
and literature of the British were their own special property and inheritance.

The argument, therefore, to be drawn from the laws of
the British becomes of great importance ; and if the proposition just laid down be correct, it would be conclusive;
and the assumption has always been that the common
law of England was of Saxon or German origin ; and shal-
low writers, who have not taken the trouble to weigh the
facts, have invariably asserted, and through repetition the
idea has become fixed and established in the English mind,
that the early institutions of Germany are precisely similar to those of England.   Professor E. A. Freeman discovered some remains of laws and institutions similar to our
own about the foot of the Alps, and he immediately jumped
to the conclusion that the English people hailed from that
spot, forgetting the fact that the contrary of the proposition was just as likely to be true, since although the Kelts
—and these were Keltic institutions which he confounded
with English—travelled over Europe from the south, immense bodies of these people came down southwards from
the north, and they may have been the planters of these
very institutions.   So, doubtless, may be found throughout
Germany traces of Keltic or Gothic laws, since at one
time the whole country was Keltic or Gothic ; but this is
a very different theory from supposing, as is popular, that
there is any similarity between modern German customs
and laws and those of the British.   We know from the
high testimony of Dr. R. G. Latham that there is no town
or village in Germany the inhabitants of which have a
language which has a common origin with the English,
and so it may be as distinctly asserted of their laws.

German institutions are essentially different from English, and they possess little in common. Our greatest legal historians, from Coke, Seldon, and Hales to our own day, assigned a Saxon origin to the English common law, simply, as it would seem, for want of a better. George Spence, in his valuable work on the "Origin of the Courts of Equity," first doubted the accuracy of this theory, and it was reserved to the author to show that the English common law was Keltic in its origin.

This idea was at first scouted as ridiculous. Legal journals, the "Law Journal" especially, vied with each other in their anxiety not to deprive the author of the credit of the discovery, but to discredit the idea. Yet unprejudiced men from the first admitted the truth and the importance of the idea, and though no lawyer has perhaps committed himself to a belief in it in print, many are ready in private to admit it, and perhaps no one will now venture to dispute it; for it is one of those discoveries which has only to be mentioned for every one easily to prove it for himself and in his own way; for it is not like the discovery of Columbus—the theory may be proved by an infinite variety of approaches. Dr. Charles Mackay has boldly adopted the idea, and he has proved it in his own way by showing the etymology of many law terms to be Keltic. The Very Rev. Canon Ulick J. Bourke, 17th December 1878, thus wrote to the author: "No doubt at all that half or two-thirds of the old Kelts remained in the country when it was said to be (by modern English historians) Saxon. They had, therefore, the old laws of which you wrote, as sure as you are in existence. St. Bede and the monks of the times did not know the state of the whole country; they went on mere rumours and first appearances, like most young writers."

It would be impossible in the space allotted to this book
to do more than point out a few leading instances in which
the Keltic laws of the British agree with those of the
Shemetic race, and it is assumed that the laws of the
latter were similar to the laws of the Israelites.

Writers upon the so-called Saxon laws have frequently
observed that these boasted codes are in reality little more
than a string of mulcts or fines for various offences and
injuries, and that the principle of these laws is very
similar in all ages.   This is true, and the grand principle
of all these laws is summed up in the Mosaic dictum—an
eye for an eye, and a tooth for a tooth.   The principle of
these mulcts is the law of compensation, which is a Mosaic
dispensation, as it is also the foundation of our law of
damages.   It may be said that such a principle is the
basis of every law of every nation that gives a remedy for
a wrong; but what nation besides the Jewish and our
own holds that for every wrong there is a remedy ?   There
is a spirit of true justice about such a law that stamps it
as being of Divine origin.

Then, again, mercy is a Divine attribute; and mercy is
the principle upon which our law is supposed to be carried out and dispensed—the mercy of the sovereign.   The
Shemetic race allowed, by the express permission of the
Almighty, cities to be set apart where certain criminals
might take refuge and escape the consequences of their
acts.   These cities of refuge became known as sanctuaries;
and the law of sanctuaries, which is founded on the law
of mercy, is well known to our law, and it was a part of
it during the tenure of the Druids.

The law of Borough English, as it is called, is simply a
remnant of the patriarchal system.   The nomad races
were compelled, in the first settlements of mankind, to

send out the elder sons to find new habitations, whilst the younger adhered to the home plots. This law is the oldest law of tenure that we possess, dating back ages before the Romans came to this country, and to the time when it was only partially inhabited. No more striking proof can be obtained of the immense antiquity of our legal system.

The extraordinary similarity that exists between many of our early laws and those of the Israelites might raise an inference that they were copied from them after the institution of Christianity, but positive evidence exists of their pre-existence; and therefore it follows that the people of this country must either have come into contact with the Shemetic race at a very early date, or have been conquered by it; or, as is very much more reasonable, and probably follows, the British people were of Shemetic origin.

# CHAPTER XXIII.

### · THE CLAIMS OF PRIORITY OF THE THREE KINGDOMS.

IT is with shame that an Englishman approaches the subject of Irish antiquities. As a nation we are profoundly ignorant of Irish history, and apparently care little to examine that treasury of learning, although there is so much within it which would enable us to unravel the history of our own country. The insensate hate of Dr. Johnson for everything Scotch seems in these days to possess every Englishman who has to treat of Irish affairs, whether ancient or modern. What is the meaning of this? Englishmen as a rule are generous enough to admit the superiority of others when they discover it. Surely it is not a spirit of envy, a knowledge that the Irish have records of infinite value compared to our own, that deters our writers from their examination. What then can it be? Is it the difference of religion? Surely not. What then can be the meaning of it? Why is everything Irish persistently kept out of sight, just as Dr. Johnson persistently ignored everything Scotch? (Though in ignorance that they were the same tongues, he had some respect for the Irish.) Why is it that we have no English-Irish histories, no accounts of our own of this singular people? We have seen that Irishmen and Englishmen are of the same race; that every settlement in England has its parallel settlement in Ireland, and we learn that this was the case from the first dawn of intelligence that breaks over us.

Thus we find the dolicocephalic or Shemetic race, who first peopled England, have their parallel in the Formorians, who distinctly claim to be of Shemetic origin. Villanouava asserts that they were Phœnician merchants or pirates; but, as it has been attempted to be shown, the term Phœnician was frequently applied to Shemetic people who reside in other countries. Then we find that the Belgic settlements of England were paralleled by settlements of Firbolgs in Ireland. Then as there were Scoti or Scythi in Ireland, there were also Saxons or Scythi in England, and the same with the Picts or Jutes. Both countries possess them. The great race of Tuatha de Dannans, undoubtedly the first race in Ireland or in England for power and intelligence, are paralleled by settlements of Damnonii in the West of England and of Silures in Wales. That the Danes settled in both countries is an ascertained fact, and subsequently the Normans, as popular history records; and if we dive a little deeper into tribal history, we shall find that the subdivision of each great wave of humanity that rolled over both countries alike were also the same. Almost every great tribe of people to be found in England is also to be discovered in Ireland.

It is scarcely necessary to determine which country first peopled the other. The answer to that would probably be given if we knew whether the Cimmerii or the Phœnicians first arrived in the British Isles. If history is accurate in the date of the first passing by the Phœnicians of the Pillars of Hercules and of their settlements at Cadiz, of which there is very grave doubt, then unquestionably the Cimmerii had reached England long prior thereto, and to the English would be credited the honour of having first sent the Formorians to the Emerald Isle; but it by

R

no means follows that earlier settlers had not preceded them. There can be little doubt that both the Belgæ and the Tuatha de Dannans passed through England on their way to Ireland. Villanouava (p. 118) admits this as regards the latter people, and he gives a curious translation of their name. He says, " Sunt qui jejunio stomacko silentio meditantu."

The Danes probably invaded Ireland originally independently of England, sweeping round Scotland, and settling on her northern and western coasts, and the Normans undoubtedly first peopled England. On the whole, perhaps, the balance of authority would accord to England the palm of being the parent of the other, but it is a point of grave doubt; and this is abundantly clear, that Ireland returned the compliment, and if she received colonies from England, she repaid her in kind, for in Scotland both the Picts and the Scots owe their parentage to Ireland, and there they became inextricably confused with the English races which receded before the approach of the Roman legions. If Scotland received that name from Magna Scotia, her name of North Britain was given to her by England. In this book Scotland and Scottish affairs have hardly been touched upon, for this very reason: Scotland has no nationality of her own. She is not, as Dr. Johnson insinuates, beneath contempt, since she numbers amongst her tribes and her people the best blood of both England and Ireland. Dr. Johnson, who, like the Oxford school, persistently ignored the Keltic element in the English language, imagined that the Scotch (which he called the Erse) and the Irish were totally different languages. He writes of the Erse: " As I understand nothing, I cannot say more than I have been told; it is the rude speech of a barbarous people, who had few thoughts to express, and were content, as they conceived, grossly to be understood; and after what has been lately talked of Highland bards and Highland genius, many will startle when they are told that the Erse never was a written language; that there is not in the world an Erse MS. a hundred years old, and that the sounds of the Highlanders were never expressed by letters till some little books of piety were translated, and a metrical version of the Psalms was made by the Synod of Argyle."

It is true in one sense that there are no Scotch MSS. over a hundred years old, but this is due to the absurd vanity and impudent unveracity of a few Scotchmen, who, just as certain scholars in England invented a Saxon language, or rather one they called Anglo-Saxon, when the so-called Saxons spoke the same English as the Britons, so these Scotchmen endeavoured to foist upon the world a language they called Scotch, which they pretended was essentially different from the Irish Gaelic; but Dr. Latham (see his philological work) disposes of this nonsense by proving their identity, and Dr. Charles Mackay bravely and honestly admits that the "Scotch and Irish Gaelic are essentially the same language, with a few orthographical differences, and more especially the substitution of a dot for the letter *h* in the mode of expressing the aspirate." And Canon Ulick J. Bourke shows still more accurately the points of difference between them; but imagine the value of the learning of the Oxford school which still adheres to Dr. Johnson and implicitly follows him! They must know by this time that Scotch and Irish are the same, and they must know that the so-called Anglo-Saxon language, of which they have actually professorships (!!!), is as great a forgery as the so-called Scotch of modern times; and this also they

must know, or, if not, they can learn the fact by reading
Dr. Mackay's excellent work, " The Gaelic Etymology of
the English Nation," how many English words are derived
from the Gaelic. It is stated, I know not with what
truth, that Canon Ulick J. Bourke has an Irish-English
dictionary ready for the press. This also will produce
immense enlightenment. Surely, with all these accumulated stores of learning, there is some hope of Englishmen coming to respect and study the true sources of
their language.

It is curious to see the dilemma into which Scotchmen
have been thrown by blindly adhering to their literary
forgeries. They are in as ridiculous a plight as those
Englishmen who would derive everything English in
literature, law, and politics from the imaginary Anglo-
Saxon. They do not know their own language; every
philologist, at any rate, differs from all his brethren.
On the curious question of the meaning of St. Filian's
Cogerach, recently mooted by Dean Stanley, no less than
ten Scotch philologists rushed into print to confound the
Dean, and each one confounded the other. Donald Clark
of Roseneath alone of the whole number gave anything
like a satisfactory solution. His knowledge of the use of
the implement enabled him to obtain a correct etymology,
so a dispute arose respecting the meaning of the word Kil-
righ-Monadh. Eight or nine Gaelic scholars each contradicted the other. Professor Blackie, who happily holds a
sceptre over this unruly coterie, referred the dispute to Dr.
Reeves, Dean of Armagh, who endorsed the view taken by
Donald Clark. The following extracts from the writings
of Mr. Clark will give a tolerably accurate view of the
state of the philological difficulties of the modern Scots.

"There are a number of Gaelic philologists who make

no distinction between old Celtic and Gaelic, and, like a drowning man grasping at a straw, they grasp at any root for a Gaelic word, if it be only like Gaelic, whereas most roots of Gaelic words in old Celtic are no more like Gaelic than black is like white. For instance, old Celtic leath pinnt (half a pint), pronounced in Gaelic seipin, and in Scotch chopin. Here is a compound word in Celtic, and the same is pronounced in Gaelic in one word and the initial changed, and the same is transformed into Scotch and the initial changed again; and so it is with most Gaelic. It is quite different from ancient Celtic. The Gaelic lexicons are but of yesterday. The Rev. W. Shaw found the words so changed, and he inserted them in his lexicon as pronounced in his day—quite different from the Gaelic of Bishop Carswell's ' Confession of Faith,' having Guaidheilge = Gael and Gaoidheilghe = Gaelic.

" Very humble guides are the lexicons, with no uniform spelling; some words having two forms of spelling and some three, and a wrong construction put on many of the words even then.

" Gaelic is modern Celtic much deteriorated, and its roots can only be found in ancient Celtic.

" Celtic has many instances of two (and more) words from one root, and these in many instances unlike each other and unlike the root."

This is tolerably clear, that there can be no Scotch MSS. older than the date of the invention of the language, just as there are no Anglo-Saxon MSS. older than the age of Marianus Scotus (the compiler of the Saxon Chronicle and inventor of the language; see the author's "Introduction to the Study of Early English History "), and most unfortunately the early Irish MSS. of the Scotch have been destroyed. There is no hope, therefore, of

much enlightenment from that country upon English
philological or ethnological researches, and we must confine our attention to Ireland.

There is one point much insisted upon by Irishmen
which ought not to be wholly passed over. Welshmen have
combined with the Irish—especially has the Rev. E. Lydd—
to give the latter the honour of having peopled England,
because they found that the names of rivers, mountains,
headlands, tribes, and people all over England more closely
assimilated with the Irish Keltic than with the Welsh.
But this is surely begging the question, because Wales
cannot claim everything English to have been derived
from herself—surely it does not follow that it is owing
to Ireland. The exact contrary may be the case, or, as it
is most probable in many instances, both countries obtained the same names from the same source. Nothing
certain can be gathered from the argument.

The Norman conquest of Ireland was a necessary consequence of the dominance of the Normans in England.
Rome found that Canute the Great, the first sole monarch
of England, was the truest friend of religion and the most
obedient son of the Church; and above all, was as powerful as he was obedient. The petty wars between conflicting countries and tribes, which disgraced England
equally with Ireland, and which brought much misery in
their train, the Popes saw, would never end unless the
hands of the strong king were strengthened, and the
sanction of religion was added to his power. Hence to
Canute, as well as to his descendant William the Norman,
the Popes gave their aid; and just as they aided the
Normans to subjugate England, they aided them in
extending their conquest over Ireland, and for the same
reason. And the Norman Conquest was successful

in both countries for the same reason, that in each the Danes and Normans found numbers of settlers of their own race who but too thankfully joined in consolidating the power of the invader. Until English as well as Irish historians recognise this fact and act upon it, their so-called histories will be as fabulous and foolish, in spite of their affectation for learning, as the works of Freeman and Stubbs, of Creasy and of Green. Irish, in their hatred of the Saxon, should remember that their subjugation by England was not done by Saxon arms, but by the arms of the Normans who had conquered the Saxons.

Curious, too, is the fact that Henry II. assigned as one of the reasons why he should conquer Ireland that she gave assistance to France; the very reason why Cæsar proposed to conquer and invade this country. Adrian IV., the Pope who granted Ireland to Henry, was the only Englishman that ever sat in the chair of St. Peter— by name Nicolas Breakspear. Irishmen should not impute to him a motive of acting solely for the benefit of his native country, since he only followed the traditional policy of his predecessors, especially that pursued towards Canute, who, and not William the Conqueror, was the true author of the Norman Conquest of England.

# CHAPTER XXIV.

## CUI BONO?

IT is a common question when the subject of this volume is mooted, and one which many intelligent and well-intentioned people put—*Cui bono?* Why disturb the historic notions we imbibed in our infancy? Will any one be a penny the better or a whit the wiser for it, even though it should be the fact and comes to be admitted that the English common law is Gallic and the English people Gauls? Well, the answer depends upon circumstances. People of poor ambition and of small imagination will probably gain little by the knowledge. The doctor will visit his round of patients, the lawyer will wrangle and quibble over his law points, and the parson will preach to his flock in precisely the same manner as they now pursue their weary, plodding ways. But will no one be better and wiser for it? The author would put this question by way of answer to the former—the solution depends upon the state of the feelings, upon the instincts and aspirations, the wills and desires, of those who will be affected by it. Is it a slight thing that England, the dominant power of the British Isles, the race supposed by the Scotch, Welsh, and Irish to be distinct from them in blood and nationality (Englishmen are looked upon as of bastard French and German extraction), seeks to show that she too is of the same blood as her compatriots, and equally entitled with them to a share in the proud inheritance of the

Gael, the distinct nationality of the Kelt, the ancient lineage of the Cimry ? What if all these families of nations should find that the English, whom they at the same time despise and envy, are of as good blood as themselves; that the hated name of Saxon or Sassenach—that term of reproach which for 700 years has been hurled at them in hate and defiance—is after all the same as Scot, their own most cherished name—that which the great Irish nation bore, not seven centuries ago, but seven centuries before the birth of Christ, and which they imparted to Scotland, although they lost the use of it for themselves ?

It is no light thing to step between the Saxon and the Kelt, each of them even now, after hundreds of years of animosity, hating each other and panting to settle their differences by a final resort to the sword. Those who think this language exaggerated should travel in America or in our own Canada and ascertain the feelings of the excited Irishmen settled in those countries towards us. To lay waste England is their cherished dream. Aye, it is no mere figure of speech to write that they hate her with a devilish and undying hatred. And why? Has England done them any real harm? is she doing in Ireland any such deeds as are daily done by Russians and Germans to their conquered subjects? Let those who doubt it visit Poland, whether Russian, Prussian, or Austrian, or even the native provinces of Prussia. If England governed Ireland as Germany governs herself, there might be truth in the cry against us—there might be reason in the hatred nourished by excited Irishmen; but Irishmen in their own country, except that they cannot govern themselves by their own Parliament, are as well off, and perhaps better in some respects, than Englishmen in England; at any rate, they have as much liberty and as little interference by the police. In Germany a man cannot even marry unless the policeman should certify that he has sufficient income to support a probable family, and hence he lives with the woman he longs to make his wife in concubinage, and but too generally ends in deserting her. Though God is good, and when such devilish laws prevail, He aids the unhappy sinner, forced into sin against his inclination, to obey as he would desire the laws of his Creator. In the eyes of God, let us hope that these unions, though unlawful according to law, are not sinful in fact. If Protestant England forced on Catholic Ireland such a national sin as this, then truly Irishmen would do well to abhor her.

Then, again, if England took her sons from the plough or from behind the counter on pretence of educating them or of training them to protect the Fatherland, and so prevented them from fulfilling the greater duties of aiding their parents, or of satisfying the requirements of the police in the matter of marriage portions, and if by so doing the trade of the country was paralysed, and it was, as is the case with Germany, turned into a huge barrack, the sanctity of home destroyed by the involuntary presence of one or more soldiers, unfit mates in a small house for a young wife or for daughters—in such a case as this Ireland might well execrate the Saxon; but she has none of these excuses. There is no country in the world where personal freedom is less interfered with, and where men can occupy themselves so completely in their own way without molestation or interference by the state; and yet the fact of the bitter hatred between Kelt and Saxon is no fiction, but a dreadful reality, and one that may hereafter produce a terrible catastrophe.

Nor is this awful state of things an unhallowed dream,

a phantasy of a perfervid imagination.  It is a stern reality;
and the one dominant idea which pervades most Irishmen,
and which nourishes this frightful hatred of us in his
heart, is that he is engaged in a struggle of a nationality
against a domination alien in language, in blood, and in
religion ; and unhappily it cannot be denied that the most
intelligent and independent people in Ireland are the most
consistently and intensely national ; that the parts of the
country where poverty is lightest and industrial and
agricultural success most palpable and enduring, are those
where the Irish population are most powerful ; and in the
districts where crimes against morality and social order
are least known, there English rule has its most inveterate
foes.   In the words of one of the most gifted and upright
of Ireland's sons now living, A. M. Sullivan, whose authority is cited for these propositions, this feeling is not a mere
empty sentiment, but the very instinct of the Irish nature,
by which an Irishman is attached to the race from which
he sprang, and feels its individuality, its life, and weal to
be as dear to him as his own.   To use his own words :
" It is not a mere empty sentiment nor instinctive feeling
unfortified by the fact of cool reason and practical judgment.   It is a wise consideration of what we find to be
most in harmony with, not alone our feelings and instincts,
but in harmony with our material interests, which prompts
us to guard our distinct national existence, and to regard
as abnormal, revolutionary, unjust, and oppressive the
domination of any foreign influence over it."
    And this same " cool reason and practical judgment " had
taught Mr. Sullivan—so blindly does one erroneous and
dominant idea overcloud the judgment—that in former
days as well as at present—certainly he does not limit
the idea to the past—" that terrible and satanic agencies

are employed, not to conquer but to extirpate the Irish
race, to break, to deaden, to kill, to crush within them
the spirit of liberty, and make them, if allowed to live at
all, a race of creeping, crawling helots, dwarfed in body,
in mind, and in soul." Surely Mr. Sullivan forgets that
in England he belongs to a profession of which a "creeping, crawling helot," Earl Cairns, an Irishman, is at the
head, and that Irishmen are judges in this as well as
in their own country; that Lord O'Hagan, sitting with
Lord Cairns and a Scotchman or two of no particular
rank, are in a majority in the highest court of appeal,
not only for England but for all her dependencies; that
a Scot is Lord Chief Justice of England and an Irishman
Lord Chief Baron; and, as his name imports, a West of
England Celt Chief Justice of the Common Pleas; that
if England's object is to dwarf the minds and souls of
Irish helots, she has not been guilty of success. But that
a man of Mr. Sullivan's intelligence and position can
allow such words to be republished at this day is proof
of the genuineness of his belief—evidence of the intensity
of his feelings.

The Irish are undoubtedly a highly intellectual race,
and keenly sensible of ridicule. Mr. Sullivan himself
speaks of his countrymen as being "the scorn of strangers,
the ill-used brute drudges of an inferior race;" yet, without
denying the fact of Irish talent, he will not, on consideration, refuse to acknowledge that some Englishmen have
been eminent in their day, and that possibly there are a
few still living who may rank intellectually upon an
equality with his own countrymen; nor can he deny that
his own countrymen, both in his own country and in
England, have an equal chance of success in every line of
life with the dominant but inferior race he despises.

Mr. Sullivan imagines that the secret why Irishmen have been able to endure (and, we may add, to keep secret too) such terrible suffering for such an unprecedented period, unflinchingly in defending its nationality— he merely dates it seven hundred years—is because their national rights and feelings were inextricably wound round the cross of faith; and he adds, " We are national to-day because our nationality took refuge at the altar of that faith, and fled with it to the cave and the fastness. Twined in holy union, they endured, and, strengthening each other, bravely met every storm of persecution." This might be true if the persecution dated from the time of Henry VIII., but it can hardly be predicated of the first English king of that name, or even of Henry II. Indeed, Mr. Sullivan is guilty of a poetical license in coupling these two matters, Irish nationality and the Catholic faith, together; for, as he himself frankly admits, the Irish Protestant is as hostile to the English union as the Catholic. Surely such illogical and inconsistent reasoning should prepare us for the fact that in Irish grievances and sentimentality there is a screw loose somewhere, and that it may turn out that Irish politicians are not wilfully but hopelessly in error; and it is marvellous that so clear and acute a people are so ignorant of their own history, and if they do not know it themselves, they must not be angry if the English fail to discover it, for the proof to be supplied by the foregoing pages is to the effect that Ireland and England have been at war together and have invaded each other, not for seven hundred years, but for three times that period, and that this first occurred at so early a period that it is almost impossible to predicate who was the aggressor and which the injured party. Canon Ulick J. Bourke, the greatest living Irish writer on history,

admits that he cannot possibly determine whether the
stream of emigration flowed from England to his country
or the reverse ; and if we conclude, as it is hoped will be
the case, that the theory of this book is correct, and that
the hated Saxon is the Scythian, it may turn out that
Ireland, as it was the brain of the British Empire, was
also the dominant factor of the union, and conquered
England by main force.

It may be urged that the fact that there was always, as
there is now, strife between the countries, is proof of their
being different nationalities ; but this is not so.    The
history of the Israelites is proof to the contrary, for they
as frequently turned their arms upon each other as upon
their neighbours; and if it should be that the Irish and
English are of the same race, the fact that they were
separated by the seas between them so long that their
relationship was forgotten, is amply sufficient to account
for their hostility to each other, if indeed it is necessary
to account for it.

Now if the Irish would but learn this one fact, that the
dominant English are of the same blood as themselves—
that they are not German, as has been supposed, but are
purely Keltic—would not many of the grievances, which
are really based on assumption of this point, melt away ?
It is not intended by this that there are no Irish grievances,
and that there is nothing to be remedied.    That cannot be
predicated of England.    There are unhappily many things
that require alteration, many laws that are repugnant to
common sense and equity, some common to both countries,
some only attaching to one.    Nor is it always possible to obtain justice in England.    Judges are often prejudiced, sometimes dishonest, and too frequently incompetent.    Again,
in England the very profession to which Mr. Sullivan

himself belongs is suffering grievous injuries at the hands
of the Irishman who presides over it. English Catholics
have no chance with Irish Catholics, or with their Protestant competitors. Only one has ever reached the
Bench, and very few are selected for the rank of Queen's
Counsel. If the trade of the Nationalist would be destroyed by an admission of the English claim to a share
in the Keltic inheritance, that of the Patriot would still
endure; and his usefulness and power would be increased
if he applied himself to the cure of real, and not of fanci-
ful, diseases. God forbid that it should be said that the
Irish have no claim for redress, no right that they do not
possess already; that were to endorse the wrongs under
which they suffer. But undoubtedly the bitter feeling
would be removed if this nonsense of alien blood were
abolished; and these pages have been written—this chapter, though the last, was, in fact, written first of all—
with the hope and aim of bringing out the truth upon
the subject, and of dissipating error, the presence of which
was unpleasantly forced upon the writer during a recent
sojourn in the United States of America. His hope and
chief aim in writing this book has been that the terrible
feeling of hatred may pass away, and that Englishmen
and Irishmen may learn to look upon each other as
brethren, and unite in action, not to destroy each other,
but to further with all their might the common good.

# INDEX.

ABARIS = Memphis, 116. ·
Abomenus of Tyre puzzled Solomon, 126.
Abraham's piety vouched for by historians, 114.
Achorus, son of Pharaoh, Irish served under him, 76.
Aco, city of, 117.
Acusilaus corrects Hesiod, 31 ; on the longevity of the patriarchs, 113.
Adoniram collected tribute in Spain for Solomon, 41, 144.
Adrian IV., Pope, an Englishman, 263.
Aedui = Hedui = Aides of the Greeks, 68.
Æschylus on Scythians, 222.
Agarthaclides corrected by Josephus, 32.
Alexander of Macedon employed the Saxons (see Occa Scarlensis), 77.
Alexander Polyhistor cites Cleodamus, 41.
Alfred the Great, his forged Life, 52.
Amber only produced in Estonia, 149 ; found in England proof of connection with Estonia, 149 ; where found in England, 149.
Ambrones, a common war-cry of the Cymry and Italians, 145.
Ammana = Rabbah, 69.
Ammanus Marcellinus, Goths = Scythæ, 210.
Ammonites held Rabbah, 70.

Amos, the prophet, accusation against the Phœnicians, 117.
Ampère, M., on Sabine influence upon Rome, 141.
Amramian canal, 97 ; = Aramean, 111.
Anagu, the lower region, 72.
Anak = Phene Anak, 104.
Anakim, see Anak, 104.
Anarcharsis a Scythian, 222 ; calls the Greeks Scythæ, 223.
Anastasius, Goth = Scythæ, 210.
Anaxagoras, expounder of Greek mythology, 59.
Ancient Germans have no Promethean works or arts, 134.
An Gael = Angle, 199.
Angelus = Anglen, according to Professor Stubbs, 168.
Angle = An Gael, 199 ; An-gielies, 202.
Angles = Saxons, Bede, 197 ; Latham, 197 ; Freeman, 197.
Angli came from an Alpine slope, Freeman's idea, 169 ; a tribe of the Swevi, 169 ; of Tacitus, 167.
Anglicyn, meaning of term, 198.
Anglo-Saxon characters like the Irish, 93 ; is not a polished, but an illiterate tongue, 184 ; no stages in language, 54.
Anglo-Saxons, the, 197-203.
Antiochus IV., coin of his age, 117.
Apion, Cimmerii are Kelts, 214.
Apollo = Baal, 124.

S

T

292        INDEX.

THE END.

PRINTED BY BALLANTYNE, HANSON AND CO.
EDINBURGH AND LONDON.

www.ingramcontent.com/pod-product-compliance
Lightning Source LLC
Chambersburg PA
CBHW031401270326
41929CB00010BA/1282